A Childhood Not Eas[y]
A History of

By Lee Woolcott-Ellis

Do Monsters really exist?

"Yes, they do"

Dedication

**I dedicate this book to Mandy Woolcott
My world, my love, my life,**

without whom this book would not have been possible.

A very special thanks to Tom Elliot, Andy Hillier, Jerry Bedford, Mark Jordan, Steve Dobson, Adem Akyol, Kevin Campbell and to many others who have supported me or this writing project directly.

A special thanks to all the friends, acquaintances and all the supportive people from Facebook forums and the general Internet, who have been incredibly supportive with positive comments, etc. It means everything.

It is good to talk.

INDEX
of Chapters

Foreword:	Tom Elliot, Chartered Psychologist	page: 5
Introduction		page: 6 - 17
Chapter 1:	So why am I writing a book?	page: 18 - 22
Chapter 2:	How did all this begin for me?	page: 23 - 25
Chapter 3:	The first day at boarding school and the lasting effect of that	page: 26 - 31
Chapter 4:	Life in the Boarding School System (1970 to 1980)	page: 32 - 38
Chapter 5:	Living with me was not easy (Childhood Sexual Abuse and Mental Illness)	page: 39 - 50
Chapter 6:	The Underwood Report And the evolution of 'Maladjusted Children' and Independent Boarding Schools	page: 51 - 61
Chapter 7:	The Search for Justice and Truth	page: 62 - 90
Chapter 8:	Closure	page: 91 - 97
Links:	Support and Services	page: 98
Appendices Index:		page: 99
Appendices:	Additional and supporting information	page: 100 - 190

Foreword

Childhood is a place in time, designed by adults ideally to nurture and help children to develop and thrive. We have memories from, but not of childhood since we are, no longer that child. We may look back on it with rose tinted spectacles for the most part, preferring or denying the more shadowy aspects and pains of growing up, Peter Pan like. Yet this book is far removed from an idealized retrospective of a boyhood in 1970's England. The author provides the reader with a first-hand account of historical, childhood, sexual, physical and emotional abuses within a total institution, set up for so called maladjusted children from the age of 6 or 7 years through adolescence.

As a psychologist, I have always been suspicious of labels and especially so of labelling the very young. So, when Lee told me that he had been sent to a 'home for maladjusted children' in the 1970's this immediately raised such suspicions. How could this friendly, kind and articulate man in my therapy room ever fit such a misguided label, or indeed that any child should have to start life with what could become a cruel self-fulfilling prophecy. So began Lee's investigation into his childhood medical notes, which revealed that his young mother with very little support was not coping. This was a turning point in terms of being able to turn away from a core belief that he was somehow responsible for being separated from his mother and belonged in a 'home'. It also meant that he was then able to objectify those responsible for the many abuses he experienced and disavow shame and blame and state a new rule for living, that there would indeed be no more secrets.

It is written with immense fortitude and will be of great value to survivors of abuse who have ever been asked the naïve question "why did it take you so long to disclose the abuse." In 21st Century Britain, Lee's hope is that we will live in a more enlightened age. We will no longer tolerate having to wait for another Saville inquiry before our public and private attitudes and level of insight change. We will look inwardly and outwardly toward the prevention of abuse in the day-to-day way we relate to each other - as beings that have lived through childhood and are nurturing of the children of our time.

Tom Elliot CPsychol AFBPsS
Counselling Psychologist
Cognitive Behavioural Psychotherapist

Introduction

Most of the deadlines I set myself for completing this book were never met. To be completely honest, the amount of drive and commitment I gave to this project, was offset entirely by the impact of writing the book had on me and those closest to me. The text is loaded with triggers for me and undoubtedly will be for others. This was something I had to learn how to manage carefully when writing the text and reading back from it.

I am confident in the knowledge, that the integrity I applied to writing this book has created an authentic and open account of my time in the private boarding school system of the 1970's, which successfully fulfils my purpose in this undertaking. Completing this book has sated the driving force that plagued me for years, telling me that it would be better for others to have a clearer, more informed opinion on what historic abuse was and more importantly, how dangerous and disturbing the perpetrators of abuse are and how wide spread and deeply ingrained the damage they wreak truly is.

The best way for people to be better informed, I believe, is from getting the information from an authentic, personal account. I am prepared to go as far as saying, my experiences chronicled in this book, are in no way unique, but they are truthful and therefore reflect accurately, many experiences young boys would have had in the 1970's boarding schools, in the UK.

It was when the Jimmy Savile child abuse scandal news broke in the UK media in October 2012, that there was a tremendous public outcry of how could this have been allowed to happen? How was child abuse so wide spread? And then followed a shocked disbelief of how depraved and monstrous Savile had been generally and more so with young children. [Appendix: M/N page 149 - 153]

Child Sexual Abuse (CSA) has been prevalent in the UK for decades, it was just hidden away and protected by a veil of secrecy. A gossamer layer of respectability covering some of the most monstrous acts imaginable, flimsy in many places yet robust enough to keep the true nature of horrendous crimes hidden away. The strength of the secrecy sturdiest in the level of protection it has been given. CSA was too wide spread and frequently reported for the system to plead ignorance of it, they just chose to. The reality was too many people of 'importance' were involved in it and because of protecting them, CSA was too damaging for the authorities to openly acknowledge. Some people would go as far as to say that child sexual abuse in the UK, especially unnatural sexual activity with young boys may have been offered hegemonic protection and as such it was 'untouchable' for many decades.

It sadly, doubtless still is to a certain extent, but slowly and surely the veil of secrecy is lifting. The Westminster abuse 'cover-up', was reported in the Guardian in March 2015 [Appendix: O page 154 - 158] and the abuse scandal in the North Wales care homes was investigated by the National Crime Agency, under Operational Pallial in November 2012. There were more than 120 suspects in that investigation alone [Appendix: P page 159 - 160].

I focus in this text on sexual activity by men with young boys and do not wish to lessen the prevalence of all types of child abuse. All child abuse being equally abhorrent. It is widely known that most ranking individuals involved in many 'scandals' were either accused of activity with, or were known to have had both pederasty and paedophile inclinations.

One of the principal things that was shaped from this appalling milestone in UK history [The Savile Case], was a public awareness that historic child sexual abuse (CSA) did happen, followed by immediate public condemnation for what Savile had been allowed to do and for justice to be seen to be done now. There was also a sense of horror at this time, in many circles, that Savile had been granted total access to whoever he wanted and whenever he wanted. I am sure any person reading this will agree with me, an individual could not possibly gain this much privilege and opportunity, without having extremely highly placed and influential contacts. I can only hope that once all the enquiries and investigations are concluded (if at all), any individuals still alive, who can be shown to have colluded with Savile, by immorally remaining silent or turning a blind eye to reports of his activities, are brought to face justice also. Their silence has been equally as destructive.

Without doubt the most important thing to come out of the 'post Savile' investigation, was the willingness of historic abuse victims to come forward to speak up about the abuse they had suffered. This was a turning point for both victims and survivors of CSA, with many more coming forward following on from media reports of other historical abuse police investigations and the subsequent successful prosecutions of historic abusers.

A sadly obvious and widely heard statement following on from the Savile exposé was – *Why have 'they' waited so long to say something*?

I will endeavour to answer that, but I would like to say here that when the Savile story broke, many victims of historic CSA had buried their abusive history. Tucked away to mitigate against the continuing pain and torture that their past presented them. Far too many of the silent victims of CSA were finding themselves being suddenly and uncontrollably triggered by mass media reporting (and many still are). This placed hundred's (quite possibly thousand's) of middle aged, proficient people with a difficult situation to manage. Hard working professionals with positions of responsibility and growing families, who now felt like the rug was being pulled from under their feet. Not knowing how to suppress these powerful echoes of their childhood and unable to control the myriad of emotions that came with them.

For some historic abuse victims, there was some reinforcement from the media reporting, or it became apparent to them, that people *were* prepared to listen to their story and to believe them. There were successful prosecutions and police forces were investigating previously 'untouchable' individuals. It was entirely possible that the police would take their allegations seriously. They bravely started to speak up and have continued to do so.

I hope that this book will help answer many of the questions you may have regarding historic child sexual abuse and more importantly, certainly for me, should begin to answer the question of 'Why did you not say anything?'

Many victims of child abuse, and I include myself here, had buried their horrific memories of historic incidents so deeply, it took powerful triggers to bring the memories back. I would say here also that although tucked away and locked up deep inside with no 'actual' cognisant memory, the ingrained effects of child sexual abuse never totally leave. They masquerade in mood and emotion, pulling and pushing the victim down a rocky road of harm, distrust and misery. Some days are easy and some days are hard. Of course, it must be said with any major trauma experience, the victim is unlikely ever going to truly 'get over' what happened to them. Emotional scars truly are deeper than physical ones.

One day and without any warning there is a trigger and back it comes to the forefront of the victim's memory. Horrified and frightened it has now become a major force disrupting the victims present life. The original pain and anguish resurfacing, because it never really went away. There is no 'tucking it' away any longer. It must be acknowledged and it should be dealt with. Changes to that person's normal behaviour, mood and character will become openly apparent. It is highly unlikely that many will still be able to continue to disguise what they are going through and what they are reliving. It becomes all consuming.

Consider someone you live with or work with. You have known this person for some time and you and many others accept that this individual has up days and down days. One day they are communicative and efficient, then on another day they are closed off and struggling to maintain the basic tasks. Unable to communicate effectively and virtually alienating themselves from everyone. We have all known that person that everyone says "oh, he is in one of those moods today, leave him to it". "Don't worry about him, he's got one of those heads on"

Admittedly, we all accept these behavioural traits and rarely do we look past the surface, do we? We never really think to ask what is this person living with? It is more comfortable for us to judge others by their character alone.

In a previous role, I worked in a busy office environment. My work required full integration with the centre administrative staff and users of a very busy educational centre. I enjoyed my job and achieved moderate success, including a 'going the extra mile award'. I enjoyed the role of technician and I had only been in post a few months when I was directed by a former Kesgrave Hall boy, to speak with the Guardian Newspaper. I received a message to contact a journalist from the newspaper.

The journalist I spoke with on the telephone, Josh Halliday, asked me whether I had attended Kesgrave Hall School, in Suffolk, between 1970 and 1990? I answered 'Yes'. Initially I became very suspicious of his motives regarding the phone call and I was immediately triggered.

After many years of burying it away, my past was suddenly very much a part of my present. I was at work and I remember going into shock. I was suddenly reminded again that I was abused as a child and that I just chose not to remember that. I felt immediately vulnerable and exposed. I do not recall saying anything to my colleagues at this point, but they must have noticed a fierce change in my behaviour. Perhaps the more perceptive ones may have done.

The contact I had with Josh Halliday of the Guardian Newspaper was a mutually beneficial relationship ultimately and I have discussed the purpose of this contact further in the book. I do not regret for one moment talking with Josh Halliday of The Guardian Newspaper, The BBC and various other regional journalists.

In all my professional undertakings from the age of 18 years and to a certain extent, in my private life also, I have been the master of illusion. I learnt at a very early age, between the age of 6 to 7 years old, that it I was offered more personal protection by not showing any emotion. I therefore grew up becoming highly skilled in masking my true feelings and emotions.

In all aspects of my life, including work, I have been productive and been able to function well, but very rarely at full capacity (100%). Over the past 30+ years, I have had my major triggers and I am fortunate that I have been able to deal with all most of what my past threw at me and move forward. Whether I dealt with it well, is open to question.

I have been fortunate to be able to speak about what happened to me as a child, in a secure and controlled environment and that has been a very positive thing for me, but the legacy of my childhood remains as a permanent scar inside my head.

Child sexual abuse is so damaging to the victims, it goes way beyond the initial harm and distress caused by the physical and mental acts perpetrated against them. It creates permanent damage that has no possible way of healing, with far reaching effects that will last their entire lifetime. Speaking of my own personal history, I can state openly and honestly that I can never forget the things that happened to me and who was responsible for them. I recall parts of my abuse every day and most nights. I see people, virtually daily, in shops, walking down the pavement or on trains, that instantly remind me of one of my abusers. I instantaneously recall the person, the abuser and what they did to me.

The most insignificant things, a word, a song, a place, a smell, etc. can take me back there. Inactivity or silence is enough sometimes for my brain to conspire against me and allow me to wander into that shadowy, foreboding forest inside my mind.

Every day I fight my mind for control over the effects of the horrors during my childhood. I cannot be alone with this. Child abuse is a self-perpetuating crime that continues to affect the victims infinitely. Many victims of childhood abuse end up taking their own lives as adults. I have considered it myself at least once in the past.

In respect of an effective and healthy mind, most days I operate at 95% efficiency, with the occasional stray thought of my past experiences intruding into the present, to potentially distress me. Thankfully these are easily dismissed and soon forgotten as I continue in my daily tasks. I have many coping strategies, for which I am eternally grateful to my psychologist of many years and my friend, Tom. In respect of 95% effectiveness, who can truly say they feel 100% everyday?

In other words, I have managed to control and suppress these thoughts mostly. Occasionally on some days (or nights), my ability to fight the sadness and anger becomes more challenging. On these days, I will attempt isolate myself as far as is possible from others and contain it.

Speaking up could involve talking to a close friend or trusted family member, a medical practitioner (family GP) and ultimately, or for some initially, the Police. An initial point of contact invariably forced upon the victim by a point of crisis. A mental health episode or a breaking point.

When a victim of childhood sexual abuse comes forward and does speak up, it must be said, it has taken immeasurable courage for that individual to do so. It is probably one of the bravest things that person has done, in my opinion, to go against this built-in desire to NEVER speak about what happened to them. They will undoubtedly feel afraid and vulnerable because of doing this, but they will have taken this course of action because they want the screaming voices in their head to stop. They will finally want the truth to be known, they will be looking for justice for the harm inflicted upon them and ultimately, they will want their abuser/s to be exposed for what they truly are/were.

The initial conversations will be highly charged and emotional. If I could offer some advice to anyone being spoken to in this situation, you do not need to say too much, you just need to 'listen'.

If you were to ask that person – 'why did you not say something before?' The answer will undoubtedly be, "I couldn't". It is likely that is all you will get from them at this point. The immediate effect of asking the 'why' question has a danger of closing any trust between the two individuals. For me, this represents the pinnacle of a 'closed question'.

For me, hearing 'why did you not say something?' still stirs emotion in me. It makes me very angry. It is an insult and I do recall clamming up as a natural response to this question many times.

A victim of abuse may feel if they tell someone about what had happened to them, they will be blamed for it or at least be accused of lying about it all.

A prime example of this was an encounter with my biological father. He, loudly shouting, accused me of lying and berated me heavily, when I told him one day in 1996 that I had been abused as a child and I was speaking to the police about it. "Oh, my God" he said, "You cannot accuse people of stuff like that". "You will end up in prison or something". As was quite usual with him, the viler, more aggressive side of him emerged with questions like - "are you doing this to get some money" or "what's your angle here". My father, a man of few words, and most of them vulgar and meaningless.

I cannot recall why I chose to tell him of all people at that point in time. I consider this to be a major sign of weakness in me and indication of my state of mind then. These outbursts from him only went on to reinforce my fears of not being believed. He was one of the first people I told about my past and one of the last for another 17 years. I obviously thought I could trust my father. I must have thought he would be there to protect me, but was then delivered this sudden realisation and stark reminder, that he wasn't there as a protective force for the last 10 years of my actual childhood, when I was forcibly kept away from my home. He was never there for me, to protect me from the indecent assaults and violence I suffered at the hands of my supposed carers. He was not a father.

I have been estranged from my real father since the year 2000. A sudden awakening in me then saw him for the real person he was. A nasty, vindictive malevolent force. A narcissist in every respect, who clearly appeared to revel in the control of all around him. I had suffered enough abuse in my life up to this point. I gladly cut myself off from him then and I feel my life was enriched as a result.

Many victims of abuse are told to keep what happened to them a secret and sadly most do. They keep it locked away deep inside for a very long time. It is very difficult for most victims to think about what happened to them, even tougher to try talk about it. For many victims, they will always be fearful of mentioning their past. There is always that possibility that their story will not be accepted or people will refuse to listen to what they have to say.

Many abusers threaten the victim, that if they tell anyone about what had been happening, they may kill someone in their family. Some abusers threaten the victim that if they talk about it, the authorities will come in and permanently break up their family.

Many victims of abuse dissociate when memories of their own abuse surfaces, to distance themselves from further pain or to even protect their loved ones from sharing their pain. Some victims may only be able to speak about their abuse once their abuser is dead; not that speaking about it becomes any easier for them at that point.

Even during the year 2012, at the age of 48, the actual act of talking about my past to someone else, was extremely difficult and it took me a good year or two to get over that difficulty.

The conditioned instinct of not talking about it meant I had to physically force the words out. This was beyond strained and very, very upsetting for me to do. When initially attempting to talk about what had happened to me, a mass of emotion flooded forward leaving me a complete wreck.

Thinking back at why this left me so raw, led me to believe it was because it brought to the forefront such powerful emotions, such as fear, sadness, guilt, disgust, anger and hatred. An extremely volatile mix indeed, that needed to be handled very carefully. You can now see why with such ingredients being present, some people cannot handle it and it becomes a recipe for disaster.

Therefore, it is so important that anyone who has been triggered and wants to talk about it, is directed towards, or is at least able to access qualified support. Without putting a system of support in place, this is tantamount to lighting a firework and placing it back in the box with the unlit fireworks.

Bringing these emotions out would be better handled in a safe and structured environment. When I started opening-up, I did not always handle it well on my own and did let things spiral out of control on some occasions. I reached numerous crisis points, some of these quite severe. This thankfully was not always so and it did get so much easier once I entered in cognitive behavioural therapy sessions (CBT) with a psychologist.

In time, it became clear to me that healing was taking place, when I could talk about certain elements of my past, without crying.

So, to answer the question from earlier in this introduction - It is easy and natural for any caring, compassionate person to say to a victim/survivor of historic child sexual abuse 'why did you not say anything?' I believe it would unquestionably be kinder and better received, if they were to say, 'No wonder you were unable to say anything'.

Many of the boys who went through the boarding schools I did in the 1970's, like me would have experienced abuse and violence at a very young age (6 and 7+). We were all extremely vulnerable and very alone, having been isolated from any family members, who possibly would be looking out for us. That for many was the root of the problem and was why they were so openly exposed to harm. There were no regular inspections or audits of our boarding schools, certainly none that I was made aware of, and the school management and carers virtually had a free hand to do whatever they wanted to do. Many of them of course, did just that.

For us, the boys of Heanton Hill School and Kesgrave Hall School, institutional abuse was a way of life, because it was 'our life'. We grew up institutionalised and knew no different. Living in this very strict and regimented way was our 'normal' and to be able to survive every day within such a regime, demanded total submission from us.

In addition to common place corporal punishment and casual violence, any attempt made to disrupt or refuse indecent sexual advances and other demands of an intimate nature, from some of the male staff members and older boys, was invariably met with further violence or just taken through superior strength or brute force. It soon became very clear that fighting against sexual advances was totally counterproductive. To truly survive, it was necessary to allow them to satisfy whatever unnatural desire they had with you and then they would at least leave you alone.

After boarding school, as a boy of almost 17 years, I was left feeling highly ashamed of everything that had happened to me. My abusers had been very skilful in transferring all their guilt and shame on to me. For many years, I believed that no one would ever believe me and if I spoke it about what had happened to me throughout my childhood. I truly believed that I would be ridiculed or hurt further if my secrets were ever to come out. This was my dirty, nasty secret that I had to keep quiet about.

Even to this day, when I occasionally think about some of the things that happened to me as a child. I still attempt to analyse or make sense of some of the acts committed against me. I occasionally still have the odd nightmare, painfully reliving some of the incidents and I struggle to believe it really happened to me. It seems so unnatural and inconceivable. I cannot understand how any man could be so depraved and derive pleasure from such acts with children. It is beyond my comprehension. I do wonder sometimes how I am sane.

I am happy to talk about my abusive childhood now and have even given talks to police officers and social workers regarding my experiences. I believe talking about CSA and raising awareness, through openness and discourse is the right thing to do. Allowing child sexual abuse and child sexual exploitation to become stigmatised and taboo subjects again, will only serve to perpetuate it through secrecy. This is one of the primary factors behind the writing of this book. It is about my journey through the abusive, boarding school system of the 1970's. I have been brutally honest about everything, but I will not talk about the actual sexual acts themselves. There is no benefit to be gained from that content and I fear such dialogue would be misused, by the monsters I despise in this world the most.

To put this book into perspective – From the age of 6, I was regularly sexually, physically and mentally abused by more than 10 different men, at two separate schools throughout the 1970's, virtually on a weekly, if not daily basis for a period of just under 10 years. These men committed indecent acts - some to me, some with me and some forcing me to do things to them. The best way for these paedophiles to manage their asset, was to keep me submissive and broken, interlaced with small, infrequent acts of kindness and thereby maintain full control of me.

Most of these men continued to do these things with me for between 3 and 5 years each. Roughly calculated, this totalled between 2,500 and 3000 indecent assaults against me. This was in addition to frequent and excessive physical violence I suffered and the constant humiliation and mental torture that eventually subdued me throughout my school days.

By 2015, I had successfully proved, with the help of other former boys of the schools, a total of 50 counts of indecent assaults against me, in the law courts. That equates to 1.666 percent of jury proved assaults, from the estimated total. I would have increased that percentage significantly if other abusers had not killed themselves or slipped through the net by way of natural death. Other individuals, like the school GP in Suffolk, escaped prosecution through the powerlessness of the legal team in securing corroborating evidence. That was always going to be a challenge in both Heanton and Kesgrave Hall cases, due to the nature of historic investigation.

The huge wave of historic abuse cases being reported to the Police forces has continued to the extent in 2017, Senior Police officers were saying that they cannot cope with the volume of abuse allegations that required investigation. [Appendix: R page 166 - 167] The judicial system is under great pressure and they continue to say that the prison system cannot effectively incarcerate the volume of convicted paedophiles coming through the Courts. Arguably in addition to the amount of victim's reporting historic assaults, that can also relate to funding cuts in the Police and Prison Services. What is inherent in the first statement, is the overwhelming recognition of how prevalent CSA was in the UK since the 1970's and how many people were directly affected by it then. Equally thousands are still affected by it today. Another indicator supporting this would be the number of historic abuse victims entering treatment with community mental health services and other therapy providers. This has created an additional burden to their already stretched services.

I should add here, if anything in this book affects you (triggers anything in you), please do seek some support for yourself. This is important and speaking to a close family member or friend is a good place to start. Speaking to your family doctor (GP) is always an option. They should be able to refer you to a suitable provider for confidential support. I have been very open with my accounts of the past and in doing so I have been triggered many times myself when writing this book.

I have not directly mentioned in the book, the names of any of the boy's I was at the boarding schools with, as I do not wish to expose them and cause them any further harm directly. I have however mentioned and named several the abusers – the paedophiles and perpetrators of violence against me and other boys and feel justified to do so. Many of these are monsters who have undoubtedly preyed on hundreds of young boys, over the decades since I had the misfortune to be ensnared by them. They deserve nothing less than being exposed for what they were.

I have used the past tense in that last sentence, because if they have not been imprisoned already for their crimes, they are already dead. Some through natural causes and some by their own hands following being exposed by some of their former victims and me.

For many years, I threatened to put the memories, thoughts and recollections of my turbulent boarding school years into writing and in effect I started writing this book in my mind in the 1990's. It was not until 2013 that I started to properly collate my memories. It was at this point that the book really took shape. It has taken a further 4 years to complete.

Between 1995 and 2015, I have intermittently been dealing with the police and the judiciary in my search for justice for what happened to me in the 1970's. I was also getting regular support by accessing the professional services of a psychologist weekly from 2013. These weekly sessions were vital to me and helped me make sense of everything that came back to me, when it came back to me. This therapy continued for a few years and I value that support greatly.

When writing this book, an autobiography in essence, I frequently asked myself - *who am I to put my story in writing?* The answer invariably came to me, this book was never going to be just about me. This book is about the failed educational and care system that criminally neglected thousands of children in the United Kingdom over many centuries. It is about the independent boarding school's that had masqueraded as centres of excellence in the support and care of disaffected young boys.
I spent my childhood in this system, it failed me badly during my time there and over the years that followed.

This book ultimately is about historic child abuse. Physical, mental and sexual abuse of young boys from the age of 6 and 7 years, which although not portrayed graphically, it is written truthfully and because of that I should warn the reader that is should not be considered easy reading. Some of the boys that attended the boarding schools (Heanton School and Kesgrave Hall School) were not sexually abused during their time there. They can count themselves very fortunate in that respect.

Chapter 1

So why am I writing a book?

In both my personal and professional life, I have occasioned many people who have either experienced historic abuse personally, or have had a family member or close friend, who was abused as a child. I have also spoken with many people or have been party to discussion with individuals that have constructed their own knowledge of this subject solely, from media reports and journalistic opinion. Previous media sensationalism and social media ranting do nothing to positively support the need for the facts surrounding historic child sexual abuse to be exposed. Witness and victim testimony are principal elements I believe, for others to learn of actual truth surrounding historic child sexual abuse.

I also believe whole heartedly, that historic CSA must be talked about widely and it must be openly acknowledged. It did happen and was happening more commonly than anyone was prepared to accept. It still happens today sadly and all of us collectively, have a duty to protect all young people from it, where we can.

The one real weapon we possess to fight paedophilia, is for all of us to accept it as a reality and to recognise that learning from the mistakes that have been made in the past is an effective process, to create change now. Covering our past up, migrating blame and living under the shadow of deniability serves nobody well, least of all vulnerable young children.

I am entirely convinced that the hegemony today (political, judicial, etc.) would attract wide admiration and the full support of the people, if they just stood up and supported the truth surrounding historic child sexual abuse. As opposed to not continue to openly cover up the wrongdoings of their peers and mentors (allegedly). This would also serve to actively support better progress of many of the thousands of investigations into historic sexual abuse against children in the United Kingdom, both cold and current. This would similarly better serve and support inquiries such as The Independent Inquiry into Child Sexual Abuse (IICSA) in England and Wales, [Appendix S, page 165] which at the time of writing this part of the book, was searching to discover why, and how, CSA was so widely covered up in the UK over the past four centuries. As an aside, I would like to say that I contacted IICSA in 2015 and submitted a written account of my institutional abuse at both Heanton and Kesgrave Hall and more specifically the failings of the Local Authorities, the School Management, etc. in preventing continuous and excessive harm to come to me and others during those years. I also wrote about the initial difficulties and barriers that were put in the way of progressing Police investigations into the actions of named staff members from both schools. I am due to be interviewed by IICSA in late 2017.

Historic child sexual abuse as a subject and a reality, cannot be allowed to skulk and fester in the seedy shadows of shame and guilt and thereby be allowed to continue unchallenged. Institutions cannot be allowed to exist again where children as young as six years were introduced to regimes that remained at their best inappropriate and at their worst cruel and shocking. Young children being exposed to extreme levels and types of sexual abuse that to any right-minded person would be deemed to be truly horrendous, leaving the victims traumatised and scarred for their entire lives.

Many independent boarding/residential schools were started up and ran in the United Kingdom during 1960's, 1970's and 1980's, that became recruiting grounds for paedophiles rings. These homes and schools were operated by private individuals solely for their financial gain and were surprisingly, fully supported by most local authorities. Regional authorities with a responsibility to protect young children within their geographical areas of responsibility, yet they willingly sent vulnerable young boys to schools in other regions, that they had no direct control over. Many of these were children who had been removed from their homes, for their own protection in many cases, or because they had been deemed to be 'maladjusted' by the local authority psychologists and needed to be cared for and carefully fostered to be able to develop 'normally'.

I discovered the term 'maladjusted' when investigating my own childhood history. Maladjusted is in an appalling word. A word widely misused. I was labelled as a maladjusted child by Kent County Council School Health Service (1969) and as such they considered my needs were to be best met by removing me from the nurturing environment of a family and placing me in a same sex environment.

The term maladjusted was and is still sadly used to identify a child who falls outside of what is perceived to be normal. A dictionary definition is: *Not able to deal with other people in a normal or healthy way. Poorly or inadequately adjusted; specifically: lacking harmony with one's environment from failure to adjust one's desires to the conditions of one's life* (http://www.merriam-webster.com/dictionary/maladjusted) © 2013 Merriam-Webster, Incorporated

We have all probably heard the phrase *'Forget your past and enjoy the future'* or many derivatives of that phrase. There undoubtedly will be some merit in that for some, but I would argue, from personal experience and ask the question - *Can you truly create a better future for yourself by entirely denying your past?* I am not convinced you can.

This is the story of my confinement into the boarding school institutions that operated in the United Kingdom in the 1970's from the age of 7 years to 17 years. This is book is about what happened to me at boarding school, how it influenced every aspect of my adult life after leaving school and how I was eventually able to lay my demons to rest.

I have never truly got over what happened to me as a child in the boarding schools and in all honesty, I do not believe I ever will. I have however been able to learn how to come to terms with everything that happened to me and learn how to live with it. I have developed comprehensive coping strategies to remind me every day that the small, scared child still screaming inside me wants me to be strong and give him the life he truly deserves. I cannot and will not let my demons win.

My childhood years, or perhaps more precisely, the injuries inflicted on me in the past, although repressed for decades, have caused me and those associated with me great harm. My decades of denial and refusal to challenge the ghosts of the past have been a negative force within me. I discovered first hand that the only way to overturn this destructive influence was to face up to those elements from my past, challenge them directly and then lay them to rest. This book is about my journey from being a victim of institutional, historic child abuse, to becoming a survivor of abuse. The book is also about my story of finding my own identity and working out who I am and how I fit into everything.

It was in April 2015 that I am fully came to terms with what happened to me as a child. After many years of searching for justice and then finally getting it and completing many years of psychotherapy, I did start living a better, calmer life. How I arrived here is the story I would like to share with others. Others like me who truly deserve a better, more peaceful life. I hope that this book can bring some clarity and support to anyone else who needs it or is looking to support others with that aim. In addition, I have confidence that others will find this text an informative myth buster and it will hopefully answer some of the questions they may have.

We are now in the 'post Savile era' and there are countless people who undoubtedly have many questions. The shroud of secrecy that had been allowed to cover-up institutional paedophilia in the United Kingdom for many decades is now firmly lifting. The truth is seeping out and more facts can be learned from individual's accounts that experienced institutional abuse first hand, than from (with respect) academics studying it.

My childhood was in no way unique, but it must be said it was not run of the mill either. I had an abusive, violent childhood. I was confined to a residential boarding school in Devon from 1970 to 1975 and the same in Suffolk from 1975 to 1980. I was six years old when I was sent away from my family. My childhood was an institutional one in an all-male environment.

Through this book, I will open a window to what happened to me as a child. It will tell of the journey I have been taking from the 1970's until now. A long journey, with many twists and turns, but thankfully and story with a happier ending than I truly expected. There have been many fears and anxieties I have had to conquer along the way and a few barriers I have broken through. With the love and support of my wonderful little family, I have become the I am today. I would also like to acknowledge a Psychologist, Tom, who practises in East Kent, who has been instrumental in my progression to living a healthy and peaceful life and the best kind of friend and ally a man could have.

This has not been an easy journey for me by far, but I can say now that after all these years, I finally know who I am now. I have an identity I can relate to and I finally understand what life is about for me and how I fit into everything. One very valuable lesson I learnt along the way is - to fulfil a better life, you need to understand what is important to you. However, to truly thrive and live a full life, perhaps more importantly, we need to identify what is not important to you. If something has a negative influence on you, if something is holding you back or dragging you down, distance yourself from that influence as soon as is practicable to properly move on.

A violent and abusive childhood does leave scars. I know I will never fully get over what happened to me as a child, but I have had to learn how to live with it. The search for the truth and justice has been the driving force of my journey.

Chapter 2

How did this all begin for me?

I was born in Ramsgate on the 24th September 1964 at the Ramsgate General Hospital, which is now a site for more modern apartments in Westcliffe Road, Ramsgate. I lived in Eltham Close, Margate with my mother, father and older sister, who was one year and twenty days older than me. I have some memories from the early years. I remember some events whilst I attended Drapers Mills School and Northdown Primary School. I remember hearing about the Vietnam War and being fascinated by the war images I saw. I enjoyed drawing and colouring and my favourite sketches, which were pictures of tanks and fighter planes bombing the ground. I loved attending Saturday morning pictures at Dreamland with my sister and other children from Elham Close.

I really enjoyed spending time with my Nan and Granddad in the Tivoli area of Margate, so in many ways, a normal childhood thus far. But, then I also recall being locked in my bedroom a lot whilst at home by my mother. My sister and I shared a bedroom. The door was invariably bolted shut from the outside at night, preventing us from leaving the room to go to the toilet, etc.

I remember my father being removed from the house by the police when I was very young, somewhere between two or three years old. He did not leave peacefully; there was a violent struggle in the house. A uniformed police officer came into our bedroom and left without saying anything. That was the last time my father was a part of our family unit.

By 1969 my father had remarried and I ran away from my mother's house and spent a short time with my father and step mother Janet at their house in Glencoe Road, Margate. I enjoyed my short time there and remember happily walking to school at Drapers Mills, through from the allotments entrance in College Road, Margate. My mother did not allow me to stay with them for long and took me back home. During 1969, I had left Drapers Mills School and had attended the then, newly built Northdown County Primary Schools for a short while. Northdown School had opened at the end our road (in Tenterden Way, Margate). I did not last long at Northdown Primary and was soon excluded from them before my 6th birthday. I was only there for a few months. I do not recall too much about the school, but I do remember the headmaster of that time, Mr Profit. He shouted at me a lot. I do remember running away from the school on a couple of occasions, running down Elham Close to the bottom alley way to watch my mother driving down Millmead Road, as she went to work on the farm at St. Nicholas at Wade.

It did appear to go very wrong for me between 1969 and 1970. Having been excluded from my primary school, I have some recollections of spending my days with Mum, playing on the farm at St. Nicholas at Wade and at Northdown Farm, Margate. My mother worked on both farms and had to take me with her, so she could continue working. There were other young children there also, periodically. I recall having had a great time on the farms, playing in the haystacks and the barns, sheltering in makeshift canvass tents when it rained and enjoying the occasional interactions with the farm animals, including cats and dogs.

By 1970, I was placed in a residential boarding school at Heanton, near Barnstable in North Devon [Appendix: B, page 101], where I was desperately unhappy, frightened and very lonely.

I have vivid memories of my first few days at Heanton School, which is now an old peoples home. I hope they are treated better than we were. Heanton School closed in 1985.

I could not work out why I was there and I did not know why I could not go home. Even looking back now, all these years later I cannot really comprehend the whirlwind of activity that took place within a couple of months, that took me away from my home, my sister and my family. One minute I was at home with Viv, my sister and then I was living with a group of other boys aged six to eleven, completely confused and extremely traumatised.

When looking back at my past and researching the system that was responsible for sending me to residential schooling, 277 miles away from my family and home, was where I discovered the term 'maladjusted'

Without doubt, in my case, the term maladjusted was used as an instrument, to label me, so that I could then be dealt with in such a way that would have been difficult to do otherwise. For example: a child that requires constant attention and perhaps lacking the care and support needed at home. A child who would undoubtedly come to more harm by being kept in the home environment. This child if labelled as maladjusted could be removed from the home environment by the local authority and would not need to be returned to the home environment until they reached the age of their own responsibility – 16 years of age.

This would adequately describe my situation in 1969/1970. Having gained access to my medical records in 2013, I found out that between the age of 5 and 6, I was labelled by my mother as a difficult child. The family GP recorded that. The letters on my medical file went on to say my Mother described me as destructive and constantly misbehaved child. A child that could not be left without constant supervision.

I certainly cannot remember misbehaving or being destructive in the way described by my mother. I would go further and say that was not the case, certainly no more than what you would expect from a young boy, at that age. With some evidence of some neglect at home at the hands of my mother and with the possibility of further harm coming to me, I was taken out of the family home by Kent County Council and placed into the care of Heanton School, nr Barnstable in North Devon.

Apart from three trips home a year for short holidays, I remained at Heanton School as a boarder until 1975, when then, at the age of 11, I was transferred to another residential boarding school in Kesgrave, nr. Ipswich. [Appendix: C page 102 – 103] This boarding school was called Kesgrave Hall School. I eventually returned home again, to live in 1980 when I was 16 years old, a few months before my 17th birthday.

Chapter 3

The First Day at Boarding School and the Lasting Effect of that

At the age of 6, I recollect one day being told I was going to a new school. Before long that day arrived and I rang my Nan to say goodbye because I was going on a trip. I was very close to my Nan. At this point I was quite upbeat about the whole thing, I naively had no idea I would be staying away from home and the family. This day all started off as a great adventure.

I had a very smart new uniform, and a suitcase full of new clothes. I said goodbye to my mum and my sister, she was getting ready for her school. A lady collected me from the house, a social worker, and we got a taxi to Margate Railway Station. The train ride to London was great fun. When we got to London, we got in a taxi and went to Paddington Station.

At Paddington, we met up with some men and lots of other boys who were wearing the same uniform as me. I now know those men to be John Downing and Roy Lester, housemasters at Heanton School throughout the 1970's.

My case was put into the back of a coach, with the other cases and we got on the coach. We left Paddington and I started to feel a little apprehensive by this stage, bewildered even. I asked Mr Downing where we were going and he told me that we were driving to my new school. Mr Downing called me over to where he was seated at the back of the coach. He sat me on his knee and told me not to be frightened. It was a long trip to Devon and I sat with him for at least the first hour of the journey.

It was at this point when I was just six years of age that I became a victim, not only of sexual abuse, but a victim generally. The actions of one man, John Downing during that coach trip to Devon from London on that day in 1970, was going to have far reaching and devastating effects on me and throughout the rest of my life. John Downing became the architect of my potential destruction. From this point, my entire life was moulded.

Everything that was going to happen to me over the next ten years of my childhood, with these people, was set in motion right there on that coach trip, on the knee of John Downing.

Was I chosen by Downing? Had he studied my personal file – sent by Kent County Council?

Was he aware that there was no father figure in my life? and that I had been sent to Heanton because of a dysfunctional relationship with my Mother?

Did I fit the right criteria for a predatory paedophile to make an immediate move against me? There was no grooming required here, I was under Downing's direct care for the next 5 years.

I believe that I was labelled by Downing, at that point, as a child who was vulnerable and as such I would be able to be susceptible to indecent assaults and inappropriate sexual activity. This of course became a reality for me, with the degree and frequency of the physical and indecent assaults against me increasing over the next decade.

For a considerable amount of the journey on the coach I was on Downing's knee. He spent much of the time rubbing his fingers across the front of my trousers and between my legs. I could not understand why he would be doing this and felt too frightened to say anything to him or even move. I was frozen in that position. After at least an hour, I wet myself, soaking his lap. He became very angry and carried me over to a free seat, throwing me into the seat.

When we finally arrived at the school, it was a getting late. I was still unaware at this stage that I would be staying here. I was oblivious to the fact that this was a boarding school. Why had no one explained this to me?

I had no idea I could not go home. Try to imagine this scenario through the mind of a six-year-old boy. A six-year-old boy who was now panicking. Vulnerable, frightened and very confused as well.

What was happening to me? In addition to man on the coach, John Downing, who was clearly gratifying himself by rubbing my genitals, I had wet myself on him, which made him very angry and that was equally traumatic for me. I was now unpacking my suitcase in this alien building, instead of making my way back home.

We had an evening meal and we were lead to a washroom, where I washed in a large, open room that had loads of sinks in it. I was led to a bedroom which housed 8 beds and told to get into one of the beds. My case and clothes were already there. I told the man present, Kenneth Scott (I believe) that I wanted to go home. He said that was not possible. The lights were turned out. I remember crying uncontrollably for hours, as did many other boys. A few hours later, quite late at night, I was led through a dark corridor and up a single, small flight of stairs to a telephone in a booth. This was in the staff quarters of the school.

There were several adults present. One of them said to me your mum is on the telephone, you can talk to her. I was relieved to hear my mum's voice and still sobbing, I told her I wanted to come home. She told me it was not possible and said she would see me when I came home for holidays. When the phone line went dead, the man told me to get back to the bedroom and said he would take me there. I was hysterical at this point and said I wanted to talk to my mum more. He said 'No' and I was carried back to my bed. I did not understand why my mother had not told me I was not going to be coming home.

Why wasn't Mum there to protect me?

Who was going the protect me?

I wanted someone to tell me everything was going to be ok. This was a living nightmare, a very, very bad dream. It was in no way made clear to me that I was staying away from home. I did not understand why this was happening and I sobbed myself to sleep that first night.

That was the one and only night I cried myself to sleep in the boarding school system. From that day onwards, I vowed never to show any emotion to these people and for the entire ten years in the boarding system, I never did. What was more tragic, I think, I also vowed never to show my mother any emotion either. I could not rely on her and I would not allow her to let me down again. I could not forgive her for abandoning me. I had resigned myself to the fact that the World was not a safe place and no one in it could be trusted.

I had gone from a happy go lucky 'normal' little boy and in one single day I had become a frightened six-year-old boy who had suddenly realised he was all alone. There was no one to support me, no one to protect me and there was no one I could rely on – only myself.

This was a life changing day for me, a milestone in my life. The catastrophic culmination of a sequence of events that transported me from juvenile innocence to cautious and apprehensive adulthood, within the rising and setting of one sun. I had to grow up in an instance to be able to protect myself and to be able to survive. No child should ever be placed in that position.

I am drawn to an article by Katie Englehart - which talks of so-called *Boarding School Syndrome* [Appendix: U page 168 - 186]. Her writing explores the syndrome and talk of Dr Joy Schaverien and Nick Duffell. A quote from Dr Schaverien, appears to resonate with what I have said above:

"Even when not mistreated, being left in the care of strangers is traumatic... A shell is formed to protect the vulnerable self from emotion that cannot be processed. Whilst appearing to conform to the system, a form of unconscious splitting is acquired as a means of keeping the true self hidden... The child then makes no emotional demands but also no longer recognises the need for intimacy. The self begins to become inaccessible; 'Boarding School Syndrome' develops. The syndrome starts to fester on Day 1; there is loneliness, dejection. But boarders learn to be stoic: they pull themselves up by their bootstraps and take it all on the chin." The article 'Shed a Tear for Britain's Messed Up Boarding School Kids' can be read in [Appendix G: page 113 – 119] other links to Dr Joy Schaverien and Nick Duffell can be found in [Appendix F: page 111 - 112].

I recently gave some thought to the feelings and emotions I associated with the three short holidays a year we were given whilst at Heanton and Kesgrave Hall in the 1970's. The holidays consisted of a total of 9 weeks a year, spread over Easter, Summer and Christmas.

What was apparent now, when putting my mind to it, was that I did not look forward to seeing my mother when having a holiday break from the school. When I returned home to Margate for the short breaks, it was a welcomed release from the violence and abuse I suffered at the schools, but nothing else. I looked forward to seeing my sister, I missed her and of course my Nan and Grandfather.

Equally, when it was time to return to the schools I did not mourn the separation from my mother. I just did not look forward to returning to the abusive environment of the schools either, or seeing the people I knew were in them, waiting for me. This is very sad on reflection, but an indication of the awareness that there was no bond between my mother and I during those horrendous years and for many years to follow.

Conditioning myself never to show others any emotion, has not always served me well throughout my adult life. I am certain this conditioning would have contributed to many of the mental health problems I have exhibited, in addition to several failed relationships.

Bottling up any emotional response, positive or negative is not good for anybody. It also gives a false impression to others and on occasions fails to deal with a situation that perhaps needs dealing with. From that early age, I had chosen to cry in private. I very quickly discovered that to be sad or upset and to show this to others was a weakness. A weakness that others can manipulate or use to gain your confidence and in doing so, you will invite them to hurt you more. Paedophiles and abusers of young boys are adept at looking for weaknesses in potential victims. Any slight chinks in a small child's armour will provide an opportunity for them to provide temporary solace or support. This is one of the main areas of approach, for them to gain a child's confidence.

Other traits I took away from my institutional past, was suffering from frequent bouts of anger and violent outburst, which included attempting to inflict damage to physical objects, I had for many years inflicted harm on myself by punching brick walls and other impenetrable objects. This caused a few relationship issues for me, as well as inflicting considerable injury to my hands and wrists.

It is little wonder I have had many issues throughout the years. In addition to the suspected, early deprivation I suffered up to the age of six and the 'boarding school syndrome' that I would have undoubtedly developed after being placed into that cold, hard regime from such an early age - there is of course the actual legacy I took with me, from the abusive teachers and carers, who had preyed on me throughout the 1970's.

The inheritance of guilt, disgust and anger that I carried within me, which for 30 years or so developed into a constant inner battle, with an inherent desire to self-destruct. This was a long battle, a daily battle entwined into my everyday professional and adult life. It was something I had learn to live with, it became part of my normal routine and something that on many occasions I got very weary of. I became the master of disguise. This was post-traumatic stress disorder (PTSD), I just did not know I had it, or a certainly gave it no credence.

Some days I was left feeling that I needed to escape and shut myself away. Being with others, speaking with others became unbearable. The need to distant myself became greater and when this is not possible to do so and then I would become moody, snappy and generally unpleasant to be around. Anyone who has known me throughout the years will probably recognise these former traits of mine. In the past, this did make me aggressive to. Wholly unpleasant to experience and I should imagine, very unpleasant for those around me.

Chapter 4

Life in the Boarding School System (1970 to 1980)

'We never lose our demons, we just learn how to live with them'

Boarding school was a very lonely and dangerous place in the 1970's. It was a place where to survive, you had to mature quickly, become less dependent on others and learn very fast, how to be fully self-reliant. Because of this, there was no natural development for me as a young boy, from the age of 6 years old. Everything about boarding schools for me was false. A veneer of respectable individuals and academia, providing a convincing disguise for a malicious institution, riddled with perversion and governed by hostility.

I had two clear choices in both Heanton and Kesgrave Hall School, as they were both run in an identical way. The regimes were in fact connected. I either conformed fully with the regime, by submitting and relinquishing all and any of my individual traits or I retained some essence of personality and rode the rollercoaster of existence that followed. A life of violence and distress where I singled myself out as a target constantly. I was, I believe, my own worst enemy in that respect. The harder they came down on me, the more stubborn I became. The more they attempted to hurt me, the less I was prepared to show any emotion to them. I was a child that refused to conform to a system I despised.

Discipline after all is born from respect. How could I respect these adults that hurt me, humiliated and belittled me? How could I respect these carers who made me do disgusting things and left me feeling dirty and frightened? This was a system that destroyed its own structure by operating under a culture of harm and criminality.

Gross mismanagement of the highest order, allowed to proliferate openly as the schools were part of a bigger paedophile movement that plague every aspect of structure and culture within the United Kingdom in the 1970's.

Both schools, Heanton and Kesgrave Hall, demanded full and unchallenged submission from the boys, as they wished for the boys to be embedded into the fabric of the school. This was easy for some of the boys and other boys were constantly drugged to keep them suppressed.

Other boys, much like myself gave a superficial impression of conforming. Creating an altered personality that served us well on many occasions, but even this essentially deployed deceptiveness, occasionally faltered. This was when the real violence erupted.

The strongest of boys had a limit to their strength and willpower, but we all had a breaking point. Eventually we our strength would fail and eventually they would win.

I do wonder, if some of the more voracious paedophiles amongst the male staff members at Heanton and Kesgrave, the alpha paedophiles - John Downing [appendix H: page 120 - 122] and Alan Stancliffe [appendix: I page 123], had a specific appetite for the untamed, spirited child. Nurturing the spirit and then breaking it. A sort of 'forbidden fruit tasting sweeter'. I think there may be some basis to this argument sadly.

Alan Stancliffe for example, a frequent and main abuser of me between 1976 and 1979 – One side of him was an 'Uncle Stan' figure, as he was also known. The jovial woodwork and technical drawing teacher. The housemaster and out of school hours' carer. Your friend who periodically gave you single squares of Bournville chocolate (slabs as we knew them) which were highly prized. Stan the Man who created cassette tapes of the Moody Blues for his 'special' boys. That side of Stancliffe changed dramatically, when he became 'Stancliffe, the sexual predator' who had an insatiable appetite for fulfilling his own sexual pleasure, by indecently assaulting young boys. Most serious attacks were at night, when most boys would be asleep and he usually came to you stinking of whisky. Out of all the paedophiles I encountered, from both schools, Stancliffe was the only one I can recall, who brought a small foot stall along with him. His comfort was clearly a serious issue for him, as he interfered with us.

The way both Heanton School and Kesgrave Hall School were run, engineered a hive of seemingly cloned, unfeeling children that questioned nothing and complied with all and any requests placed on them. As previously said, that did not mean they got that from all the boys that were sent to the schools, indeed there was a small faction of non-conformists in both schools. Boys that paid a high price to retain some of their character and spirit.

I for one truly believe that I never gave 'them' all of me. It was because of this of course, that I suffered more than some. It was because of this, naturally that I was singled out by the Alpha's. It was because of this, that my mental health had suffered for many decades following on from my time at the schools. I suffered a combination of mental health illness, born from a complex and lengthy trauma.

To summarise – 1970's boarding school was a hard place to survive in and to be able to do so, you had to be either extremely hard or totally submissive.

The school's themselves, controlled principally by Vivienne Davis, Director/Headmaster of Heanton and Director of Kesgrave Hall [Appendix: B/C pages 101 - 103] were marketed as centres for excellence in the field of developing maladjusted boys, through the employment of innovative pedagogical methods and 'good old fashion' discipline.

The reality, as widely known today, was that Heanton School and Kesgrave Hall School concentrated too much emphasis on maintaining discipline and any good practices that were achieved there, were to be completely subverted by the resident paedophile ring.

Heanton School and Kesgrave Hall School were not that distant from what you would imagine a military academy to be like. A highly structured, dictator led environment, that had strict uniform codes and enforced practices. The motivation driving the Schools ethos, was created from fiercely adhering to custom borne rituals, like everyone had a place and everyone had a part to play in its structure. I often liken it to something between the 1972 to 1974 BBC television series of 'Colditz Castle' or the Hogwarts School of Wizardry from Harry Potter, without the sorcery of course.

We slept in dormitories, generally housing 5 to 8 beds spread out in an open room, apart from senior rooms at Kesgrave Hall School, where older boys had cubicles, with beds, lockers and desks for writing and studying on.

In the mornings, we were woken collectively and after grabbing your wash kit, each dormitory was taken to a wash room or shower room, for supervised washing. Likewise, in the evening. In the evening following on from collective showering, each dormitory would be settled into bed and a period of reading would be given before lights out. During the night, a 'duty' housemaster would patrol the upper landing area and would sleep in the staff quarter on the same floor of the school.

Breakfast, Dinner and Teatime meals were all eaten in the Dining Hall. This was a very regimented process, with heads of table being responsible for serving out meals and maintaining discipline.

Morning assembly saw the headmaster and senior management team appearing in front of the assembled school in full black gown and mortar board headdress. Hymns were sung from hymn books and directed from numerical signage displayed at the front of the hall, much the same as in most CofE churches and a daily motivational speech would be read out also. Another specious facade of a seemingly decent and reputable school, with an historic culture that was worthy of maintaining.

The senior management team were entirely complicit in the abuse that took place, both sexual and physical. Apart from actively being part of it, on many occasions, they were frequently told of it by both boys and other appalled staff members.

There were occasions when the police were informed of sexual and violent assaults, by some boys and staff members. These individuals had a habit of disappearing shortly afterwards, never to be seen at the schools again and no explanation being given for their disappearance.

Music really was a life saver.

There were not many things I had control of whilst in the boarding school system, but one thing I did have, no one could take away from me. I had music. From my early school's days in Devon, through to the Kesgrave Hall years, I lost myself in music. It was comforting, it was at times forbidden, but most of all, I could call it 'mine'.

I have included here a blog I wrote in February 2015, which really captures my thoughts back then, on the importance of music to me:

Posted my WordPress Blog on February 14, 2015 by lwe1964:

1969 was a dark time in my history. One day in late September 1969, at the age of 6, I went on an adventure. I was sold this vision of 'you are going to see your new school'. What I was not made clear of, was that the school was a privately-owned boarding school in Heanton, North Devon and I would not be returning to my life at home with my sister and family for another 10 years. Short visits home were going to become short holidays, in contrast to what was normality for other children. Being 275.4 miles away from home is quite a shock to a 6-year-old boy.

The indecent assaults started on the very first day, on the coach trip from Paddington Station to Heanton. The beatings and humiliation was not far behind. This soon became the norm. It was only a few days in the system before I started to cut myself off from all those around me. Withdrawing into myself for my own protection. Disassociating myself from all that was happening to me and around me. OCD soon set in.

This was my way of retaining some control for myself, in the chaos I had been plunged into. I had a small transistor radio, not dissimilar to the one in the blog picture. I cannot recall if I brought the radio with me from home, or if I swapped or bartered for it from one of the other boys. The radio was my best friend and listening to music became the best distraction ever. I was at Heanton School until 1975 and the attended Kesgrave Hall School, Ipswich until 1980. The radio was always with me and night it served to transport me to another world. A world of great music and lyrics that helped me forgot my life.

At night, we slept in dormitories which held between 6 and 9 pupils. I placed the radio under my pillow and lost myself in the music. The early seventies were a great time for music, with Fleetwood Mac, Pink Floyd, Deep Purple, Blue Oyster Cult, Uriah Heap, to name but a few bringing some pleasure to my life. Some of the European Stations were great then and easily accessible in the medium wave band. The indecent assaults happened virtually every night, with the assailants being male members of staff. You knew when they were coming and you remained silent whilst they were with you. It was not worth trying to stop events, it only made things worse. These men were physically bigger and stronger. Let events progress quickly and then they would leave you. That was the best way, it was going to happen anyway.

The radio served you well when these things were happening to others in the room. Pressing your ear into the pillow, with the radio secreted underneath, you could ignore what was happening to another boy and concentrate on the music. I could not have imagined how I would have coped back then without music to lose myself in. In the same way, over the years since leaving the last school, I have still enjoyed music and enjoy a wide spectrum of genres today.

The blog I wrote for a short while **No More Secrets,** [Appendix: K page 126 - 145] was a forerunner to this text. I enjoyed writing the blogs and found that to be helpful to me. Towards the latter blogs, I was involved in the court processes with John Downing and decided to concentrate my writing in the book project.

On the music theme, I have recently had some tattoo's done on my left forearm. Truly symbolic symbols that celebrate one of the main albums I lost myself in, all those years ago and the closure of my journey today. The album of my childhood, Pink Floyd's Dark Side of the Moon, still very much rates as my number 1 album today and always will do. The tracks themselves soothe and transport my mind into total submission. When listening to it, on headphones preferably, all conscious thoughts and stresses are instantly replaced with relaxation and no agenda. A chillout and lose yourself in the music moment.

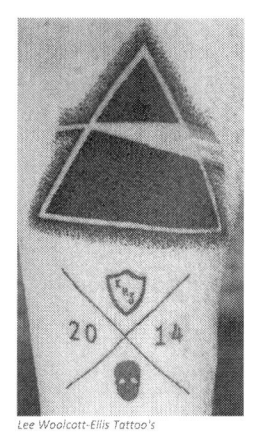

The lyrics and sense of the album itself connects with me, in a meaningful way also. The description of it provided in Wikipedia explains this well for me:

Lee Woolcott-Ellis Tattoo's

'*The Dark Side of the Moon is the eighth album by English rock band Pink Floyd, released on 1 March 1973 by Harvest Records. The album built on ideas explored in earlier recordings and live shows, but lacks the extended instrumental excursions following the departure of founding member and principal contributor, Syd Barrett, in 1968, that characterised their earlier work. It thematically explores conflict, greed, the passage of time, and mental illness, the latter partly inspired by Barrett's deteriorating mental state.*' https://en.wikipedia.org/wiki/The_Dark_Side_of_the_Moon

We all have a dark side. The second tattoo, a symbol I designed whilst sitting on a train one day. Once again, a very symbolic of my journey. The diagonal crossed lines signify 'the end' [X], closed off. Finished.

'2014' was the year I properly exposed John Downing to the nations press and we got him into Exeter Crown Court, to face up to his crimes; the completion of my Heanton School journey.

'2014' was the year I completed my Kesgrave Hall School journey also. My active part in Operation Garford came to an end with the deaths of Alan Stancliffe, Kenneth Scott (Wheatley), Michael Lafford and David Brockman.

The 'KHS' shield is self-explanatory and is there to represent the school blazer badge.

The 'skull', as much as it could represent the deaths of the individuals mentioned above, has a far more important and meaningful part to play in the tattoo. The most important part. The Skull symbolises the overcoming of the challenges I faced when dealing with my past, including my own looming death, which I faced at the lowest moments. It symbolises strength and power, and offers me protection (some people who know me may note that I have many skulls on me, mainly in jewellery). It is said that the skull symbol can symbolise the death of an old life, a past that has been defeated and a change for the better has occurred. A rebirth so to speak. I would say that was highly appropriate.

My mother recently uncovered a school report of mine [Appendix: W page 188], from Kesgrave Hall School, Summer 1979. This was from the middle term, leading up to my final year at Kesgrave Hall – The forerunning term of my GCE and CSE preparation work. The validity of that report, in fact any school report coming out of that establishment is difficult for me to comprehend the rationale in play.

My academic abilities and effort have been graded by school teachers, many of whom in addition to playing their part in the pedagogical process, were also sexually abusing me or mistreating constantly. It is hard to believe that any learning took place at all and that this educational establishment was brash enough to continue the facade of respectability. The comments and marks provided by the majority of teachers in that 1979 report mean absolutely nothing. They have no basis in reality and if anything, are an indication of how the staff were able to continue in the farce that was Kesgrave Hall School, ignorant of the impact of the actions and any potential damage these caused. For those staff members, their own personal desires and perverted pleasures far out-weighed any responsibility the bore.

I achieved well in my GCE and CSE results, remarkably and excelled much further academically, when attending further and higher education, as an adult. I attained GCE's in English (Lit/Lang), Wood Work, Art, Geography, Religious Education and CSE's in Maths and Technical Drawing, surprisingly. Academically, I flourished on leaving the boarding school system. I shunned any educational establishment for many years, but attended a number of courses at Thanet Technical College (no East Kent College), where I studied Law (GSCE) in 1997 and Web Design and Counselling Skills training from 1999 onwards.

In 2000, I went to University (Canterbury Christ Church) and signed up for four years – completing a HND in Multimedia Technologies & Development, a BA (Hons) in Digital Media (RFTV) [2:1] and a PGCE, specialising in post compulsory education (IT and Public Services).

Chapter 5

Living with me was Not Easy
(Childhood Sexual Abuse and Mental Illness)

For far too many years of my adult life, I never thought I could be happy. A truly horrifying attitude to live with. Worse than that, I believed I was not allowed to be happy either. This installed mindset is one of the typical consequences for an adult who was continually abused sexually, as a child.

An interesting blog I read, by Gloria Siess – entitled *'Childhood Sexual Abuse Causes Physical Brain Damage: An Alarming New Study'* suggests that the extensive sexual abuse I suffered as a child, may have damaged my brain and made me permanently unhappy. This article, I believe has some merit. I have added it for reference purposes and it can be read in [Appendix: E page: 109-110]

I had post-traumatic stress disorder (PTSD) for 32 years, but I did not fully recognise this or understand it, until a psychologist explained it to me a few years ago. I knew I was different from other people and behaved differently, because I constantly avoided the company of others and channelled most of my energies into striving to be on my own.

I did not feel like a proper man and I have always hated socialising as an adult and rarely did so. Because of this, virtually over 30 years of this, I still do not find it easy to socialise in large groups and frequently make excuses not to go to events. This is habituated behaviour.

My 10 years at boarding school had stripped me of any identity, recognisable or fashioned. I did not know who I was and I had no understanding of how I fitted in with everything else and everyone around me. Because I left the boarding school system in 1980 without any real-life experience, communication or interpersonal skills, I floundered around for decades, experimenting with all and every type of relationship I encountered, professional and personal.

Thinking back, when I left boarding school a few months before my 17th birthday, I felt angry and distrustful of everything and everyone. I felt very sad and alone. I suffered from a continuous raging pain in my head. Not so much a headache type pain, it was as though voices were shouting constantly at me, inside my head. Loud and undefinable noise that constantly drove me to distraction. I found back then that only additional and immediate physical pain offered instantaneous respite from these angry demons inside me.

I found myself punching brick walls and physically destroying things with my hands and feet, often leading to physical injury. Headbutting doors and walls was frequent and undertaken in conjunction with very strong compulsions to do so. I had obsessive compulsive disorder (OCD), with compulsion being more prominent than obsession. I was also very skilled at building things up, from every facet of my adult life, so I could purposely destroy them. This of course was another form of self-abuse.

When I left the boarding school/care system in 1980, I had not been properly equipped by that system to deal with 'adult' life in any fashion. I had no idea how to properly interact with others at all, as I was not equipped with the necessary and broad interpersonal skills required by a young adult. I did not possess any confidence to help with any of life's everyday experiences.

I think what was even more worrying was, that I did not hold any profound value of any kind, to my life. The need for self-preservation was missing in me. Quite terrifyingly the desire to survive and thrive was not something I left the institutions of the 1970's with. If anything, thinking back, I had always harboured a realisation, that one day I would end up killing myself and through the darker periods of my early adult life, I would have willingly welcomed it.

The later becoming highly apparent, as I muddled my way through my 20's into my 30's. I was always angry and would recklessly enter into dangerous situations, without any forethought of the consequences to myself and on occasions to others with me or around me. I had for many years, whilst serving with Kent Police, gone into volatile and violent situations, when it would have been wiser to have waited for back up, without considering the potential impact on my safety and gave no thought to the consequences of that.

It was whilst watching a documentary in 2013, on one of the Sky TV channels about OCD, I suddenly realised that I had exhibited many indicators of this condition, from the age of six. It was present in me, it would seem from my first few days at Heanton School in 1970. I had no recollection of any traits prior to that. I am guessing it was my way of maintaining some control in my life, as it was clearly being dominated by my school masters and others in my new life.

The effects of attending boarding school and the historic abuse I suffered throughout those years, affected me very badly and followed me into my adult life, establishing as a very complex trauma, later to be better classified as PTSD. In addition to OCD, this also manifested in me continuously, through the following character traits:

- Aggressive mood swings
- Deep and very dark depressions
- Lack of emotion
- Being very distant
- Self-harming
- Damaging property
- Anxiety and Sadness
- Bereavement issues (loss of innocence and childhood)

When giving the subject much thought, I could not imagine for an instance, what it must be like to live with me over the years since I left the boarding school system. But then, I also realise now, that I had even had trouble living with myself throughout those post boarding school years.

It has only been over more recent years, that I have had some clarity of thought on these matters and a better understanding of them. Some perception of what I had done, over the years and why I had been compelled to act in those ways. It is only been a few years since I started to really start to understand who I am now and what life is about for me. I am now comfortable in the knowledge that I am loved by my immediate family and that I can love them back as well. It is very sad that it has taken me nearly 40 years to get to this point and although I was very embittered by this, I have since been able to move on from that.

My behaviour and the origin of that, can only be contributed to a direct effect of being mentally, physically and sexually abused by individuals, in the boarding school system operating in the UK in the 1970's. Boarding school syndrome [see Appendix: U page 168 - 186] itself is destructive enough to a young boy's development and ability to fully interact in their adult, post-school world, without the added developmental complications created by the abuse.

I received extensive cognitive behavioural therapy (CBT) [see Appendix: V page 187] sessions, between 2013 and 2015, which has without question helped me. This in conjunction with facing my demons (pursuing direct justice through the criminal justice system) has also played a big part in shaping my true personality and my future happiness.

Those deep, darkest secrets that had remained locked away for such a long time were carefully brought into the forefront of my mind – into the here and now. The cognitive therapy I had undertaken for just over two and a half years worked better than I ever imagined it would. For this to have worked so well, I was clearly committed to the process, revealing details of things that had been tucked away tightly, to the psychologist. Details of things that happened to me, recalling by whom, where and when these things happened and recounting how these made me feel then and now. Really very difficult at times and very upsetting, but so very necessary for the improvement to the quality of life it offered.

My partner and the children were very tolerant of my 'moods' as they called it. For that I have always been grateful and love them the more for it. Thankfully, those days and the dark moods are a thing of the past. Granted I still have some down days occasionally. Days when my mind conspires and schemes against me, but I always try very hard to rein these thoughts in and not let it impact on my daily tasks. I will after all never be able to forget much of what had happened to me, as a child.

I did receive some counselling from the NHS Mental Health service in the late 1990's, at Westbrook House, which I attended on and off for a couple of years but, as I recall now, I do not believe I fully committed to that. I certainly didn't open-up as much or reveal nearly as much detail of my abusive past then, as I did with the Psychologist sessions I received a few years ago.

The psychotherapy was of immense benefit to me. I would recommend psychotherapy to anyone who is considering taking the path of speaking out about what happened to them as a child. NHS mental health services as opposed to other, privately run organisations. The main reason I site NHS services is that their Psychologists can generally offer an open-ended course of CBT (or other therapies), instead of time restricted counselling, usually 7 to 9 sessions. Historic abuse is unquestionably a complex trauma, with far reaching mental health implications that condition the victims to be untrusting and evasive. Speaking from personal experience, it took me longer than 7 sessions to build a full relationship with the Psychologist I was seeing. A trust based relationship where I was happy to talk about my deepest thoughts and issues. I believe it would not have been possible for me to have revealed any substantial information of my past, or discussed how it made me feel to just anyone. I knew I needed a more committed approach and it took me a fair few sessions with Tom, before I properly opened-up. The commitment to this therapy must be open and equal from both parties of course.

The best advice I could offer would be for anyone speaking out, is to seek the assistance of their GP initially and ask for help. This is the best way to ensure a supportive network is put in place to help them deal with reliving the ordeals they suffered as a child. The process to see a professional psychiatrist/councillor is generally through referral only and the easiest and quickest route would be via a doctor. It is worth bearing in mind however that regional mental health services are generally oversubscribed and there is likely to be lengthy waiting list. The referral process can be expedited if other factors are present, such as a danger to the individual's welfare, etc.

Professional Lee

On reflection, when thinking about my professional undertakings from 1980 to 2014, I know that my mental health would have impacted on my professional relationships, on many occasions.

I can imagine that working with me throughout the past three decades could not have been easy for my close colleagues, at times. That is not to say it a major issue. I have of course had many positive experiences at work over the decades, achieved considerably and may many, lifelong friends. There would have been times when my mental state would not have been entirely healthy and numerous occasions when some components of my PTSD would have been triggered. On these instances, as much as would have attempted to hide my symptomatic, behavioural traits, there would have been numerous occasions where I would not have been able to.

My mood swings would increase and decrease in response to other influences being present, leading me to occasionally over-react to the smallest of things, displaying some aggressiveness and thankfully only occasionally, exhibit a destructive temper that must have shocked more than a few people. I would note here, with most outbursts, this was always followed by feelings regret and remorse from me, although I very much expect this atonement was invariably, always missed by those who deserved to really see it.

It is evident that since leaving the institutional educational system in 1980; the professional engagement choices I made and the employment roads I had followed, had certainly helped me mask the psychological disorder and deep emotions that drove me daily. I invariably chose a uniformed profession, or aimed to be undertaking a role that gave me some authority over others. This altered-persona allowed me to be someone else, to escape from the unhappy and lonely person I really was and to create the Lee I wanted to be. In my career path, I have worn a police uniform, a railway uniform, a security uniform or a smart shirt and tie. In most cases, these roles allowed me to create a more confident and successful Lee, where during a lot of these times, I was principally anything but.

I think it is important also to note that, not all situations can be 'controlled' effectively by us. Over the years there have been plenty of individuals I met on a regular basis, at work, who clearly would go out of their way to ruin my day. This would be their agenda impacting upon mine and as much as I am prepared to put my hands up and admit, at times I reacted badly, I will not accept fully that my poor mental health, or conditioned behaviour was solely responsible for given situations arising. I have a low tolerance to bullies and will always challenge them, most of the time when I observe the bullying of others. This has not always served me well and made me a target on occasions. Whether adopting this position is the right thing to do, or not, I believe it is a matter for my conscience. The stand I have adopted against bullies is a characteristic element, that has been fuelled by my past.

Many years ago, someone said to me 'You don't have to like everybody' and as much as I have remembered these words, I sadly cannot remember who said them to me. This small comment or off-hand remark has remained with me for decades and it is something that have used frequently to protect my inner peace.

I am sure I cannot be the only person who can say honestly, that there are some people, who after 5 minutes of meeting that person for the first time, you just know they are 'not your kind of person'. This is not intended to signify a self-imposed snobbish characteristic or indicate an air of superiority, it is merely a snap judgement based on a dynamic assessment of the person or persons present, in each scenario. This verdict can and sometimes does, change with time.

I believe you should always trust your own initial judgment and in my experiences, that has rarely proved me wrong. It has taken me too many years to realise that I had wasted so much effort and time, in trying to win certain people over. The same goes for endlessly trying to engage with people, who clearly did not like me or refused to acknowledge me, for whatever reason they had. That was of course their prerogative. The outcome from tireless perseverance on my part, in most cases did not win them over and left me feeling angry or upset because of the negative influence of all of that wasted time and energy expended in the process. The moral of the story here, is that no one is worth compromising your own mental well-being.

This is more than just worrying about what people think about you. I had suffered from this poorly constructed sense of correctness for many years, but thankfully I do not do so today. For many years, following a career of police and security training, I have always relied on snap judgements, when time constraints did not allow an intelligence informed approach. When engaging in a situation or with people, I was trained to undertake a 'dynamic risk assessment' to quickly gauge all factors influencing the situation and to identify potential dangers. This is a process I try to employ when dealing with people also. It sadly doesn't always work, but then we cannot always factor in influences external from our control. Even with a clearly defined, operational internal radar, set to identify those caustic to me, I still allow some into my influence my wellbeing. Is that human nature?

Negative people like any negative influence should be avoided at all cost. When that is not possible, keep engagement short, sharp and on a business level and do not divulge any personal information, to better protect your mental wellbeing. Look after your mental state and don't let others pull you down.

My partner's perspective
(Living with an historic abuse survivor and their PTSD)

This section has been written by my partner of 17 years, Amanda Woolcott.

The book represents the truth about what happened to me as a child and what effects this had on me, so I felt it was important for Mandy to write about what is has been like living with me for the past 17 years. As expected it has not been an altogether pleasant experience for her. The love and support she has shown me over the rough times has cemented her commitment to our relationship. I truly do not think that I would be here today, to write this book, if it was not for the love and support of Mandy.

Lee asked me to write a small section of his book for him and although I was hesitant at first, once we discussed the reason for the request, I was happy to support this. Lee asked me to write an account of how child sexual abuse can affect a victim beyond the years of abuse taking place. This of course relates to my relationship with Lee over the past 17 years.

The harm that is caused by these horrific monsters who prey on children affects more than just the victim. The harm they create has an enduring effect on the victim's family and loved ones also.

We have lived together for 17 years and I love Lee very much. I could have quite easily have left him though, many times over the years we have been together, as it hasn't always been an easy or comfortable relationship and I have written below a small summary of why this was.

Living with a victim of historic child sexual abuse is not easy at all on a relationship and it takes a lot of patience to fully understand what they are going through and how that is impacting on you.

Being supportive of someone who has major trust issues, means sometimes you should leave them alone and wait for them to come back to you. Reading the signs, listening to them and being there for them is the key. This naturally, takes a lot of getting used to and it is completely different from what I would call a 'standard' relationship. The rules are completely different. Lee for example is a very loving and caring person, but then at times, he can be completely cut off and totally uncommunicative. The therapy Lee had with the psychologist was a great help and it is nice to have the loving Lee back again. I know Lee will never truly get over what happened to him and although he has probably told me more than he has told anyone else, I cannot imagine for an instance what he went through as a child and how that made him feel.

When I first met with Lee in early 2000, I knew he wanted to be very open and honest with me about what had happened to him in the past. He found it difficult to tell me about his schooling, but gradually told me some of his experiences. He said this was important for him. He said he trusted me and he wanted our relationship to last.

Lee had come out of a very tumultuous and abusive relationship and was feeling very raw. He had not long appeared in Court where he had succeeded in getting a conviction against Alan Stancliffe for numerous indecent assaults against him. He told me all about Alan Stancliffe and I grew to despise this man for everything he had done to Lee and the additional ordeal he had made Lee endure with three Court appearances. Lee also had some counselling therapy at the Westbrook Centre and the last thing he was looking for, by his own admission, was another relationship. Lee had been on and off antidepressant tablets for many years.

Looking back at those early days of our relationship, it would be fair to say neither of us was looking for a relationship, but we were seemingly thrown together and we both found it impossible to ignore the feelings and chemistry between us.

The first six months or so of our relationship was ok. The honeymoon period to coin a phrase, even though we were fighting off considerable external interference from many quarters and then we moved in together.

It was then Lee's real personal traits came to the forefront. He was highly regimented in every respect of daily life. He had anger management issues, some OCD problems and was totally unable to manage finances. When trying to talk to Lee about the issues that were coming to the forefront of our relationship, he became very angry and closed off. Explosive rages and running off were common, followed by periods of feeling very sorrow for the way he had behaved and being over apologetic. He was self-harming also and frequently punched walls. I was attempting to manage this while keeping the house and looking after four children. Three who lived with us and another who came to stay every other weekend.

Despite all this Lee could realise a lifelong ambition and attended Canterbury Christ Church University, when they opened their Broadstairs Campus. Feeling a bit cautious at first, at the age of 36, Lee felt supported enough to take on a full time HND course in Multimedia Technologies and Development and a BA (Hons) course in Digital Media, as a full-time student.

Looking back, this career move of Lee's was a major additional strain on our relationship. We lived on the breadline throughout the time Lee was studying and we relied heavily on University grants and bursaries to keep the house and support the children from the year 2000 until the year 2004, as Lee also signed up for an additional PGCE course at Christ Church.

In these four years, there were good times, where we were close and Lee was the most loving partner. Then there were the periods where Lee descended into full self-destruction and became insular and totally cut us all off. During these 'dark' periods, as Lee called them, I virtually became a single parent. I took everything on and managed everyone, including Lee.

It was during this time, another major event occurred. Lee's Son who lived with us asked to go back and live with his mother. He had been with Lee since 1996 and Lee had looked after him as a single parent. Lee had been granted custody through a Court order and gained full parental rights over his Son, following a very acrimonious divorce from his former wife (in his words). Not wanting to stand in his Son's way, and complying with his Son's wishes, Lee allowed him to go and live with his mother in 2003. This was a major blow for Lee and he suffered greatly for it. Lee's dark moods became more prevalent and Lee became more distant. Lee was again taking antidepressant tablets.

Lee's general health suffered, as did his mental health. He put considerable weight on and he clearly had no respect for himself and at times sadly, for us too. Our physical relationship became intermittent and was always on Lee's terms. Although there were no physical issues, in that area, there were mental health problems.

Lee was working at the Queen's Centre for Clinical Studies at QEQM Hospital, Margate in 2004. He got the job of Audio Visual Technician and enjoyed the role there. Sadly, it was a pro-rata position and the 18 hours a week put us into financial difficulty once again. Lee applied for numerous other, fulltime positions, and successfully gained a position as a CCTV Manager working with Southeastern Trains (Engineering) in 2005. Lee was pleased to be back on the Railway, as he had previously been employed by British Rail as a Train Guard. There were many people still there he knew.

Our financial position started to improve, but Lee's hours were very long. As his role with Southeastern progressed, he became lead manager for On-Train Surveillance and was constantly on call out, day and night. Reacting to major incidents and national security issues, Lee was hardly ever at home, or when he was, he was tired and distant. Lee's spending habits spiralled out of control and he got tangled up in many credit agreements that he could not manage properly.

In late 2005, we had a daughter. Lee adored her and still does. Having the baby was a positive thing for both Lee and our relationship. Lee threw himself into his work shortly after and on many occasions, this was to the detriment of both me and the children.

Because of the debts Lee had accumulated, he took on additional work at Amadeus Night Club in 2008, which meant we saw Lee even less. Lee's mental health was very poor during this period and he was completely neglecting me in every respect and the children. He was totally neglecting himself also. Living on the edge of sleep and relying heavily on caffeine tablets and energy drinks. Lee was addicted to the Gym. He was burning himself out.

It was as though I was a single parent again. Lee could not be relied on for anything at home. In 2009 things really spiralled out of control for him and his mental health was very poor. He was on anti-depressants for a short period again and I became overly concerned for his health.

Lee was having suicidal thoughts in 2009, but thankfully he cried out to me for help. A culmination of years of fighting with his mental health. It stunned him and for a while he seemed to shut down.

Thankfully, this was a turning point for him. A crisis-point with his mental health that certainly grounded him. He came back to me and we became close once more.

Things generally stabilised until late 2012, when Lee was thrown back into the deep end, having received a phone call from a Guardian Newspaper reporter. The immersion back into his past threw him completely and although he willingly wanted to help expose both Heanton and Kesgrave Hall Schools, he paid highly for it and so did we.

Lee was back into therapy and he put up barriers again, in every respect. It was another two and half years of emotional turmoil before Lee came out of both therapy, court appearances as a witness and got over general health related issues.

Where we should have been repairing things, and settling into a better life post 2015, having put John Downing in prison, and seen off Stancliffe and Scott, etc.; we are still waiting for final adjudications from the Criminal Injuries Compensation Authority (CICA).

It has been nearly five years (as I write) that Lee has been in contact with his solicitor, who has subsequently been dealing with his case against Kent County

Council. We have yet to see some action being taken in that area. All of this is preventing Lee from getting full closure.

We are closer in many respects and Lee, although settled and happy, is not entirely back with us, all the time there is unfinished business in respect of both of those horrendous schools.

Chapter 6

The Underwood Report
And the evolution of 'Maladjusted Children' and Independent Boarding Schools

The Underwood Report - Committee on Maladjusted Children (1955) Report of the Committee on Maladjusted Children (Chairman: J. E. A. Underwood) London: Her Majesty's Stationery Office.

This chapter provides a precis of the Underwood Report (1955), in which I make comparison to my schooling and the failures of the systems therein. A link to copy of the actual Underwood Report can be found in [Appendix: A page 100]. This chapter also includes a breakdown of The Education Act 1944.

During my research into writing this book, I also studied the educational and schooling system of 1960 into 1970, to include the models and policies that the respective Governments would be adopting. My early childhood was during an era, when there were many changes to social history of the Country (1950's to the 1970's).

Prior to the 1950's, the Second World War was responsible for tearing families and communities apart, this undoubtedly creating more instability in children than the previous decades. Father figures had been absent and there was the evacuation of children to 'safer' parts of the country. Over 500,000 women also served in the Armed Forces during WWII.

1945 to 1950 was a time of Austerity in the country, under the Clement Attlee Labour Government. The 1950's seeing the re-emergence of prosperity. Family centred Britons we're undertaking more leisure activities, which became more accessible to more people after the war. Holiday Camps became popular holiday destinations in the 1950s — and people increasingly had money to pursue their personal hobbies

The Underwood Report (1955), was ordered by Labour Minister of Education, George Tomlinson. He appointed a committee which was led by the then Principle Medical Officer to the Department of Education, Dr JEA Underwood (in post 1944 to 1951). The reason for the committee was to enquire into and report upon the medical, educational and social problems relating to maladjusted children, with reference to their treatment within the educational system.

The report which was presented to the Conservative Education Minister David Eccles in October 1955, who wrote in the Foreword that the committee had 'covered much ground' and 'made many interesting suggestions'. The report was finally published in 31 December 1959, the same year the Dr Underwood passed away. The procedures arising from recommendations made in the report are still practiced today by Kent County Council and other Local Authorities.

The Underwood Report was the first national study of maladjusted children, 'maladjusted,' being a term introduced by the Education Act 1944, as a stigmatising catch-all term for children who were not doing well at school, but did not present with learning disabilities. 'Maladjustment' was a kind of 'handicap' needing 'special educational treatment' in the regulations following the Education Act, 1944. A link to a copy of the Education Act 1944 can be found in [Appendix: A page 100].

In 1944, there was a huge shake up of the education system in England and Wales. This shake-up didn't arrive to Scotland until 1945 and Northern Ireland until 1947.

During 1944, the act saw the Board of Education in England and Wales being replaced by a Minister, who had direct control over the local education authorities. This was perceived at that time, to be a way of creating a more level standard of educational opportunity throughout England and Wales.

The act of 1944 created essential educational reforms, one being the requirement of secondary education for all. The requirement element of that meant that no school fees could be charged in any school being maintained by a public authority. Another reform saw the replacement of the former distinction between elementary and higher education, by a new classification of three progressive stages which we still know today as primary education, secondary education, and further education. The act also saw the creation of the grammar school, the secondary modern school and the technical school.

The Underwood Report of 1955, highlighted some provision should be made for maladjusted children in 'ordinary' schools and off-site units known as tutorial centres. The report made many recommendations, which it would appear from my own experiences in the 1970's, were partly implemented by successive Government educational policies, but perhaps the more important ones were not. I will discuss these further throughout the chapter.

The report encouraged more mainstream and community based provision for 'maladjusted' children, who were inclined to be a group apart from and generally educated outside the mainstream schooling. This of course was to prove to be more destructive to these isolated, institutionalised children, than to any perceived disruption to the children in the mainstream schooling. The report advised that there was the danger that these children would fail to develop suitably, by being isolated from their peer groups and their families. This of course was the case. I can certainly stand as testament to that.

The report recommendations to prevent this from happening, being that there should be more involvement with family members during compulsory boarding and regular day release to local, 'mainstream' schools, were not introduced at all by Heanton School or Kesgrave Hall School. With more family involvement being encouraged to our daily boarding school lives and with scheduled day release being incorporated also, one should question here – because sexual and physical abuse was so common for us, on a daily and nightly basis, would the school have struggled to keep it covered up, with such openness and transparency?

Does this then not go to show that all levels of the school management may have been complicit in the routine and institutional abuse?

As much as I do not like or agree with children being labelled as 'maladjusted', it is important to understand the evolution of the so called 'maladjusted children', as I was labelled as one of these and my life was extraordinarily altered because of that marker. I do not for an instant believe I deserved the label at all and I have been able, I consider, to have shown this clearly to be the case, in this book.

However, my institutionalisation in the 1970's, as with many other unfortunate children throughout the decades of the 20th Century had been enabled through us being considered to be maladjusted. To better understand how the authorities have been able to do this, I found The Underwood Report (1955) highly pertinent to my enlightenment in this respect. For this reason, I have included references to the Underwood Report in this book. I am sure it will prove equally helpful to many others and certainly as informative [Appendix: A page 100].

I strongly believe my early years, aged 3 to 6 years of age, where turbulent for me due to many factors being present. I believe as an intelligent child, I required challenges that were not offered to me. I required love and support of 'both' parents, but only had my mother's influence, as there was no father figure present and due to circumstances plaguing their relationship during these years. I was undoubtedly neglected and poorly treated on occasions by both parents. I believe that the only real voice I had in my early years was behavioural and is it any wonder that I used that to make my feelings known. My nonverbal communication being completely misread and misunderstood by everyone I encountered. This clearly played into the educational psychologist's hands and using 'maladjusted' I was clearly, very quickly labelled. This coupled together with my Mother's pleas to have me removed from my home and her possible veiled threats that my safety may be compromised if I was to remain in her care, my fate was sealed. My future was to be significantly disrupted and path of my life permanently altered from that point.

The Underwood Report itself describes maladjusted as *'involving a failure of personal relationships; maladjusted children find receiving and giving difficult; they do not respond to love, comfort or reassurance and are not readily capable of improvement by ordinary discipline. Maladjusted children may not necessarily be troublesome; they may be passive but insecurity and anxiety may lead to aggression as a means of relief. This however does not mean that all delinquents are maladjusted. Pupils receiving special education for other reasons may also be maladjusted.'* [Source: http://www.thetcj.org/child-care-history-policy/the-underwood-report-chaired-by-jea-underwood.]

I believe I eventually became maladjusted, but I would argue strongly that in my case, the behavioural traits described by the report, above, where not entirely present in me prior to attending Heanton and Kesgrave Hall Schools throughout the 1970's. These behavioural traits however would entirely accurately describe me on leaving the boarding school in 1980, a few months before my 17th birthday and for that matter, for much of my adult life.

Boarding school disorder, or syndrome as it is now widely accepted to be, has been fundamental in making me fit more closely the standard description of a maladjusted person.

To further support this supposition of boarding school syndrome making me fit the report's description of being maladjusted post institutionalisation and not prior to being removed from my home, would be my early and later relationships with my sister Vivienne and my Nan and Grandad on my Mother's side. I loved them very much before the age of 6 and missed them greatly throughout the ten years of being away from home. The love and affection I attached to these individuals was present before and equally after the boarding school years. I recall clearly how I was easily disciplined by my grandparents and would conform and respond quickly to instruction from them. During the psychologist's assessments of me during 1969 and 1970, they failed to establish that I not only craved love and support, but I also able to give it freely.

I was wrongly labelled as being 'maladjusted'. My parents were therefore both responsible for any neurosis I had as a small child. They both engineered it and maintained it. The Underwood Report recommended that Child Guidance Clinics should work with children, their families, their schools and school health services to prevent maladjustment. It is fairly evident in my case that the Kent County Council, CGC in Ramsgate failed in all these respects.

In 1955, in the report from J. E. A. Underwood, the word 'maladjusted' was not a new term, but it was not until then that it had become more widely used. The terminology 'being maladjusted' did have an evolution from the development of intelligence tests by Alfred Binet. Binet was a French psychologist who invented the first practical IQ test, the Binet–Simon test, in 1904 for the French Ministry of Education.

The 1944 Education Act re-introduced the term 'maladjusted'. Under the 1944 Education Act, children with special educational needs were pigeon-holed by their disabilities, as defined in medical terms. Many children were considered to be uneducable and pupils were categorised into groups such as maladjusted or educationally sub-normal and given special educational treatment in separate schools. Many evacuee hostels were set up during the Second World War and continued as hostels for maladjusted children after the end of the war. It was Post-War regulation that placed new responsibilities on health and local education authorities to provide child guidance clinics and support children in special schools. The main ages for referral to a child guidance clinic were between eight and nine.

I was referred to the Newington Road Child Guidance Clinic, in Ramsgate in 1969, at the age of five. I was taken away from home at the age of six. The process of removing me from my home and family was apart from being entirely floored, was expedited astonishingly fast.

The Underwood Report recommended that Special Day Schools and classes should be expanded and Residential care should provide a 'temporary' home during treatment, with local authority reception centres being used for observation and assessment. Boarding schools should focus solely on educational treatment and should not have wholly separate teaching and care staff. Boarding schools should have links with other associated services and families; there should be an expansion in their provision, especially for children with low or high IQs. The vast majority of the recommendations made in the Underwood Report were **not** introduced by Government or local authorities and all the reasons requiring such safeguarding to be put in place, became a reality because of this, especially so for my boarding school peer group and me. Many of the 'historic abuse investigations' currently being undertaking are as a direct result of this narrow-minded and short-sighted governance.

The refusal by the governing bodies of that time, to accept the reality of wide spread paedophilia and uncontrolled violence being metered out to vulnerable, institutionalised young people under their control was criminally negligent. This of course would be even more horrific if some knew what was happening, but chose to ignore it.

Principally the avoidance of both organisational and cost implications of ensuring proper and effective measures were put in place to protect all young people being sent away from home, for extended periods (boarding), far outweighed the possibility of immediate or long-term harm becoming them. Extended exposure to individuals, house-parents (carers) and live-in teachers allowed for the creation of culture of violence, the proliferation of paedophile activity and the formation of established paedophile rings. Heanton School and Kesgrave Hall School were amongst these with predatory paedophiles like John Downing, Kenneth Scott and Alan Stancliffe having a free hand and regular supply of young boys to prey on and abuse.

The Underwood Report recommended that Local Education Authorities should be responsible for after-care, which might include a hostel or support from a child guidance clinic. The reality of this, for long-term boarders was there was no after-care provided at all. Once we outgrew the system and fell outside of the parameters of compulsory educational age, we were unceremoniously thrown back out into the big, wide world and expected to manage on our own. With no established interpersonal or communicational skills, many boys including myself, struggled to make sense of the 'adult' world or how we fitted into it and how to survive within it. This would undoubtedly have been where the recommended after-care programmes would have helped us.

The Underwood Report of 1955 stressed the need for school psychological services and the role of school health services, but regretted that there was currently no obligation to provide child guidance clinics. The recommendation was for all children, including those at independent schools. This never happened and throughout ten years at boarding school, I was never seen by any external professional, apart for the School GP.

I made allegations of indecent assault against the school GP in 2012, following my recollection of at least three indecent assaults by him, that took place at Kesgrave Hall School between 1975 and 1980. The former Kesgrave Hall School GP from the late 1970's, was arrested by Suffolk Police during 2014 and questioned regarding the alleged assaults. Because it was not possible to corroborate these allegations by witness testimony, the former GP was not charged.

The Underwood Report made many, very sound and suitable recommendations to support young children considered to be maladjusted. Most of the recommendations were ignored completely by Government and failed to be implemented by County Authorities. The rest is history, as they say.

It is entirely beyond comprehension that Government, Local Authorities and other major entities, such as the NHS, the BBC, the Cadet and Scout organisations, etc., throughout the 1970's and 1980's failed to observe the manifestation of paedophile activity and the propagation of paedophile rings, that spread epidemically through their organisations. There were of course many connections here. For example, what was happening to us in Heanton School, North Devon and Kesgrave Hall School, in Suffolk, was going on in boarding schools all over the British Isles. Paedophile rings were highly established, well supported and protected at the highest levels. The Paedophile Information Exchange (PIE) [Appendix: D page 104 - 108] shows evidence of that.

Individuals from all organisations where young people were present, were reported for inappropriate sexual activity and much worse, at the time of the incidents. Children did tell what was happening, but no one listened and if they did take it on board, it failed to progress fully through to the proper channels. This is a story we hear time and time again in nearly all historic abuse investigations and Crown Court trials. It became evident very early on for me, as a victim of the abuse, that it was futile trying to tell about what was happening. The consequences of this were too high a price to pay.

The protection offered to high profile paedophiles, Judges, Celebrities, Politicians, etc. was very commanding. No one could break this protection net for many decades. Jimmy Savile is a casing point here. What the monster Savile was doing with young people, whilst in the BBC and in Birch Hill Hospital, Rochdale, Scott House Hospital, Rochdale, Bethlem Royal Hospital, South London, Shenley Hospital, North West London, West Yorkshire Ambulance Service, St Martin's Hospital, Canterbury, Queen Elizabeth Hospital, Gateshead, Meanwood Park Hospital, Leeds and Calderdale Royal Hospital, Huddersfield, Leeds Infirmary, Stoke Mandeville Hospital in Buckinghamshire and the Royal Victoria Infirmary, Newcastle, failed to surface as any active investigation at the time, following allegations being made, that progressed to his arrest. With a list that long, gleaned from current investigations, it is not hard to understand now how the system protected itself and why so many people have come forward today. I call it the Paedophile Hegemony, akin to any clandestine organised crime syndicate that protects its members, whilst fulfilling their every need.

The individuals still alive today, who knowingly failed to follow up on any report of indecent behaviour and criminal acts committed against children, to protect either the person being accused, or their organisation, are, in my opinion beyond detestation. In the BBC and the NHS during the 1970's, the senior management, the decision makers heads of department, the programming directors would have known about Saville. They would have had to make decisions about 'the best way foreword' following repeated allegations of indecent assaults committed against young people.

Being complicit in a child's sexual abuse is as bad as the act itself. Any such person is guilty of complicity, having knowingly allowed a child to be abused, continued to be abused or allowed the paedophile to continue abusing other children. In 2015, 261 celebrities and politicians, including sports, TV and music stars, were being investigated for alleged child sex abuse. They are among more than 1,400 men suspected by police of being sexual predators as the then Home Secretary (Theresa May) warned it is only the "tip of the iceberg". This list included 135 TV, film and radio stars, 43 musicians and seven sports figures as well as 76 politicians. In number is in addition to the hundreds of schools, religious institutions, children's homes and sports clubs being implicated.

There were thousands of additional allegations made to police in 2015, involving families and other types of child sexual abuse. These figures, from the police coordinating hub Operation Hydrant, reveal for the first time the massive scale of inquiries in to historic and current sex abuse cases, which unquestionably would have since increased in number further. [Source: http://www.telegraph.co.uk/news/uknews/law-and-order/11617789/Scale-of-child-sex-abuse-revealed-in-new-police-figures.html - 12:19PM BST 20 May 2015]

In 2015, Mr Simon Bailey, the head of Norfolk Police and lead on child sex abuse for the National Police Chiefs Council (NPCC), said the scale of child abuse was "stark". "The referrals are increasing on an almost daily basis so the numbers I refer to today are a snap shot in time." Chief Constable Bailey said reports of child sex abuse were increasing on a daily basis and expected police to receive some 116,000 allegations before the end of this year. Theresa May (Home Secretary), Speaking at the Police Federation annual conference in Bournemouth in 2015, said: "We will need to face up to the changing nature of crime and the impact on police forces, including the much greater reporting of previously ignored or under-reported crimes such as child sexual abuse".
[Source: http://www.telegraph.co.uk/news/uknews/law-and-order/11617789/Scale-of-child-sex-abuse-revealed-in-new-police-figures.html - 12:19PM BST 20 May 2015]

Two years later, this 'need' emerged as massively over-stretched police forces, suffering from major resource and financial cut backs, transpiring in many historic abuse investigations faltering and others failing to get past the intimal starting blocks or move forward. Extremely devastating to any victim of historic abuse who drummed up the courage and came forward to give evidence. Feeling let down, exposed and highly vulnerable, many will not be capable of pursuing the justice they so deserve. Many paedophiles slip justice in this manner.

In February 2017, Chief Constable Simon Bailey has said that paedophiles who view indecent images should **not** be charged and taken to court unless they pose a physical threat to children. Theresa May, as Prime Minister in 2017, could push forward her changes to the 'changing nature of crime', in this case by allowing Chief Constable Bailey to effectively decriminalise the downloading and viewing of child related pornography. Simon Bailey reported that "An individual who is not in contact with children, who doesn't pose a threat to children and is looking at low-level images ... when you look at everything else that's going on, and the threat that's posed of contact abuse to children, we have to look at doing something different with those individuals."

[http://www.telegraph.co.uk/news/2017/02/28/police-chief-calls-low-risk-paedophiles-spared-jail-officers/] - 28 FEBRUARY 2017 • 8:05AM]

As much as I agree that police resources are stretched and perhaps a smarter way can be found to manage these investigations, like recruiting additional officers, we should be a little concerned at the nativity of the senior police officer responsible for child protection in the UK. I apologise for being graphic here, but to fully understand what is going on, we must explore the reality Internet based child pornography. Any person actively viewing or downloading child related pornography (mainly images of adult males undertaking sexual activity with children) is doing that through personal desire. They have entered the search terms to find images of naked children and this sexually arouses them. Many of these men have either scrutinised the image or downloaded and saved it for constant personal use.

We hear time and time again, that these individuals do not view/download just a handful of images, it is usually thousands of images of children, some as young as infants. The purpose for viewing or having these images, is for that individuals own sexual gratification – there can be no other reason. For the senior child protection police officer, to follow the Governments desire to decriminalise online child pornography as 'low risk', is quite shocking. The complicity I previously spoke of continues into another era.

There cannot be such a thing as a low risk paedophile. Any person capable of viewing children being sexually abused, for their own sexual indulgence, presents a real danger to all young people, without question. It is also proven that many men who download child pornography will migrate to other attempted, or actual psychical sexual assaults on young children, either related to them or otherwise. It is my opinion that this UK Government policy of decriminalisation is total madness and an agenda for enhanced maltreatment, placing thousands of young children in harm's way. It is a policy that fails to tackle the core issues of this hideous crime. The police should focus on the facts in front of them, where every single available image of a child being sexually assaulted, is a crime scene.

I am reminded of a successful investigative outcome in the early 2000's. Whilst studying Digital Media at Canterbury Christ Church University, I lectured occasionally, to the Criminology and Policing courses in New Technology and Internet Based Crime. I also helped design a digital resource to assist Kent Police in rolling out training in Intelligence Led Policing (ILP). Kent Police were one of the forces trialling this now, widely used Policing model. Collaborating with former Chief Constable Sir David Phillips and the Head of Crime and Policing at CCCU, I was also involved in trialling some useful software (KFD) Known File Database, which listed 10's of thousands of 'known' digital signatures of child pornography images. This database was used when any computer or hard drive was seized by the Police, during an investigation. Even when child pornographic images had been deleted from a computer hard drive, it was possible to partially reconstruct the binary strings and identify what images had been present on the device. Robin Bryant, head of Crime and Policing (CCCU), had liaised with the National High-Tech Crime Unit (NHTCU) and working with Romanian and Russian Police units, via an Interpol operation, they had identified that many of the young boys being abused in the captured Romanian images, were street children who had been reported as missing in Russia. Great collaboration that proved it was possible to identify the real victims that are directly affected by this abhorrent crime.

Chapter 7

The Search for Justice and the Truth
The Police and the Courts

"It is good to talk"

"You know, sometimes all you need is twenty seconds of insane courage. Just literally twenty seconds of just embarrassing bravery and I promise you, something great will come of it."
Benjamin Mee
We Bought a Zoo ©2012 20th Century Fox

A few weeks before my 49 birthday I wrote to my GP, who incidentally was also the practice manager at my local GP surgery. I made a formal, written request to view my medical records. I was particularly interested in viewing the older, hand written and typed notes from my birth in 1964 until 1970, when I was sent away from home to Heanton, North Devon.

After a short consultation meeting with the GP, he agreed to initially go through my medical file on my behalf and see if there was anything that would be of use to my search for information. A few days later I received a telephone call at work from the GP. He told me that although there is very limited information contained in my old medical file, he had located several letters that would provide some information for me. He explained to me that in the late 1960's the doctors did not keep such extensive records as they do today. He also confirmed that for the period from 1970 to 1980, my file did not present any information. I did expect this, as I was under the care of the two boarding schools during that 10-year period.

In total, they were four letters disclosed to me [Appendix: T page 166-167]. Sometime later, I was able to view my medical records in person and confirm that there were only these four letters that proved to be pertinent or of interest to my quest. I thought there should have been more letters and wondered if others had been removed from my file. The copy of letters I had were from the Kent County Council School Health Service (Child Guidance Clinic, Newington Road, Ramsgate) to the family GP of that time (Dr G.M.S. Keogh) and from Dr Keogh to the Consultant Psychiatrist Dr K.M. Frazer.

In a letter dated 29th July 1969, Dorothy C. Wall (assistant to Dr. Frazer, Consultants Psychologist at Kent County Council School Health Service) wrote to Dr Keogh (family GP) to confirm his referral of me to the Child Guidance Clinic.

Ms Wall goes on to say that whilst in the play room at the Newington Road, Ramsgate, Child Guidance Centre, I showed no signs of the disturbed behaviour my mother had complained to the GP about. Ms Wall goes on to say that I was active, friendly and amenable.

I had always been led to believe that I was sent away from home because I was an uncontrollable, badly behaved child. I had in some ways always accepted that the abuse happened to me at those schools, because they were just abusive environments. I had always believed then that it was my fault that I was treated so badly, because I had given the authorities no other course of action in 1969 but to send me away. The logic that my mind had followed was, if I had not have behaved so badly, I would not have ended up at Heanton School and Kesgrave Hall School.

These accepted realisations had allowed me to repress all conscious memories of attending the schools in the 1970's and the abuse I had suffered, whilst at the schools. I feel that by partly accepting some responsibility for being sent away, this subconsciously allowed any recollection of the school time to be locked away. Of course, this was not entirely locked away, but manifested in my behaviour in general, in my relationships with others, in many of my activities and in my mental health condition throughout the decades that followed.

Hindsight is a wonderful thing and looking back now it is more than obvious that the effects of the violence I suffered as a child, both physical and sexual have shaped and moulded me as an adult. Not always obvious, but having had counselling sessions in the late 1990's and then therapy from 2013 onwards, it has been possible to conclude why, on some occasions throughout my adult life I felt a certain way, I behaved a certain way or I reacted a certain way.

The truth offers an altogether different perspective. The information contained in these letters initially, was a bombshell. The kind of life changing event that stops you dead in your tracks. They did just that.

I had for many years often wondered - why I had been sent away from home, for an entire decade and my sister had not been? I had on a few occasions asked my mother why this had happened. She was always very quick in terminating any talk or discussion of that. The only explanation she offered was 'that it was taken out of her hands'. A line I have heard her say many times over the past five years. My Mothers argument now easily dissuaded by the evidence that came light through the letters, discovered on my medical records.

As a child, I was a victim of the worst kind of mental cruelty, including physical punishment and bullying. I was also a victim of extensive and frequent sexual assaults. Throughout my adult life I have, to a certain extent become a survivor of this childhood abuse, although I would note here that the damage this caused me or more precisely, the effects of it are something I have had to live with every day of my life.

The memories, the nightmares and the inadequacies I have, together with a strong, integral desire to self-destruct were with me every day. I say 'were', because thankfully after 30 + years wanting to explode, that part of my life has effectively been left behind now. When I go to sleep every night and I wake up every morning, I remind myself that I am 'normal' and everything that happened to me in the past, was not my fault. It is fair to say that some periods are worse for me than others, but extreme mood swings and feelings of anger are two powerful emotions I battle with still, occasionally.

A big part of my journey through dealing with this, throughout my adult life, has been a search for the truth. What happened in 1969 and 1970? Why was I sent 277 miles away from home? Why did I stay away from home for 10 years?

I already had my suspicions on what may have occurred all those years back in 1969 to 1970 and the letters I now had copies of, put the truth on the table.

I was already aware that my father, whom I have been estranged from since

1999, was not around when I was a young child. I was told by my late grandmother that he had been taken away from the family when I was very young. I had some previous knowledge that he had been removed from the house by the police when I was two or three and he had been taken to St. Augustine's Psychiatric Hospital in Chartham, Kent. I vaguely remember the police coming to the house during the night and a lot of commotion. He never returned to the family after that.

I was always led to believe that I had been sent away from the family, to a residential school, because I was disruptive and extremely badly behaved. I was told by my mother, over the years, that I was prone to eating out of dustbins, destroying things and completely hyper active to the point of causing danger to myself and others. She went on to say that I was fascinated by fire and had unacceptable sanitary habits. I have always struggled to accept these alleged revelations from mother and have not been able to recall events in my mind to support this. My sister agreed with me a few years ago, during a very candid conversation, that she also could not recall any such behaviour from me.

What made the authorities (Kent County Council) take children aged six out of the home environment and place them in residential schools many miles away? What policies or procedures were in place in 1969/1970 (in Kent) that gave them the vehicle to do this? Why would my mother, like many others in a similar scenario say 'I had no choice – the decision was taken out of my hands'? I believe some answers to this question can be found in The Underwood Report 1995 (MINISTRY OF EDUCATION - Report of the Committee on Maladjusted Children) [Appendix: A page 100].

The practicable recommendations from this report, although not entirely taken up by any UK Government, would have provided the government of the time (A Labour Government under Harold Wilson) some policy guidelines and advice. The Underwood Report on maladjusted children would have been used to mould social services policy and procedures for local education authorities. This report maintained that if a child or young person was deemed to be in danger of harm within the home environment, or unlikely to thrive and develop normally – thereby being 'maladjusted', then the child should be removed to an independent school setting, external to mainline schooling.

I do believe, more so from my own situation as a prima facie case, this 'maladjusted' child labelling used extensively in the 1970's especially, was fundamental in preventing a child from being fostered, adopted or put into the care system, which ultimately may have benefited the child more suitably, in the long term. It was believed by the authorities then that placing the maladjusted child in special, residential, independent schools, the child would be cared for and educated in a protected and nurturing environment. On reflection was this blinkered, naive or just criminally negligent? when examining the outcome some 40 plus years later.

This supposition of mine currently remains to be legally unproven. At the time of writing I am still waiting for my case against Kent County Council in the High Court to be heard. If successful, it will show in my case that Kent County Council were responsible for the abuse I suffered, by failing to ensure it didn't happen – through a non-delegable duty of care. Although they were not directly responsible for the acts themselves, measures and systems were clearly not in place by them, to prevent the paedophiles from having free and open access to me. Another question to be answered by the High Court action is whether my five years spent at Kesgrave Hall School was in fact legal? or was it false imprisonment?

The maladjusted label given to me as a six-year-old boy, by a Kent County Council Educational Psychologist – supposedly due to my inability or failure to build or maintain relationships and being unable to conform to boundaries and discipline would have been adjusted suitably by the time I reached 11 years of age, you would think. More so, with the regime at Heanton School being of military academy standard. Under that premise, would it not appear inconceivable that at 11, having also been considered to be of high intelligence, I was then sent to Kesgrave Hall School, in Suffolk for the remainder of my compulsory education. As a boarder, I remained away from home for a further five years.

I do not recall ever being asked by anybody, if I wanted to go to Kesgrave Hall in 1975. I was not once asked if I wished to go back home and to be integrated back into a normal secondary school, in Margate during 1975. My mother professes that she was never consulted regarding Kesgrave Hall. She maintains she was just told that I would be going there. I do recall however being informed that I was highly intelligent by the head teacher at Heanton School, Mr Vivian Thomas Charles Davies. He explained to me at time that Kesgrave Hall was a school that catered for children of high intellect, so I would be best suited to continue my schooling there.

Many years later I discovered of course that Vivian Davies was a director of Kesgrave Hall and he naturally had a financial interest in filling the school places. The Local Authority cheques would have been most welcomed, naturally.

The alpha paedophile at Kesgrave Hall was Alan Stancliffe, but many of the other abusers at Kesgrave were also paedophiles I had occasioned at Heanton School, years before. The Heanton alpha paedophile, John Downing visited Kesgrave Hall a few times every year. He did not attempt to interfere with me at Kesgrave. Shockingly this was undoubtedly because at the age of 11 years plus, I was too old for his taste in young boys. This fact being established during the Downing trail at Exeter Crown Court in 2014 [Exhibit H: page 120-122].

I felt it was an important part of my journey for the truth, to have a better understanding of the influences that affected my mother in the late 1960's. In no way, as to attempt to mitigate the responsibility that she should bear for the destruction of my childhood, in its entirety. It is fairly evident from what I remember and from many discussions of over the years, that she may have suffered from mental health issues herself, during those early years. My biological father certainly did. He was sectioned in an asylum at one stage, due to his psychotic and violent behaviour. He too must accept a share of the responsibility for the abuse I suffered. He too failed badly as a parent.

Another element in my Mothers failings in respecting of raising me normally, would be the violence and aggressiveness she suffered during her marriage to my father. That undoubtedly would have impacted on her.

People have often asked me how is my relationship with my mother and father now? I have no relationship with me biological father. He clearly still has many personal issues and drove me away many years ago. To date it has been 17 plus years since we last spoke. I have no desire or inclination to see him or want him to be part of my life, or that of my own family.

I love my Mum, like any son would love his mother. She is Mum after all. I can never forgive her for what happened to me in the past and I do hold her wholly responsible for that. She could have kept me at home. She could have prevented it all from happening. I choose a long time ago, not to talk to her about any of it, partly because when I have tried to in the past, I have found her stance and attitude to it all as derisory and offensive. The reality is, for my own mental wellbeing, I allow Mum to live in complete deniability of all responsibility for my horrific childhood. Where she is fully accountable for it, the last thing I need is to lose a Mother's love, now I finally have that.

A Private Investigation
Contacting the Police and Attending Court

I felt it was important to detail in the book how I went about tracing the men that harmed me in the past and what happened when I did find them. This section also details my contact with various police forces and what it was like attending court. I hope the recounting of my experiences here will help others by answering any questions they may have about associated matters.

A combination of the breakup of my marriage in 1995 from my first wife, which resulted in her taking the children from that relationship away from me to live with another man and the death of my Grandmother, Ina Madge Weller, in 1996, I suffered greatly in many ways. My mental health had begun to spiral out of my control. This was the first real trigger for recollection of the abusive childhood I had endured.

Recollections and realisation manifested through nightmares increased over the weeks and eventually the full horror of what had been happening to me all those years back started to come back to me. The early recalled memories focussed mainly on an individual who was a teacher and carer at Kesgrave Hall School. His name was Alan Stancliffe, from Pontefract in Yorkshire. [Appendix: I page 126] Stancliffe was my last main abuser, and as such, he was undoubtedly the most prominent in my mind. Stancliffe was relentless in his attacks on me and many other boys. He had a cruel sexual appetite that could only be satisfied by unnatural sexual acts being performed by him and having them performed on him.

There are many types of paedophile, but for this text, I will focus on only two types, predatory and opportunist. Stancliffe was a particularly nasty, predatory paedophile who continued to haunt my dreams after leaving the boarding school system and had unknown to me for many decades, affected my life and relationships. I was sexually abused by Stancliffe over a three-year period during late 1970's at Kesgrave Hall School. This was on a daily and nightly basis. Stancliffe never used violence in his attacks, but he would use his superior body strength to force things to happen. He was different from other abusers at the schools because he would indecently assault me during the normal school day, when and where he could. These attacks included classrooms, corridors, school grounds and toilets. A disturbing feature about

Stancliffe was the lengths he would go to satisfy his sexual appetite.

A prime example was when I was 'fortunate' to be selected by Stancliffe for a weekend treat away from school. This was to attend a band contest at Dagenham in the late 1970's, in which I joined Stancliffe and another boy from the school [MS]. Before driving down to London, we first had an overnight stay at Stancliffe's mother's house in Pontefract, Yorkshire. I was given a double bed in a guest room, which initially was a great treat compared to the barracks style conditions I was used to at School. This later turned into a nightmare scenario with a full on, undisturbed night long sexual attack by Stancliffe, with his mother a sleep in the room next door and the other boy, a sleep downstairs.

After leaving the school system in 1980, I joined up with the 2nd Royal Tank Regiment Army Cadet Force in Margate. I had enjoyed being part of the cadet services in Suffolk, whilst at school, where I attained privilege and rank.

It provided a good escape from the abusive conditions I lived in daily and when I was with the cadets, I felt protected and free to be just me. It was outside of the school regime and could not be infiltrated by school staff. During the summer of 1980, I went away for a weekend exercise with the Army Cadet Force. It was a battalion exercise in which we were pitted against the Kent Sea Cadets in manoeuvres in Margate, Dover and Sandwich, Kent. It was a great weekend and I remember for once, I had let my hair down and enjoyed every part of it. When I returned home on the Sunday afternoon, I was horrified when my mother told me that I had missed some visitors earlier that day. She told me that an Alan Stancliffe, a former house parent from my school had called to see me at our house. He had been accompanied by a former pupil of Kesgrave Hall School called Mark Whale. Mark Whale was a former friend of mine at school and he had left Kesgrave early in 1979. I was very angry to think Stancliffe had abused the school records to find my home address. He was the last person I wanted to ever see again and I could not fully understand why Mark Whale was with him. What were their motives for this visit? I was very angry and told my mum that if he ever called again, I did not want to see him at any time. I remember going back into shell after this and remained there for some considerable time.

That probably was the last time Stancliffe, Kesgrave Hall School or Heanton School surfaced in my conscious mind. It was all to be buried away very deeply in my mind and to be ignored whenever it filtered through.

During 1981, I joined the Kent Police in Margate and that allowed me to become a new person. An altered persona in which I became a confident young man. I continued police service until 1990, when I joined a local private detective agency (Tallan Investigations ltd) and became a partner in the company. I spent five years working with Tallan, tracing missing persons and serving legal process and collecting corporate dept.

It was roughly another 15 years before I started thinking back to the past. Back to the days when all those 'unspeakable' things happened. The decision for me to come forward and speak to the police about Alan Stancliffe started for me in 1995. It wasn't until 1996 that I truly opened up about him. It took a year and a lot of counselling before I could face up to that.

I would note here that I have had two main contact periods with the police regarding making allegations of sexual assaults and violence against me. This was during 1995 and 1996 and the year 2012. I have grouped 95 and 96 together for the purpose of this text, but it is important to note that these were two entirely different experiences. The way the police and the judiciary, for that matter, have evolved over those decades, understand the needs and security required by adult victims of child abuse, to be able to attend court and give evidence. The legal system is far better suited now for that purpose then was 20 years ago.

1995

I did not contact the police, as a first port of call, I initially went to see my GP and spoke to him of the nightmares and the recollection of indecent assaults and beatings I had lived through as a child. We spoke about this. Not an in-depth discussion, more of a fact-finding mission for the GP, I guess.

The GP diagnosed me with depression and it was evident to me then that I was not capable of undertaking the simplest of daily tasks. Just getting up in the morning was very difficult for me.

During this part of my life, I was no longer with the Police, my wife was living with another man and I was a single parent with my son Christopher, who had come back to live with me. I was not working. The responsibility I had caring for Christopher kept me fairly grounded. I took that responsibility very seriously and to be perfectly frank, it undoubtedly stopped me from killing myself. I fought myself constantly to keep my emotional state from Chris and for that matter, from everybody else around me at that time and believe I succeeded fairly well with that. Some mind-numbing medication from the GP did help.

Looking back on this now, I truly believe if I had not have had my children, Christopher and Carina in my life at that point, I would have killed myself. I was a like Frankenstein's monster in a sense, a complete mishmash of personalities, not truly understanding which was actually me. Most of my friends at this time, although not that many, were controlling factors in my life, almost to the point of being abusive relationships. I did not sleep much, because I had no control over my sub-conscious mind. My mind ruled the night for me and I was just very angry, all the time.

I had gained a reputation in the Police as a go getter – the first man in. I was always one of the first to get stuck into a violent situation and invariably placed myself in dangerous situations, unnecessarily on some occasions. This was not so much bravery, it was more a total disregard for my own life.

Thankfully I saw sense and when I asked my GP for help, he suggested I should see a counsellor and he referred me to the Westbrook Centre in Margate (NHS Community Mental Health Services). This was stage one of my recovery process. The first real big step.

I do recall that I attended the initial assessment appointment at the Westbrook Centre in 1996 and I spoke with two people, a man and a woman. This was a screening appointment, an assessment. I gave them a sketchy outline of my issues, but did not feel able to speak openly about my past. They recommended that I saw a counsellor, called Jerry and an appointment was made.

I attended The Westbrook Centre for the initial visit with Jerry, but after sitting in the waiting room for a few minutes, got up and left rapidly. I guess I was not ready at that time. After a few more weeks of miserable days and nights, my brain bombarding me with memories of the violence and sexual abuse that I had been subjected to, I went to the Westbrook Centre reception, without an appointment and asked if it was still possible to see Jerry.

They happily allowed this and I was shown into a waiting room. It should be said that initially I found it difficult to open up and although I wanted to be there, I was very guarded about talking about, what was after all my very deepest and darkest secrets. This unquestionably was a difficult process for me to enter, because from the age of 6 until 16, I had been conditioned not to talk about anything and instilled with a huge amount of guilt because of the things I had done and had allowed to be done to me. I had self-stigmatised my own abusive past.

Jerry was a fantastic man and a highly skilled counsellor. I respected him and trusted greatly. I was never able to open up to him fully and tell him what had actually happened (the actual details of my past injuries), but I was able to speak enough to get myself back on track and off medication. I am sure Jerry perceived enough. I had suffered physical, mental and sexual abuse at the hands of numerous male members of staff from both schools. There had been some very violent women staff members also at both schools also, but Alan Stancliffe was the most prominent person on my mind at that time. It was Stancliffe that I initially needed to deal with. It was Stancliffe that was haunting me.

I attended a weekly counselling session at the Westbrook Centre and had been for some time, when I felt the time was right for me to deal with the monster Stancliffe.

I used my investigative tracing skills and soon located Stancliffe's home address. I also set about securing a positive identification from Stancliffe's mother, of his address location Pontefract, West Yorkshire. This confirmation was achieved over the telephone. I also contacted a number of other boys from Kesgrave by phone and letter, some by email - whom I knew had been abused by Stancliffe at the same time as me. Emailing was still quite new at this time and everyone wasn't sign up to an Internet Service Provider. The Internet and people's access to it was still fairly limited in 1995/96. Hand written letters and follow up phone calls were the order of the day.

To assist the police into starting an investigation into my allegations against Stancliffe and others at Kesgrave Hall School and Heanton School, required corroborative evidence. Any historic investigation, very much like a cold case enquiry, relied heavily of witness testimony and the validation of that by further witnesses. The only way I was going to Stancliffe in a Crown Court, was to get other boys to step forward and corroborate what I was saying. It was already 15 years since we left Kesgrave Hall, but there was one salient fact, a weapon in my armoury. If I get other boys to speak to the police. Other boys I know Stancliffe had abused, I could get the police investigation started. The main thing about both Kesgrave Hall School and Heanton School, no one spoke about the sexual abuse, but EVERYBODY knew it was going on and generally, who was involved.

I explained to other boys I had contacted, that I was going to the police and I invited them to do the same.

There was a dilemma I faced. A moment of potential weakness in me I suffered at this time. I had tracked Stancliffe down and confirmed his identity, what was to stop me now listening to that voice in my head? The voice telling me to go and pay him a personal visit and having 'a chat'. Common sense and reason kicked in. That part of my mind was more powerful than the emotional side. This stopped me taking things down that route. After all, any immediate satisfaction to be gained from metering out physical pain on this former teacher/houseparent was far outweighed by my desire to see him exposed, humiliated and incarcerated, for what he had done to us all. He needed to suffer hard and long. He needed to experience how we felt.

I am sure that if I had gone to visit Stancliffe, it would have been more than just a chat and it would have likely have led to me doing a long stretch in prison. I certainly did not crave further imprisonment. I had served enough time with this monster already, I wasn't about to serve more time because of him.

The first steps I took in my search for justice, was a visit to my local police station, at Margate (Kent Police), where I made a formal complaint against Alan Stancliffe. This was recorded by an officer and followed up swiftly by a male and female officer from the child protection unit came. These officers round to my house and I gave a very full and open statement about Kesgrave Hall School and Alan Stancliffe. I also mentioned in my statement from 1995, other staff members also and also spoke briefly about abuse at Heanton School in Devon. I carried on seeing the counsellor at the Westbrook Centre weekly, during this time. This was very helpful to me and eventually I made a further, more detailed statement to Kent Police, regarding Stancliffe, Downing and others during 1996.

Both statements were sent to officers at Suffolk Police, who were handling the case and I was contacted after a short period by a detective sergeant who told me that Stancliffe had been arrested and was being questioned by Yorkshire Police. I was told that it was highly likely that the CPS would be supporting a prosecution against Alan Stancliffe, as other boys had come forward and made statements.

In due course Stancliffe was charged with numerous offences of indecent assault against me and two other boys. There was a fourth witness, but he dropped out before trial. The case eventually went to trial at Bury Crown Court in May 1999. Stancliffe was imprisoned for 12 months at Bury Crown Court in June 1999.

This case, although successful, had taken its toll on me. I remember coming out of the court room, after giving evidence against Stancliffe for the entire day (apart from the lunchtime adjournment). I sat down in the foyer at Bury Crown Court and could not physically move. I was drained emotionally and physically. The police sergeant from the case came over and sat by me. He told me I had done well and asked if I was ok. I wept uncontrollably for what seemed like hours. I could not stop. All those tears I had not shed as a child suddenly came flooding out. I was, for a short while, that small child again.

2012

I should say that 'stepping back into the ring' so to speak, was not something I entered through my own volition. I had no desire in 2012 to revisit the legal processes of dealing with my past, but the circumstances of my involvement I guess, was going to be inevitable. It would have had to be faced up to at some stage.

During the Stancliffe case, which started in 1996 and subsequent trial of 1999, I came in and out of my second marriage, as quickly as I went into it (1997). A disastrous and abusive relationship of two years, that only served a real purpose of substantiating my neurosis. I concentrated on my life with Christopher and had regular contact with Carina. I met my current partner Mandy in 2000 and threw myself into my academic studies and professional undertakings. I had no actual memories of the abuses I had suffered or the people responsible for that. It was there of course, in other ways as previously discussed, but I was not dwelling on it daily. My mental health and behavioural issues became prominent in the years 2000 to 2011, but I had not consciously associated everything together.

The moment I was contacted by a former Kesgrave Hall School boy in 2012 and introduced to Josh Halliday of the Guardian Newspaper, I stepped back into the arena of legal processes and police statements. The media were going after the abusers from Kesgrave Hall School. I could not walk away from that. I had to play my part. I had unfinished business too.

I made my video statement to Kent Police about Kesgrave Hall School, this time I was ready to spill to the beans fully. It was time to get this out. I was aware of other successful cases following on from the Savile case. I wanted to talk about Scott, Lafford and Brockman and a few of the other abusers from Kesgrave. It was also at this time I contacted Devon & Cornwall police regarding John Downing. If I was going to be dealing with the past, I had to deal with all of it.

The processes of contacting the police in 2012, in respect of tackling historic assault allegations was an entirely different animal than in the late 1990's. No direct contact is arranged by the police, where possible, until a support network is put in place for the victim. This is essential, for the victim and also for the judicial process, should it go that far. A major improvement to the process. Especially when you consider the average interview time I had, when making video statements was 2 to 3 hours. A long time to talk about the injuries you received in the past.

Whilst Operation Garford, was underway, investigating historical abuse allegations at Kesgrave Hall School from the 1970s to the 1990s, the Devon and Cornwall police investigation into allegations against John Downing at Heanton School, North Devon was proceeding also.

By the end of April 2014, it was confirmed by the Witness Care Officer at Exeter Crown Court that I would be required to give evidence at the trial of John Downing at Exeter Crown Court on Tuesday 10th June 2014. The prospect of going to Crown Court to give evidence once again, in an historic sexual abuse trial, was not something that I was looking forward to, but it was something I knew I had to do. The way I saw it, there would be no real moving forward and or putting things behind me, unless I properly dealt with it and apart from that, with Downing going to Court, I would never be able live with myself, if I walked away from that. I wanted justice for what he had put me through. He needed to be exposed for what he was and I had to play my part in that process.

The videotaped interview I gave to Kent Police during 2013, in which I made my allegations against Downing of indecent behaviour and indecent assaults against me, will be played to the court prior to my being called in to the courtroom, to be cross examined by the legal teams, on the basis of the evidence I presented.

There were a number of additional choices to be made when I gave evidence at the Downing trial in June 2014. Different when compared to my witness experience at the Alan Stancliffe trial of 1999, in Bury Crown Court. Changes for the better. When I gave evidence against Stancliffe (May 1999), I was standing in the witness box in full view of the court and facing Stancliffe himself. It was a very lengthy, draining experience to the point of being highly traumatic. I recall the uncomfortableness of feeling Stancliffe's eyes burning into me whilst I was standing in the dock and whilst I was talking, almost as though he was willing me to stop talking. On occasions, our eyes did meet across the courtroom. It is difficult to explain the horror that I felt every time this happened, I do also recall feeling disgusted by the smug look on his face. Not a very pleasant experience, but well worth it in the long run.

That was back then, in the 1990's the difference with this process now is wide spread. The police are better experienced to work with victims of historic child abuse and that is apparent from my dealings with them over the past few years. Communication with Devon & Cornwall Constabulary and Suffolk Constabulary was good and I recall early on in contact process, they were quite happy to wait for me to get some specialist psychiatric help prior to meeting them to make my statement.

When it came time to arrange for my day in Exeter Crown Court, as a witness against John Downing, I was given the choice of whether I wanted to be seated in another room on the day, and have my cross-examination video conferenced into the courtroom, for the whole courtroom to see or to have screens placed up in the courtroom, so only the judge, jury and barristers can see me. Downing and the public gallery would not be in my view.

The second option, being the preferred option and the one I selected. The video statement I made would be played to the court initially and following that, I will enter the court to be cross examined, in the witness box. There will be screens between me and Downing. On the day's I undertook this, both in 2014 and 2015, I asked to make a statement to the Judge and the Jury. I said them that I had asked for the screens to be put up in the courtroom for a valid reason. That reason being that to be able to speak openly and freely, I did not want to look at Downing directly. I explained It was not a case of being intimidated by him, it was more a case of being distracted by Downing. I explained to the court that I did not want to look at Downing because he disgusts me.

A court attendance as a witness today in an historic abuse case is a better experience by far than it was in the 1990's. A lot of lessons have been learnt and the witnesses, regardless of age are treated much better.

The weeks leading up to the Downing trial of 2014 had been stressful. I was naturally a little anxious of being cross examined in the court regarding the finer details of Downing's indecent assaults and acts of gross indecency against me. After all, this was something I had not spoken of very much in over 40 years and I have only confided in a hand full of people with any detail, in fact only two people fully. The biggest cause of anxiety to me at that time was the thought of getting on a train in Ramsgate and travelling to Devon via London Paddington to confront Downing. This journey reflects my returning to Heanton School during the early 1970's, after one of the short holidays back at home. A mirror image of that and the emotions ran high. It seemed an entirely inconceivable journey to be taking then, as an adult in June 2014.

I remember being pleased to be in the Hotel eventually. The White Heart Inn in Exeter, not far from the Cathedral. Before I could settle down and prepare for the following day in court, I went for a walk. I wanted to explore the city more and the Cathedral, but I couldn't concentrate on much else but the trial and I needed to plan my route to the courthouse. I needed to know what time to leave the hotel, to get there in the morning. I ate at the hotel and settled in for the night. I didn't sleep well, in fact hardly.

It was whilst I was in my hotel room in Exeter, following giving evidence against John Downing, that I did one of the craziest things imaginable. It certainly felt so at the time. Having kept everything secret and locked away for so many years and hidden the reason why I was in Devon and not at work, I decided it was time to 'go public'. I decided to post a Facebook status. I felt it was time to tell everyone who I really was and what I was about to do. I was not sure why, but it felt like the right thing to do. This is the text from that post (June 10, 2014):

I am a survivor of historic child sexual abuse! I have posted a picture of me from 1972. I was between the age of 7 and 8.
I am in my school uniform and travelling home from North Devon to Margate. By the time this picture was taken I had already been subjected to over 1 year of systemic, institutional maltreatment, involving mental, physical and sexual abuse in

The Author – Heanton School c: 1972

the independent, residential schooling system. For me this abuse was to continue for another 9 years, only ending when I left the boarding school system in 1980.

I was removed from my home in 1970 by Kent County Council and handed over to Heanton School Ltd, a privately run boarding school in North Devon, where I remained until 1975. In 1975, instead of coming back home to Margate and mainstream schooling, Kent County Council allowed Heanton School Ltd to keep me and they transferred me to Kesgrave Hall School Ltd near Ipswich, Suffolk, from 1975 to 1980. Kesgrave Hall School was owned by Mr. Vivian Thomas Charles Davies, the headmaster and Director of Heanton School.

Why have I chosen to reveal this now?
The secret of my 10 years of being a victim of historic child abuse has been a destructive force that has eaten away at me for over 4 decades. Although buried deeply inside me, it has affected my moods, my behaviour and relationships, both private and professional since leaving school in 1980. It has made me angry, it has made me aggressive, it has made me unpredictable, it has made me suicidal and it has made me sad. I have had extensive therapy and treatment for depression over the decades and unbeknown to many, I have had to force myself to go to work (daily) and to try to be 'normal'. It is only through my perseverance and strong will and the unconditional love and support of Mandy, that I have been able to build any sort of life. In keeping quiet and internalising the assaults and violence that I suffered as a child, I have in part created my own mental health problems, in addition to protecting the identity of the paedophiles and sadists that controlled the violent, independent school system that I attended in the 1970's. I have elected to speak out.

The veil of secrecy that has hidden the abuse I suffered at boarding school has been something that I have felt ashamed of and guilty about for the majority of my life. This secrecy has also protected the monsters that preyed on me and many others for decades, allowing them to continue with their seemingly respectable lives, hiding behind the church, other schools, etc. After a lot of support and help over the past few years, I am now conscious of the fact that I had nothing to feel ashamed and guilty about. I had done nothing wrong. I was a child and I was trying to survive!

I do not feel that I have to explain my behaviour to the people that have known me for any amount of time, but I want to. I do hope now that some of you will understand why I have behaved in the way I did, why I reacted in the way I did or said things that may have been uncalled for. I apologise if I have offended anyone. Where I am today, is the culmination of a long, long journey that will give me some peace of mind and allow me to enjoy the rest of my life, my family and my friends freely and without agenda. I have met some truly remarkable people over the years and made many friends from colleagues and acquaintances who I value greatly. And like many of you, over the years I have also met some people who have been false and destructive to me, which undoubtedly is part of the human condition. These negative people have tested my resolve and in their own way have given me the drive and ambition to better myself and make things work.

Over the past few years, I have investigated my past and traced many of the men and women who have injured me as a child. This information was handed over to the police and is being thoroughly investigated. I am currently part way through writing a book detailing *my 10 years in the residential schooling system of the 1970's. It has been a good form of cognitive therapy for me and I hope it will be able to help others, when completed. The research I have undertaken in writing the book has also looked at educational and social policies in the UK from the 1960's to the 1980's and how this impacted on me. I hope this will be completed during 2015.*

I may now be coming to terms with what happened to me from the age of 6, but this is not over for the perpetrators of the violence and indecent behaviour levelled at me as a child during the 1970's. Their nightmare has only just started.

Yesterday I travelled down to Exeter to give evidence in Crown Court today. On Trial is John Downing (aged 72) a house parent/teacher (carer) who was entrusted with the care of me, from 1970 to 1975. Downing is on trial for 25 charges of indecent assault and acts of gross indecency. The trial will go on until Friday 13th, when the verdict will hopefully be a good one. I went to court today to seek justice for the little boy you see in that picture.

In 1999, I attended Ipswich Crown Court and gave evidence against Alan Stancliffe (aged 65 now) who had indecently assaulted me over a 3-year period at Kesgrave Hall School, Ipswich, Suffolk from 1976 to 1979. He was imprisoned and subsequently re-imprisoned in 2007 for similar offences at the same school.

In respect of both boarding schools, there are others who have come forward and made statements and there are other arrests being made and to be made. There will be other trials in the near future. In the last few months, a man who I made a police statement against, has died prior to be arrested and another took his own life the day after being arrested.

Now is the time (post Saville) for others to come forward and to speak out. It is the secrecy that surrounds child abuse that protects the wrong people. It should not be a taboo subject anymore, it is repugnant and evil and shrouded by corruption. If more people spoke out and stood up for what is right, the tables would start to turn. The monstrous Jimmy Savile achieved one decent thing in his pathetic excuse for a life, he created a public awareness and outrage regarding institutional child sexual abuse. The media storm that followed the revelation of his crimes encouraged numerous victims of abuse to speak out (both men and women). In the time that has followed, the momentum for this remains and we, as a society should not let this go. Let us start to dismantle the protection and secrecy that protects the abusers. We should continue to encourage others to come forward and speak out, ensuring that there are mechanisms in place to support these people. One of the driving forces behind my investigation into the abusers of my past, was the thought 'Are these men still in a position to hurt young people?' Unless their past is uncovered and they are highlighted for what they are, they will still pose a danger to young people.
I would like to answer one question which I know a lot of people like to ask in these cases, or would like to know – Why did you wait so long to say anything?

Please understand that when a victim of childhood sexual abuse comes forward and does speak out, it has taken a huge amount of courage for that person to do so. It is probably of the bravest thing that person has done. They will be frightened and vulnerable because of this, but they have taken this course of action because they want their abuser/s to be exposed and in doing so, they will be stopping the abuse from continuing. If you ask that person initially – why did you not say something before? They will say "because I couldn't". At that point that's all you will get from them. The real reasons come out later in the healing process. Here are some of the answers to that question:

For me and the numerous other boys being subjected to this abuse, it started when we were very young (6+). We were vulnerable and alone. There were no inspections or audits of these schools and institutional abuse was a way of life for those it had entrapped. This was normal everyday (and night time) activity and it demanded total submission from us. Any attempt made to subvert or refuse advances was met with violence and brute force. It became very clear that fighting against it was counterproductive. You are left feeling shamed and the guilt of what has happened is transferred to you. You are made to be believe that no one will believe you and if you talk it about it, you will be ridiculed.

A victim of abuse may feel if they tell someone, they will be blamed for what had happened or be accused of lying about it. My biological father accused me of lying, when I told him in 1996 that I had been abused as a child and I was speaking to the police about it. He was one of the first people I told and one of the last for another 17 years.

Many victims of abuse are told to keep it a secret and sadly most do keep it a secret and keep it locked away deep inside for a very long time. It is very difficult having to think about it, even more so trying to talk about it and for some, they will be fearful of mentioning it, in case it is not accepted or listened to. I know from my experience, the actual act of talking about it to someone else was very difficult. The conditioned instinct of not talking about it meant I had to physically force the words out. Thankfully this does get better after time.

Many abusers threaten the victim that if they tell, they might kill someone in their family or threaten that the authorities will come in and break up their family.

Many victims of abuse dissociate when memories of their own abuse surfaces, to distance themselves from the pain or to protect their loved ones from the pain. Imagine the position of a 30 or 40-year-old man, with a wife and children, having to tell them that he was sexually abused as a child. The pain and anguish he is suffering in the act of telling them about it, will be transferred over to them! Some victims can only speak out once their abuser is dead, not that speaking about it becomes any easier for them.

That is just some of the reasons why that person may have not said anything for such a long time. For me, the healing process properly got underway when I started telling the medical professionals and the police what had happened to me. It has taken over 40 years to build the courage to do this. Justice has been my driving force. I am doing this for the little boy you see in my picture.

I recall feeling extremely apprehensive following posting this on Facebook. I had over 200 contacts on there. But on reflection, this was one of the best things I could have done. Apart from projecting my fears and anxiety and believing people would judge me, the entire opposite happened. Before long, the responses started coming back and numerous private messages, with words of support and comfort. In a way, I wished I had done this a long time before. I slept well that night. In all my future endeavours, I would be going into court with an army of supporters. I felt empowered.

Giving evidence in court, as a witness against one of your childhood abusers is an all-consuming event. It is as though your life is on hold and time itself stands still. There is nothing else at that point, only the impending court date. I can only imagine that Downing himself must have lived a similar experience. There was after all more at stake for him than I. This gave me great comfort. I wanted him to suffer greatly. To recap - towards the end of May 2014, just a matter of two weeks away from the Downing trial, I found that my life was consumed with thoughts of the trial. Every waking moment that I was not occupying my mind with activity or conversation, I was being constantly drawn into the impending Court activity. The same could be said of my night time thoughts too. Every night I experienced vivid dreams which blended places and people from the past and present. My brain was going into overdrive.

I went up to Margate Police Station on Wednesday 4th June 2014, after work to view my evidence video. Devon & Cornwall Police had sent a copy down to Kent Police to allow me to review what I had said in the interview a year and a half back. This was going to prove helpful to remind me what I had said and I suppose on the other hand, it had given me an idea of what line of questioning I will face when I am in the witness box on the 10th.

I did note that the video interview I gave had been edited down to some extent. There would undoubtedly have been erroneous information and equally unnecessary information. Many of the people I had talked to the officer about in my interview, had been omitted from the final draft. The indecent abuse I suffered at the hands of Mr Burrow, for example, was removed due to his death some years back and I had also spoke of the numerous indecent assaults I suffered at the hand of a former boy (Initials DC). It was deemed that the likelihood of those allegations passing the rigorous CPS grading procedures was unlikely to lead to a successful prosecution. I was informed however that the allegations against Mr Burrow and DC would be recorded and investigated, thereby allowing those details to be correlated against any future police investigations, where these individuals are named.

Mr George Burrow was a housemaster and crafts teacher at Heanton. I experienced him from 1970 to 1975. He was a former fireman and by all accounts, a man of repute on the surface. He was also violent man who did not think twice about beating us with the sole of a shoe – a specifically chosen, pliable sole, purposely removed from the original footwear, to be used for administrating punishment, through physical contact. He was also an opportunist paedophile, who gained personal pleasure from forcibly masturbating boys, he had woken and taken to the toilet cubicle in the early hours.

Thursday June 5th, 2014 – less than a week away from the trial in Exeter. I was ready to do it and although I felt that generally, I had my 'business head' on, during moments of quite reflection I failed to stop fears and doubts to creep into my head. I had constant butterflies in my stomach and most days felt like I was waiting outside of a room for a life-changing job interview, but the call never came.

The case in 2014 against John Downing fell apart. The jury failed to reach a verdict (or were unable to reach a verdict). It is suspected that perhaps the case was directed that way. It was a strong case, with excellent prospects of being successful. The corroborative evidence was sound. Maybe the influences directing the trial were pro-paedophile?? Maybe!!

A retrial for the John Downing case was scheduled for April 2015 at Exeter Crown Court. This time, a new jury was to be sworn in and an essentially important component was put into play, a different judge would be hearing the trial. Judge Graham Cottle was invited out of retirement, to manage the Downing trial.

I gave evidence on Wednesday 1st April 2015 and this time I had taken Mandy with me. The Crown Prosecution Service had agreed with the value that Mandy would bring to supporting me and booked a double room for us at The Marriott in Exeter. Having Mandy with me was always going to be winner. I was confident and I was ready.

This was my Facebook post 1st April 2015:

*This was my business face **Mandy** said - as Downing was waiting in the Court reception for us, in a weak attempt to intimidate I hope it scared the shit out of him. It was to be expected in Court. I was in the witness stand for just under 1.5 hours and felt it went well.*

Lee Woolcott-Ellis 2015
Copyright © Amanda Woolcott

They covered everything I expected. Waiting for the verdict now. 8 more witnesses after me. Should know next week sometime - that's my last court appearance which is a relief!!

The outcome of the second trial was breath-taking. More than we could have hoped for. Downing was found guilty, unanimously, of 39 counts of assault and gross indecency and was sentence immediately to 21 years in prison. I think the best epilogue to the Downing trial, was provided by Judge Graham Cottle, who summed up thus:

" It is many years since these crimes were committed but you must now answer for the catalogue of sexual abuse that you perpetrated on the seven complainants.

"I strongly suspect this case has no more than scratched the surface of the extent of the abuse of children at Heanton School for which you were responsible, but I only sentence you for the offences of which you were convicted.

"These boys came from unfortunate and disadvantaged backgrounds from which they were plucked when they were six or seven and taken to this school in North Devon.

Judge Graham Cottle
Copyright © Associated Newspapers Ltd

"They arrived no doubt as bewildered, frightened and abandoned children. On any view, they were exceptionally vulnerable. They were introduced to a regime that was at best inappropriate and at worst cruel and shocking.

"Excessive punishment of boys was routine and in that climate, you, as deputy head, took the opportunity to regularly, repeatedly and over many years abuse small boys as and when you pleased.

"The level and type of abuse was to right minded people truly horrendous and the victims have been scarred for life as a result. They were all required to relive their experiences by your denial.

"They were exposed to humiliating and embarrassing ordeal of having to tell their experiences to a room full of strangers. Nobody could fail to be moved by seeing them struggling to cope with that ordeal.

"They were demonstrably truthful but they had to contend with accusations of lying and fabrication.

"As a teacher and deputy head you subjected them to very serious sexual abuse. The regime at the school gave you licence to do whatever you wanted to these vulnerable and defenceless children and that is precisely what you did.

"For years you abused one boy after another after another. Apart from anal penetration you committed every form of sexual assault on one or more of them. One act of indecency would now be charged as rape.

"You made boys engage in sexual activity with each other for your sexual gratification and entertainment.

"At this trial, you have maintained an arrogant and defiant stance in the face of overwhelming evidence. I have to arrive at a total sentence that reflects the enormity of these crimes against vulnerable young children over many years.

"Your victims have tried to make something of their lives but drugs, alcohol, depression and imprisonment are common features. They are deeply scarred by and the majority of the blame for that can be lain at your door."

http://www.devonlive.com/devon-headmaster-organist-jailed-cruel-shocking/story-26320051-detail/story.html#gI5YWE5mfADZlwJz.99

This Downing trial saw the end of the investigation into abuse at Heanton School and the investigation was closed by Devon and Cornwall police in 2015.

Most of the people at Heanton School responsible for violent assaults against young boys, merciless mental torture and indecent activity with or to young boys were either dead, or there was a lack of corroborating evidence and witnesses, thus preventing any further investigation being taken. John Downing by far, was the alpha paedophile at Heanton School.

Operation Garford, Ipswich and my part in that investigation was still on going in 2014, when I attended the first John Downing trial in Exeter. By the time I saw Downing being sent down in 2015, my part in Operation Garford was over.

I made my statement for Suffolk Police in 2013. The processes with Suffolk police was very similar to that with Devon and Cornwall police, apart from I had more actual face-to-face contact with officers from Operation Garford than I did with those from Devon. I am guessing the geography involved would have played some part in that. The key developments from Operation Garford for me were my initial involvement in it.

I actively supported The Guardian Newspaper reports and gave interviews to them, to the regional newspapers and to the BBC. The reports and interviews can be seen in [Appendix J: page 124-125].

The media exposure was handled well and it worked perfectly. We had a rocky start to the police investigation, but with support from Dan Poulter, the Conservative MP for Central Suffolk & North Ipswich, he urged Suffolk's Chief Constable, Simon Ash to reopen the Kesgrave Hall School abuse investigation from early 1990's. With many additional witnesses coming forward to support the police investigation, Suffolk police had no choice but to open it and to widen the investigation to cover the allegations of abuse at Kesgrave Hall School, from 1975 until 1993. Additional names were thrown into the mix and Kesgrave Hall School was thoroughly looked into. In all 17 individuals were investigated and over 100 witnesses were spoken to. No stone was left unturned by Suffolk Police and I found all my dealings with them thorough and highly professional.

Key occurrences for me in Operation Garford:

Two men were arrested by Suffolk Police Officers from Operation Garford on 11th April 2014 and questioned regarding allegations of his indecent behaviour and alleged sexual assaults, whilst they were staff members at Kesgrave Hall School in the 1970's. One of the men was Kenneth Wheatley, known to us at Kesgrave Hall School as Kenneth Scott. Scott was also questioned the same day by officers from the National Crime Agency in respect of Operation Pallial (Historic Abuse Investigation in North Wales). The believe the other man was Alan Stancliffe.

On Tuesday 15th April 2014, I finished work and got home at the normal time of just after 5.00pm. At approximately 5:30 pm, I received a phone call on my mobile from a Suffolk Police detective. They wanted to come and see me at my house. About 1 hour later, the two Suffolk Police officers whom took my video statement on 26th September 2013, came to the front door.

We settled into the lounge and after the pleasantries the officer's told me that following the arrest of two men on Friday 11th April. One of the men was Mr Scott, the houseparent (carer) I had named regarding Kesgrave Hall School. I was told that Kenneth Wheatley (Scott) from Barnsley was found dead beside a railway line in Barnsley on Saturday 12th April 2014.

I do have to say that I was shocked to hear this and when asked how I felt, I had to say I had mixed emotions. I know what the Kesgrave/Heanton monsters were capable of and I knew of the damage and harm they can cause. Taking all that into consideration, I think I would have preferred him to have faced justice and rotted in a living hell, rather than have taken the cowards route and decide not to face his accusers, me being one of them.

As they days went on from this revelation (it took a few days to process the information properly), I concluded that I was unhappy about his death. I would not entirely mourn him as a person, but I am reminded of a line from a poem by **John Donne** – *"Any man's death diminishes me, because I am involved in Mankind; and therefore, never send to know for whom the bell tolls; it tolls for thee"*

After all it is these Christian morals that separate normal human beings from these debased, creatures that prey on young children for their own sexual gratification.

As the weeks went on, it became known through the media that the man found dead on the Railway track on 12th May was Kenneth Wheatley (62) from Barnsley [Appendix: X page 189]. They made the connection to Operational Pallial and Operation Garford. Kenneth Scott, very much like John Downing and Alan Stancliffe was a predatory paedophile, in every respect.

A further bit of digging suggested that Scott had changed his surname in the early nineties when he was released from prison, to protect his identity. Scott was jailed for 8 years in 1986, having been found guilty of gross indecency and buggery whilst a house-parent in the North Wales Care Homes [see Appendix: P page 159-160]. From my own personal experience of Scott and knowledge of his interactions with other boys at the school, it is evident of his progression from a mild pervert in the seventies, to a full blown predatory paedophile in the 80's. There is a seriously lesson to be learnt here, especially with the current trend to decriminalise certain, so called 'soft' activities, like downloading and storing pornographic images, involving the abuse of children.

During the afternoon of 13th May 2014, I received a mobile phone call from an officer on the Operation Garford team, to tell me that they had located David Brockman, a former house-parent from Kesgrave Hall School, that I had named in my recent statement them. He had been questioned by officers from Operation Garford, but they had received further information that he had died from a heart attack during the week of 5th to 9th May 2014.

David Brockman was a particularly nasty man and I doubt very many that had encountered him at Kesgrave Hall School would mourn his passing. It is a great shame that he had escaped a court trial and full exposure for what he really was. He should have faced my allegations of indecent assault and physical assault. The truth about Brockman's past would be buried with him, if it was not for text like this. This was the *real* David Brockman.

The picture portrayed of Brockman in an obituary published by Russ J. Graham of Transdiffusion (8th May 2014) [see Appendix: Y page 190] made out that he was a public spirited, self-made broadcasting expert that supported youth causes and public enterprise. I can talk from personal experience here, I would suggest that anyone who had the misfortune of being under the care of Mr Brockman at Kesgrave Hall School would know him as a pathetic paedophile and a sadistic monster, who relished the suffering and discomfort of young boys. He was a monstrous man who touched and groped boys indecently. His favourite trick was standing in a doorway, forcing boys to exit having to squeeze past him and as you passed through the doorway he would thrust himself forward causing you to rub against his genitals as you hurried past. He frequently kicked, slapped and punched boys as young as 11 years old.

Brockman was hiding from his past in the Huntingdon Community Radio - HCR104fm, hiding from what he used to be. I would question his credentials also, to my knowledge David Brockman was a full-time houseparent at Kesgrave Hall School certainly throughout the later part of the 1970's into the 1980's, so there has to be some question to his claim that he was working at the BBC and writing for the Radio Times throughout the 1970's.

Alan Stancliffe died on 17th September 2014 in a hospice of liver disease. He had been interviewed by Suffolk police and was on bail [Appendix I: page 123]

Alan Stancliffe, of Pontefract, west Yorkshire, was arrested earlier in April 2014 for suspected assaults on three pupils at Kesgrave Hall School. I was not a complainant in this matter, I had achieved my justice on the Stancliffe front in 1996 and was party to his incarnation back then. I was reliably informed that Stancliffe (65) was being treated for advanced liver disease, at the time of his arrest for fresh allegations against him. Following this he had appeared to refuse his medication for the treatment of alcoholic hepatitis. He allowed himself to die sooner than later.

Stancliffe was a raging alcoholic back in the 1970's, when he stank of whisky most nights, when he visited my bed. There was one occasion he was so drunk, he had brought a footstall to sit on to assist him. He indecently assaulted three of us that night in the dormitory and had vomited on the foot of my bed also. If you are wondering if he had cleaned up after the vomiting – no, he did not. The bedding would have been changed during the day by the cleaning staff.

Since Stancliffe's arrest earlier this year it is understood a fourth man has contacted police to make allegations about him. However, at the time of his death Stancliffe had not been arrested in relation to these allegations. He had been due to answer police bail on December 9.

During late September 2014, I received a phone call from the Detective Sergeant (Operation Garford) Suffolk Police, mid-afternoon whilst at work at the Queen Elizabeth the Queen Mother Hospital, Margate, with some updates of from the Kesgrave Hall investigation. Confirmation, that out of the five persons I had made allegations against in my last video statement to Suffolk Police, in relation the Kesgrave Hall School 1975 to 1980, only two persons remained active in their investigation. Brockman, Scott (Wheatley) and Stancliffe had recently died, so that finished any possibility of justice achieved in their case.

The forth man I made allegations against was the Kesgrave Hall School doctor. A General Practitioner from Martlesham Heath. I remember attending his surgery when I suffered a broken collar bone in 1978. He sent me to Ipswich A&E. Apart from that, my main recollection of the GP was his annual visits to the school, when we were stripped naked and laid on a bed in the infirmary for him to give us an annual MOT and injections, etc. My allegations were what else happened whilst I was in the room with this man all the time being watched by the headmistress Mrs. Shepherd.

The DS informed me that they had identified and located the former school GP. He had been arrested and questioned in a police station regarding the allegations I had made. I got the impression that there may have been other allegations from another witness, in the same vein. The man had denied all allegations and it was considered that this matter would not stand up to the Crown Prosecution processes and therefore it could not be followed up. There was some gratification to be gained I guess, from the knowledge that the former School GP had been arrested and questioned in 2014. I expect he had not for once believe that is actions in the 1970's would have come back to bite him.

So, by late 2014 only one person remained viable, in respect of my allegations made to the Police in 2013, that was Mr Michael Lafford. At this stage, I was told his case was with CPS awaiting a decision.

On November 18, 2014, another phone call. The last man standing, so to speak in my part of Operation Garford, Michael Lafford had taken his own life – also.

67-year-old Michael Lafford, French and German teacher and house-parent at Kesgrave Hall School was dead. He had been quizzed by Operation Garford detectives, but on that fateful day, he was at his home in Oxfordshire and officers from Thames Valley Police were banging on his door. They were there to question him on 'other matters'. After barricading himself in, to prevent his impending arrest, he swallowed many tablets. When officers finally gained entry into his property, they found him slumped on the sofa. Lafford died in hospital later that day. Another monster gone. He cheated justice in this world, but will atone for all his actions – they all will.

Following Lafford's death, a spokeswoman for Ofsted confirmed the he had been employed as an additional Ofsted Inspector, but had been employed by Tribal, one of its inspection service providers.

By mid-November 2014, my active participation in Operation Garford had now concluded. The only part I could now play was possible corroboration and validation.

Operation Garford finally concluded in May 2016 following the conviction and imprisonment of John McKno, a teacher from Kesgrave Hall School, whom I never had the misfortune of meeting. McKno worked at Kesgrave between 1986 and 1987, but his history of offending took place in two of his previous schools also - Beam College in Devon (where he taught from 1978 to 1979) and St Michael's College in Worcestershire (where he taught between 1979 and 1985).

Operation Garford was more successful than anyone could imagine. The officers involved should all be very proud of what they achieved. They gave a voice to many of the boys, who had buried away the horrific experiences they suffered, whilst detained at Kesgrave Hall School. Many of the disgustingly violent and sick men, that preyed on young, vulnerable boys were exposed and several of them faced their final judgement as a result.

By stepping forward and speaking to the police about their historic experiences, a lot of the boys would have been given the opportunity to unburden themselves of such haunting memories. Many would have been given the opportunity to get proper support and treatment in that respect. That is a winning scenario.

I would like to quote from Detective Constable Wendy Leah. I got to know Wendy Leah over the few years I was involved with Operation Garford. I found her, like all her colleagues at Suffolk Police, highly professional, exceptionally well communicative and motivated in the case, to the point of obsession.

Wendy Leah, when reporting after the McKno sentencing said:

"Time should never be a barrier in achieving justice. I hope the sentence passed today provides some level of closure and allows the victims to continue to recover from these traumatic experiences."

That sums Operation Garford well. Thank you to all officers and support staff involved in the lengthy and convoluted investigation into Kesgrave Hall School. Now fully exposed for the hell hole it was. I would also like to thank all the former boys who came forward and supported the police investigation.

To all those boys that appeared to survive fully and progress through the school, without incident, you certainly can count your blessing and to all the former teachers and staff, that did me harm – may you all rot in hell. ☠

Chapter 8

CLOSURE
Positive Mental Health and recognising who Lee is

The year 2014 was highly significant to me. The year I saw the last of my childhood tormentors facing a jury in Crown Court. John Downing a truly horrific and dangerous man, who was subsequently sent to prison for 21 years in April 2015. His last year of freedom, the time between the Crown Court trials of 2014 and 2015, were undoubtedly the worst year of his life, thinking constantly whether he would be sent to prison. This would be for him a life sentence because at the age of 72, he would unlikely be coming out again.

The year 2014 was the year I identify as the end of my abuse journey. Downing was in the system and he was not getting out of that again. He had been exposed and he was going to face a jury, which he subsequently did. Downing is now serving his sentence in Parkhurst Prison. In my blog, I wrote the following piece:

Copyright © 2015 Devon Live

A caged monster
Posted on April 11, 2015 by lwe1964

On Friday 10th April 2015, after 3 years of legal hurdles and a few twists and turns, we have finally put an extremely evil paedophile away. Together with other men of great courage, former Heanton School boys who have suffered violence and abuse at the hands of John Downing, we finally got a jury to find him guilty of gross indecency, indecent acts and violence against boys from the age of 6 to 11. The jury took just under three hours to return guilty verdicts on 39 counts against John Downing. Within hours, he was sentenced to a total of 21 years in prison and taken away. The former teacher/carer of Heanton School, nr. Braunton, North Devon (1968 to the 1980's), now a 73-year-old man will unlikely ever see freedom again.

This is a realistic sentence and in a small way, it has helped me to find some closure for the 5 years I was sexually and physically abused by John Downing at Heanton School, from 1970 to 1975.

This is a proper, appropriately lengthy sentence that will send a message out to the other surviving abusers from Heanton School and Kesgrave Hall School. It is just a matter of time before your day comes. I would like to say to any other former boys that suffered sexual, physical and mental abuse at either of these (or other schools) this has been a good thing to do, a worthwhile thing. It was not always easy to undertake, but I would encourage other former victims (survivors) to follow the legal path. There is a considerable amount of healing to be gained from it. Expose your abuser/s and improve your life and your mental health. It can work, the system will support you and listen to you. Justice can be achieved.

A message to John Downing *– There is no more hiding in St. Michael's Church in Torrington behind the veneer of respectability anymore. The true John Downing is now exposed to the whole world. You are a vile, depraved and violent creature who will now rot in prison for the rest of your days. You know what you did to us and you know you have only had to answer for a small fraction of your actions. You are disgusting and you know it. Think back to Wednesday 1st April 2015, at approximately 09:35 hours. You were sitting in the Crown Court at Exeter and clearly waiting for me to enter the Court. You knew I was being cross examined that day, because you had viewed my evidence the afternoon before. When I entered the Court with my partner, Mandy, you stared at us. I was not intimidated by you, I saw a sad, lonely old man. Can I remind you of what you saw - A confident, professional man who has achieved well in his life, being supported by a loving, beautiful woman.*

I would like to explain why I requested for the blinds to be put up in Court when I was cross examined. I was in no way intimidated by your presence in Court. The reason for my request was that I did not want to look at you, because you disgust me.

You did not ruin my life Downing. You and others made it difficult for me for a few years. You humiliated me, beat me, you did disgusting, abhorrent acts to me and in my presence, but I am better than you. I have a life, yours is now officially over. I feel no pity for you. I hope you rot in prison and one day you will have to answer properly for your sins against all those children.

In Court, you misguidedly said that your actions and the violence you used 'was of the time' – if that could in anyway mitigate your actions. Well, it is you who is now doing the time Mr Downing!!

Blog Reference: https://leewe15.wordpress.com/2015/04/11/a-caged-monster/
Devon Live reference: http://www.devonlive.com/devon-headmaster-organist-jailed-cruel-shocking/story-26320051-detail/story.html#1

In 2014, Alan Stancliffe was also now dead, but not before I had my final say about him and he was interviewed by Suffolk Police once again. Other boys also had the opportunity to have their say about his crimes towards them and hopefully start their journey to find some inner peace.

It was also the year that David Brockman died from a heart attack, undoubtedly assisted by his arrest for historic abuse allegations. The year Alan Stancliffe, Kenneth Scott (Wheatley) and Michael Lafford all died, by their own actions because of the impending court trials they faced and we, former Kesgrave Hall School boys had played some part in those deaths. By contacting the police and making statements, these individuals died indirectly because of just that. Their past cruelty and crimes against us caught up with them.

Historic abuse is still featuring in the media and more people that come forward, I am convinced will encourage more people to come forward. I truly hope that the Independent Inquiry into Child Sexual Abuse (IICSA) does impact on policy and procedure, to not only help to prevent CSA continuing unchecked, in all parts of our society, but also helps to encourage more victims to come forward. [Appendix: S page 165] I do wonder though how far the 'system' will allow itself to become exposed 'paedophile hegemony'.

Real development would see the failure by Clergy, School management, Social workers and Police officers, historically and currently, to act positively to reports of child sexual abuse being criminalised. Failure to act and even worse, allowing it to knowingly continue, is as bad as the act itself. These factors are a big part of the problem and allow it to proliferate openly through their inaction and agendas.

In all the years of my turmoil, anger and sadness and really feeling that something was missing in my life, it was just me. The real Lee. I had no identity from the moment I was taken away from home at the age of six years. From that instant, my life was controlled by others and any spark of personality was quickly extinguished. Even to the extent that on leaving the institutional system I only found comfort in abusive friendships and situations. There was some comfort to be gained from feeding off other people's agendas. After seeking support and accepting that things had to change, there was a eureka moment and a realisation that the thing I was searching for all your along, for most of my life, was right there by my side from the start. I didn't need to crave the attention of others and certainly not the negativity of that.

Going back to face my demons, real evil individuals and reliving my past horrors was my saviour. Opening my mind and letting the screaming child come out, in a controlled environment, gave me the vehicle I needed to support the numerous police investigations into the crimes committed by former teachers and housemasters. Not an easy road to follow, but the path I had to take to get to the morning after the prison van doors slammed shut on the final person I had to deal with, John Downing.

Ironically, Downing was the genesis of all my troubles and the final solution to my happiness. Being told he was removed immediately from the Court room to a prison van was an insanely happy moment. A happiness so powerful it took the breath out of my lungs. It was over. Justice had been served. The truth was told and people listened and acted. They had all been dealt with in one way or another. The small, frightened children, that had lived for years in complete terror had stood up and said to their masters 'enough, you now have to answer for what you did'

I no longer had unanswered questions or unfinished business. The job was done and although there was no need to look back any further, the memories and horrors of what had happened to me as a child, are still there. The difference today is that they no longer control and direct my life. They are contained and as such given some respect by me. I needed to be comfortable in the knowledge that there is no real 'getting over' what happened, I had to accept this fact and then learn how to live with it.

I am reminded of what the psychologist first said to me on day one of my therapy 'imagine that your mind is currently an overfilled airing cupboard, the doors continuously bulge open and because the contents are all jumbled up and essentially just thrown in there, it is not possible to close the doors of the cupboard. What we are going to do, is carefully start to remove the contents of the airing cupboard and one by one, we will fold them up neatly and start to place them back into the airing cupboard, in such a way that we can successfully close the doors of the cupboard'. We did just that.

In conclusion:

We are all a product of our experiences, but equally we do have some control over our life journey. We can effect real change for ourselves, through positive actions. I have had, to use the vernacular, a 'fucked up' life. Although at times, an all-consuming nightmare that impacted on every sphere of my existence and those dear to me – but, by accepting all that happened, did happen and wanting to do something about dealing with that, I did just that. I effected positive change and returned my demons to the pit of hell they came from.

Child abuse in every respect, is destructive far beyond the initial acts themselves. The perpetrators of such devastation have no real conception of the extent of harm they are causing their victims. They are lost in the pleasure of the moment itself and that about sums them up - self-centred, despicable creatures who have no humanity left in them. To be able to perform such abhorrent acts on a fellow, vulnerable human being, without any thought or concern for their victim's wellbeing, current or future, just about describes what debased, and worthless creatures they are. Paedophiles have no part in our culture and in my opinion, should be removed from society, permanently, for the safety and security of all young people.

My story is in no way unique, but the outcome is something worth talking about. Historic child sexual abuse and violence I endured as a child, like an extreme trauma, is something no one who experienced it can ever truly forget. It will always be part of us and it will always be there. We have a responsibility to ourselves to learn how to live with our pasts and make the most of our lives.

There is still more to do, to get child sexual abuse openly spoken about and acknowledged as a major concern in the UK. It has significantly changed post Savile and many people have come forward and spoken of their past abuse, but stigma and taboo remain.

Male mental health continues to be a particularly difficult area to impact upon and male suicide still shockingly, accounts for the highest suicide rate in the UK, this being for men aged 40–44 (*The Samaritans – stats 2015*) [Appendix: F page 111-112 for link]. Convincing men who are adult victims of child sexual abuse, especially those who remain in total denial, that they need to talk about what happened to them, is always going to be difficult. The 'system' still needs to adjust more to support this.

The media has done so, in most cases sensationalising of abuse stories is non-existent now, with too many previously 'getting their fingers burnt', the McAlpine story comes readily to mind. The Police and the Judiciary have improved procedures and are ensuring witnesses have appropriate support in place, during different parts of evidential processes being applied.

Recognising that it is not easy for adult victims of child abuse to speak openly to a courtroom has been covered by blinds being made available to support the witness and video conferencing also. The video statement, when compared to the written statement, is a major move forward. The length of time these interviews take place, still needs to be addressed though. Anything over 1 hour, is going to be an issue for some people. My videoed interviews went up to nearly 3 hours on occasions. This is very exhausting, mentally and not having a trained professional present, to close the boxes being opened, can be problematic.

'Stepping into the arena' as I have called it previously, when making a police statement and delving back into your mind, recalling all the harmful memories that have dwelled in the nightmare regions of your brain, is abusive. I have stood in the witness box many times and the first thing that has happened on every instance, is a defence barrister standing up, addressing me and then telling the whole courtroom that I am a liar and that everything I said in my evidence statements or video was pure fabrication. Some would argue that this is just part of the judicial process. Others may say that this is abusive. Loudly accusing the victim of lying about the abuse itself potentially unsettling an exposed and vulnerable person. The defendants being found guilty generally refuted the barrister's indictment.

I believe the process of getting a guilty plea in a crown court trial, for a serial or predatory paedophile is generally better now, certainly a quicker process. There are undoubtedly pro-paedophile individuals frustrating the systems, where they can, but the more we can encourage, brave victims of child sexual abuse to speak about what happened to them, the more we can expose the paedophiles and disrupt their networks.

The 'paedophile hegemony' as I have named them do exist, sadly. There are networks of paedophiles, that have members of high rank or privilege, and these are protected by likeminded individuals. Secret organisations if you like, that operate in the shadows, but I firmly believe that with every successful case, that exposes the truth about paedophile activity, dissolves their power and importance, bit by bit. Disrupting any network will cause it to cease to function effectively.

I am glad I decided to face my past and deal with all that happened to me and to those that harmed me. It may not have been an easy task, at times, but it has been the making of me. I found my identity and I found inner peace. The monsters that took much of my life away from me, were forced to face up to their pasts also and all, one way or another, have paid the price for their actions.

To close, I would remind any person triggered or affected by this book, in any way to speak to a close friend or family member or get some support. Links provided on the next page.

Without wanting to appear cavalier, if anything in this book 'of truth' offends anyone – you need to deal with that. Some of the people named in the book may have appeared to be decent people in some circles, but behind closed doors at Heanton or Kesgrave Hall, they were violent, sick individuals, that should never have been left in charge of any child.

It is good to talk.

Help & Support

The following pages provide some links to places for help and support of victims of abuse.

Support

NAPAC - The National Association for People Abused in Childhood
https://napac.org.uk/

MIND
https://www.mind.org.uk/information-support/guides-to-support-and-services/abuse/sexual-abuse/#.WZ_TUiiGNPY

A-Z List of NHS Mental Health Trusts in England
http://www.hp-mos.org.uk/a-z-list-of-nhs-mental-health-trusts-in-england/
(Google 'Mental Health Services' for all other countries/regions)

The Survivors Trust
http://thesurvivorstrust.org/

NSPCC - National Society for the Prevention of Cruelty to Children
https://www.nspcc.org.uk/

Survivors' Voices
http://www.oneinfour.org.uk/wp-content/uploads/2015/11/Survivors_Voices_Report_November_2015-2.pdf

Finding a doctor (General Practitioner)
http://www.nhs.uk/NHSEngland/AboutNHSservices/doctors/Pages/NHSGPs.aspx

Advice:

Samaritans
https://www.samaritans.org/

Citizens Advice
https://www.citizensadvice.org.uk/

Government/Legal:

Bolt Burdon Kemp is a national law firm specialising in claims for loss and injury
http://www.boltburdonkemp.co.uk/

Victim Support
https://www.victimsupport.org.uk/going-court

POLICE
Contact your local police station or police force to make allegations of historic abuse.
https://www.police.uk/information-and-advice/reporting-crime/

Other:

The UK & Ireland (Paedophile) Database
https://theukdatabase.com/

No More Secrets (Facebook – Child Sexual Abuse Awareness Page)
https://www.facebook.com/No-More-Secrets-809446972476085/

Survivors of Abuse
http://survivorsofabuse.org.uk/low-child-abuse-csa-chris-tuck-founder-director-s-o-b-www-survivorsofabuse-org-uk/

APPENDICES

The appendix section of the book, provides a reference point to parts of the text, in the book, as directed by the book section. It also contains additional research materials, that I either used or referred to. I have included such research in the book, as I am sure other victims of historic abuse, may also find interest in those pieces.

Appendix A:	The Underwood Report 1955	page 100
Appendix B:	Heanton School	page 101
Appendix C:	Kesgrave Hall School	page 102 -103
Appendix D:	Paedophile Information Exchange	page 104 - 108
Appendix E:	CSA and Physical Brain Damage	page 109 - 110
Appendix F:	Links to research sources	page 111 - 112
Appendix G:	Boarding School Syndrome - Katie Englehart #1	page 113 - 119
Appendix H:	John Downing	page 120 - 122
Appendix I:	Alan Stancliffe	page 123
Appendix J:	Lee Woolcott-Ellis Media Links	page 124 - 125
Appendix K:	No More Secrets (The Blogs)	page 126 - 145
Appendix L:	Boarding School Syndrome – Wendy Leigh #2	page 146 - 148
Appendix M:	Jimmy Savile	page 149 - 152
Appendix N:	The Dame Janet Smith Review (Jimmy Savile)	page 153
Appendix O:	The Westminster Abuse Scandal	page 154 - 158
Appendix P:	Operation Pallial	page 159 - 160
Appendix Q:	Operation Garford	page 161 -162
Appendix R:	Police under pressure	page 163 - 164
Appendix S:	(IICSA) Independent Inquiry into Child Sexual Abuse	page 165
Appendix T:	Lee W. Ellis – The Doctor's Letters	page 166 -167
Appendix U:	British Journal of Psychotherapy – Boarding School Syndrome #3	Page 168 - 186
Appendix V:	CBT Cognitive Behavioural Therapy	page 187
Appendix W:	School Report – Summer 1979	page 188
Appendix X:	Kenneth Scott (Wheatley)	page 189
Appendix Y:	David Brockman Obituary	page 190

Appendix A: The Underwood Report (1955)

The Underwood Report - Committee on Maladjusted Children (1955) Report of the Committee on Maladjusted Children (Chairman: J. E. A. Underwood) London

http://www.educationengland.org.uk/documents/underwood/underwood1955.html

The complete report is shown in this single web page (**link above**). You can scroll through it or use the following links to go to the various chapters.

(page numbers in brackets)

MEMBERSHIP OF COMMITTEE
(Appointed by the Minister of Education by Minute dated 4th October 1950)
Chairman: Dr. J. E. A. Underwood, C.B.E., M.B., D.P.H. (Principal Medical Officer, Ministry of Education, until 30th June 1951).
Dr. A. F. Alford, C.B.E., M.B. (Senior Medical Officer, Ministry of Education).
Miss E. M. Bartlett, Ph.D. (Psychologist to the Education Committee, Essex County Council).
Miss S. Clement Brown (Director of Child Care Studies, Home Office Children's Department Inspectorate).
Dr. H. M. Cohen, M.D., D.P.H. (Principal School Medical Officer, Birmingham County Borough).
Dr. E. M. Creak, M.D., F.R.C.P., D.P.M. (Physician in Psychological Medicine, Hospital for Sick Children, Great Ormond Street).
Dr. P. Henderson, M.D., D.P.H. (Principal Medical Officer, Ministry of Education).*
Mr. R. Howlett (Under Secretary, Special Services Branch, Ministry of Education).
Mr. W. F. Kemp (Headmaster, Bredinghurst School for Maladjusted Boys, London).
Mr. J. Lumsden (H.M. Inspector of Schools).
Mr. E. D. Marris, C.B. (Under Secretary, Special Services Branch, Ministry of Education, until 30th September 1951).
Mr. E. W. D. Ray, O.B.E. (H.M. Inspector of Schools until 15th September 1951).
Dr. W. Rees Thomas, C.B., M.D., F.R.C.P., D.P.M. (Senior Commissioner, Board of Control).
Mrs. M. J. Robinson, J.P. (Member of London Juvenile Court Panel).
Dr. W. P. H. Sheldon, C.V.O., M.D., F.R.C.P. (physician, Hospital for Sick Children, Great Ormond Street).
Dr. A. Torrie, M.B., D.P.M. (Medical Director, The Retreat, York).
Mr. E. W. Woodhead (County Education Officer, Kent County Council).

Secretary
D. Neylan (until September 1952) (Ministry of Education).
M. A. Walker (from September 1952) (Ministry of Education).

*Dr. Henderson succeeded Dr. Underwood as Principal Medical Officer of the Ministry of Education on 1st July 1951 and was co-opted as a member of the Committee at their ninth meeting on 6th July 1951.

Appendix B: Heanton School

Heanton School
Heanton Hill, Barnstable,
North Devon EX31 4DT

Copyright © http://www.heantonschool.org.uk

Heanton School Limited
Company Number: 00978502
Company Type: Private limited with share capital
SIC Code: 6523
Inc. Date: 30 Apr 1970
Annual Returns: Unknown
Annual Accounts: Unknown
Change of Directors: 26 July 1985
Final Dissolution: 07 Jul 1992

Mr. Vivian Thomas Charles Davies
Born: Mar 1928
Director, School Master
20 Nov 1990 — Close

Mrs Mair Buddug Davies
Born: Apr 1929
Director/Company Secretary
20 Nov 1990 — Close

Registered Address: Trading Address:

The Priory
Stradbroke
Diss Norfolk
IP21 5HU
United Kingdom

Heanton School Limited was registered on 30 Apr 1970 with its registered office in Diss, Norfolk. The business has a status listed as "Dissolved "and it had 2 at the time it closed. Heanton School Limited has no subsidiaries.

[Information source: © 2009-2013, DueDil Ltd https://www.duedil.com/company/00978502/heanton-school-limited]

Appendix C: Kesgrave Hall School

Kesgrave Hall School
Hall Road, Ipswich, Suffolk IP5 2PU

Copyright ©Archant

Kesgrave Hall School Limited
Company Number: 01259517
Company Type: Private limited with share capital
SIC Code: 7011
Inc. Date: 20 May 1976
Annual Returns: Unknown
Annual Accounts: 30 Apr 1996

Change in Registration Office: 14 Jan 1994
Change in Share Capital: 21 Feb 1987
Change in Mem & Arts: 21 Feb 1987
Change of Directors: 12 Jul 1985

Mr Nigel Robert Kennard Mr Vivian Thomas Charles Davies
Born: Jul 1944 Born: Mar 1928
Director, **Chartered Accountant Director, Schoolmaster**
11 Jan 1991 — Close 11 Jan 1991 — Close

Mrs Doreen Ann Brunning
Born: Unknown
Company Secretary
11 Jan 1991 — Close

Registered Address: Trading Address:
Garland House
Garland Street
Bury St Edmonds
Suffolk
IP33 1EZ

Kesgrave Hall School Limited was registered on 20 May 1976 with its registered office in Suffolk. The business has a status listed as "Dissolved" and it had 2 at the time it closed. Kesgrave Hall School Limited has no subsidiaries.

[Information source: © 2009-2013, DueDil Ltd
https://www.duedil.com/company/01259517/kesgrave-hall-school-limited]

Appendix D: Paedophile Information Exchange

How did the pro-paedophile group PIE exist openly for 10 years?

By Tom de Castella & Tom Heyden BBC News Magazine

27 February 2014
http://www.bbc.co.uk/news/magazine-26352378

Former KGB spy and PIE member Geoffrey Prime (left) and PIE Chairman Tom O'Carroll (Image copyright PA/REX FEATURES)

The Paedophile Information Exchange was affiliated to the National Council for Civil Liberties - now Liberty - in the late 1970s and early 1980s. But how did pro-paedophile campaigners operate so openly?

A gay rights conference backs a motion in favour of paedophilia. The story is written up by a national newspaper as "Child-lovers win fight for role in Gay Lib".

It sounds like a nightmarish plotline from dystopian fiction. But this happened in the UK. The conference took place in Sheffield and the newspaper was the Guardian. The year was 1975.

It's part of the story of how paedophiles tried to go mainstream in the 1970s. The group behind the attempt - the Paedophile Information Exchange - is back in the news because of a series of stories run by the Daily Mail about Labour deputy leader Harriet Harman.

The Daily Mail has revisited the story of PIE to ask how much Harman and her husband the MP Jack Dromey knew about the group during their time working at the National Council for Civil Liberties, now Liberty, in the late 1970s. PIE was affiliated to the NCCL from the late 1970s to early 1980s.

Many of the revelations are not in fact new. The story's return to the front pages demonstrates the shock people feel about how a group with "paedophile" in its name could operate so openly for so long.

PIE was formed in 1974. It campaigned for "children's sexuality". It wanted the government to axe or lower the age of consent. It offered support to adults "in legal difficulties concerning sexual acts with consenting 'under age' partners". The real aim was to normalise sex with children.

Journalist Christian Wolmar remembers their tactics. "They didn't emphasise that this was 50-year-old men wanting to have sex with five-year-olds. They presented it as the sexual liberation of children, that children should have the right to sex," he says.

It's an ideology that seems chilling now. But PIE managed to gain support from some professional bodies and progressive groups. It received invitations from student unions, won sympathetic media coverage and found academics willing to push its message.

It's wrong to say that PIE was tolerated during the 1970s, says Times columnist Matthew Parris. "I remember a lot of indignation about it [PIE]. It was considered outrageous."

The group's visits to universities were often opposed. In 1977 PIE's chairman Tom O'Carroll was ejected from a conference on "love and attraction" at University College, Swansea after lecturers "threatened not to deliver their papers if Mr O'Carroll stayed", the Times reported. The May 1978 issue of Magpie, PIE's in-house newspaper, records how O'Carroll had been invited to address students at Liverpool and Oxford University but that the visits were cancelled after local opposition.

Protestors and police outside Conway Hall, London, where PIE was holding its first open meeting in 1977 (GETTY IMAGES)

One of PIE's key tactics was to try to conflate its cause with gay rights. On at least two occasions the Campaign for Homosexual Equality conference passed motions in PIE's favour.

Most gay people were horrified by any conflation of homosexuality and a sexual interest in children, says Parris. But PIE used the idea of sexual liberation to win over more radical elements. "If there was anything with the word 'liberation' in the name you were automatically in favour of it if you were young and cool in the 1970s. It seemed like PIE had slipped through the net."

Some have suggested that the nature of the debate was different then. "In this free-for-all, anything and everything was open for discussion," said Canon Angela Tilby on Radio 4's Thought for the Day. "There were those who claimed that sexual relationships between adults and children could be harmless." Homosexuality had only been decriminalised in 1967. There was still prejudice and inequality. The age of consent was 16 for heterosexuals but 21 for homosexual men.

Wolmar had first-hand contact with PIE. In 1976, he began working for Release, an agency helping people with drug and legal problems. Its office at 1 Elgin Avenue in London was a mailing address for PIE. Nobody knew much about them, Wolmar says. "They used to drop in once a week to pick up their mail. They were greasy men," he recalls, people who fitted the stereotype of the "dirty mac" brigade. After Wolmar raised questions about PIE it was decided to bring them in for a meeting.

Wolmar's colleagues pressed the man from PIE on the age of consent. Wolmar says that the man said there should be no age of consent. Shocked at the idea of a group advocating sex with babies, he and his colleagues unanimously decided to "boot them out".

It was easy to join PIE. According to a Times legal report on a blackmail case from February 1977, there was no need for subterfuge, just an application and a cheque for £4. In the report, the prosecutor in the case stated: "He said on the form that he was a paedophile, male, married, 29 years old and attracted to girls between the ages of seven and 13 years." The judge proclaimed himself "horrified" at the existence of PIE.

Unsettlingly for a modern audience, the PIE member received anonymity (as is typical in blackmail cases) and there is no mention of any prosecution of him. Meanwhile, the blackmailer was jailed for three years.

The brazenness could be shocking. Keith Hose, one of PIE's leaders during the 1970s, was quoted by a newspaper saying: "I am a paedophile. I am attracted to boys from about 10, 11, and 12 years of age. I may have had sexual relations with children, but it would be unwise to say."

When Polly Toynbee interviewed O'Carroll and Hose in the Guardian in September 1977 she heard men incredulous at the lack of support from the press. They seemed genuinely aggrieved at what they called a "Fleet Street conspiracy". One of them told her: "We would expect the Guardian, a decent liberal newspaper to support us."

Labour politicians Harriet Harman and Patricia Hewitt have come under fire for the NCCL's links to PIE (copyright PA)

In a Guardian piece from 1975 it's clear "paedophile" was still not a widely used term and the opening line explains it - "one who is sexually attracted to children". In the piece, Hose is treated as a reliable source throughout.

There were divisions within progressive circles. In 1977 the Campaign for Homosexual Equality passed by a large majority a resolution condemning "the harassment of the Paedophile Information Exchange by the press".

When Peter Hain, then president of the Young Liberals, described paedophilia as "a wholly undesirable abnormality", a fellow activist hit back. "It is sad that Peter has joined the hang 'em and flog 'em brigade. His views are not the views of most Young Liberals."

And when a columnist supported Hain in the Guardian he was inundated with mail from people - many willing to give their name - who defended sex with children.

Reading the newspapers of the time there is a palpable anxiety that PIE was succeeding.

A Guardian article in 1977 noted with dismay how the group was growing. By its second birthday in October 1976, it had 200 members. There was a London group, a Middlesex group being planned, and with regional branches to follow. The article speaks of PIE's hopes to widen the membership to include women and heterosexual men.

Toynbee talked of her "disgust, aversion and anger" at the group but added that she had "a sinking feeling that in another five years or so, their aims would eventually be incorporated into the general liberal credo, and we would all find them acceptable".

There was a battle raging over free speech. Some, such as philosopher Roger Scruton, felt that freedom of speech had to be sacrificed when it came to groups like PIE. In a Times piece in September 1983 he wrote: "Paedophiles must be prevented from 'coming out'. Every attempt to display their vice as a legitimate 'alternative' to conventional morality must be, not refuted, but silenced."

A Times letter writer, Peter Cadogan, took a different line, defending PIE from the National Front despite loathing them. "Yet again, they assaulted me with stink bombs and sundry soft fruit when I was defending the freedom of speech of another group I abhorred, viz, the Paedophile Information Exchange." He continues that the way to cover "nasty people with nasty ideas" is to "give them all the rope they want and then hang them with it every time they practice what they preach".

But during the 1980s, PIE came a cropper. Its notoriety grew in 1982 with the trial of Geoffrey Prime, who was both a KGB spy and a member of PIE. He was **jailed for 32 years** for passing on secrets from his job at GCHQ to the Soviet Union, and for a series of sex attacks on young girls.

A short article from the Daily Mail in June 1983 records how a scoutmaster in Castle Bromwich, Birmingham, resigned after being exposed as a member of PIE.

PIE critics: Head teacher Charles Oxley, who infiltrated PIE, Mary Whitehouse and Geoffrey Dickens MP (copyright GETTY IMAGES)

In August 1983 a Scottish headmaster, Charles Oxley, handed over a dossier about PIE to Scotland Yard after infiltrating the group, **the Glasgow Herald wrote**. He said the group had about 1,000 members.

But the NCCL continued to defend having PIE as a member. As late as September 1983, an NCCL officer was quoted in the Daily Mail saying the group was campaigning to lower the age of consent to 14. "An offiliate [sic] group like the Paedophile Information Exchange would agree with our policy. That does not mean it's a mutual thing and we have to agree with theirs."

The authorities debated ways of shutting PIE down. O'Carroll was sentenced to two years in jail for "conspiracy to corrupt public morals" and PIE was disbanded in 1984.

It's hard now to believe the group existed for more than a decade. "Even then the word paedophile was pretty taboo," says Wolmar. "I do find it slightly astounding that they were able to use that name."

This article is copyright © BBC Magazine - http://www.bbc.co.uk/news/magazine-26352378

Additional source of information on (Wikipedia):
Paedophile Information Exchange (PIE)
https://en.wikipedia.org/wiki/Paedophile_Information_Exchange

Appendix E: CSA and Physical Brain Damage

Childhood Sexual Abuse Causes Physical Brain Damage: An Alarming New Study
http://garnetbird.hubpages.com/hub/Childhood-Sexual-Abuse-Causes-Physical-Brain-Damage-A-New-Alarming-Study#slide3122854
(Sourced May 2014)

By Gloria Siess, {"Garnetbird"}

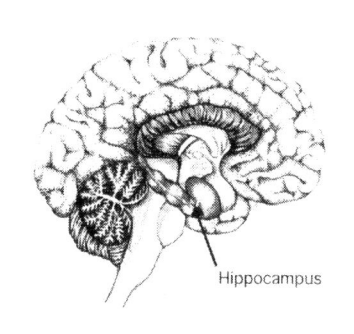

It is estimated that childhood sexual abuse affects over 40 million people yearly, just in the United States alone. To those of you, like myself, who struggle daily with symptoms and defence mechanisms acquired from childhood incest, this study will prove especially enlightening. It will also, hopefully soften the attitude of family members and close friends who must endure the drama of the survivor. So many times, I have heard well-meaning people state, "Just move on and forget about it," or the more judgmental, "You're just CHOOSING to be unhappy."

The problem is not that survivors want to stay miserable--new research indicates that childhood sexual trauma causes actual shrinkage and damage to the part of the brain called the hippocampus. This finding in itself is shocking and astounding. The hippocampus deals with learning, stress responses and memory. When brain stressors such as early sexual abuse and incest impact its development in children, the lasting effects into adulthood can be profound. Pop-up memories, intrusive, negative thoughts, flashbacks and a kind of over-all numbing called disassociation are just some of the symptoms this causes. To anyone who like myself has experienced incest recall "popping up" while they are pushing a grocery cart, this can be devastating and difficult to treat even with the best of therapists.

Some of the symptoms associated with the shrinkage of the hippocampus feed into what is known as Post Traumatic Stress Disorder. This bag of disturbing "tricks" the mind plays on survivors includes flashbacks, feeling uneasy and "on edge," and on guard constantly, nightmares, and general problems associated with memory. Gaps in memory can also occur, for a few minutes to a few days. This may well explain the emergence of abuse memories suddenly "popping up" at a later age in a survivor's life. The hippocampus also affects the part of the brain called the prefrontal cortex, where stress responses are absorbed and dealt with.

Incest survivors have a far more serious response to stress than those who have not experienced severe childhood abuse. I, for one, have to get more sleep than what is normal in order to function in a stable manner. I also need down time in which to think, dream and generally detach from outside stressors. This need can appear to others as being "lazy" or even "spoiled." Think of the Incest Survivor as a very sensitive child in an adult body. The child has to be protected constantly in order to thrive and feel "safe. "Again, this is not coddling oneself. With brain damage as a side effect of such abuse, all survivors need to watch and monitor their stress responses carefully. One of my favourite sayings is, "I'm not hiding from life...I'm healing from it."

We all admire injured or disabled athletes for jogging or walking at their own pace. We think of them as brave and heroic. In this same manner, the Trauma Victim needs to be viewed in a positive light, not judged for pulling away when they need to. Quiet "down time" can be very healing and soothing. Or as a friend of mine said (who experienced Satanic Ritual Abuse as a little girl} "I don't need dramas or roller coasters. Inside, I AM a roller coaster."

The work Dr. Bremner conducted took place at the Yale Psychiatric Institute, and has been met with interesting reactions. Many Incest survivors find his work to be liberating and validating; others are disgusted and think it's "hogwash," in so many words.

Note: For many of us--myself included--extensive therapy is very helpful and can be life-saving. However, for those of us who do not possess the health coverage and means for regular therapy, a local Incest Survivors Group may provide a supportive, healing environment. Groups may differ, and you may have to shop around for the appropriate setting in which to heal. I personally hooked up with a powerful group in Southern California and am the better person for it. Our Group Moderator was a ritual abuse survivor who was literally tortured sexually for many years and now teaches other survivors to let their "inner child" play and heal.

Dr. Bremner is still on the Faculty at Yale--I recommend his article, "Does Stress Damage the Brain?"

http://garnetbird.hubpages.com/hub/Childhood-Sexual-Abuse-Causes-Physical-Brain-Damage-A-New-Alarming-Study#slide3122854

Copyright © Hubpages

Appendix F: Links to research sources and other articles of interest:

The Guardian: The Westminster child abuse 'coverup': how much did MPs know?
https://www.theguardian.com/politics/2015/mar/17/westminster-child-abuse-paedophile-ring-failure

The Guardian: Convicted paedophile arrested in Kesgrave Hall and north Wales child abuse inquiries took his own life two days later, inquest told
http://www.eadt.co.uk/news/convicted_paedophile_arrested_in_kesgrave_hall_and_north_wales_child_abuse_inquiries_took_his_own_life_two_days_later_inquest_told_1_3899644

The East Anglian Daily Times: Kesgrave: Three-time convicted paedophile teacher Alan Stancliffe dies while on bail facing fourth set of child sex allegations
http://www.eadt.co.uk/news/kesgrave_three_time_convicted_paedophile_teacher_alan_stancliffe_dies_while_on_bail_facing_fourth_set_of_child_sex_allegations_1_3796796

The Guardian: Operation Pallial: 37 suspects in care home abuse inquiry
https://www.theguardian.com/uk-news/2014/feb/18/operation-pallial-suspects-care-home-abuse-north-wales

The Guardian: Jimmy Savile: timeline of his sexual abuse and its uncovering
https://www.theguardian.com/media/2014/jun/26/jimmy-savile-sexual-abuse-timeline

The Guardian: Timeline: a history of child protection
https://www.theguardian.com/society/2005/may/18/childrensservices2

The Guardian: Timeline: a history of child protection
https://www.theguardian.com/uk-news/2015/mar/16/police-watchdog-investigate-claims-met-covered-up-child-abuse

Derek Gillard: Education in England: a brief history
http://www.educationengland.org.uk/history/chapter06.html

The Underwood Report (1955): Report of the Committee on Maladjusted Children
http://www.educationengland.org.uk/documents/underwood/

Oxford Mail: Ex-teacher died after swallowing pills during police raid, inquest told
http://www.oxfordmail.co.uk/news/11655764.Ex_teacher_died_after_swallowing_pills_during_police_raid__inquest_told/?ref=mr

Joy Schaverien – Lost for Words
http://joyschaverien.com/wp-content/uploads/2015/04/LostforwordsTTApr11.pdf

Nick Duffell: Boarding School Survivors
http://www.boardingschoolsurvivors.co.uk/about-us/

The Guardian: Boarding School Syndrome review – education and the pain of separation
https://www.theguardian.com/books/2015/jun/08/boarding-school-syndrome-joy-schaverien-review

The Society of Analytical Psychology: Author Schaverien Discusses Boarding School Syndrome
https://www.thesap.org.uk/author-schaverien-discusses-boarding-school-syndrome/

The Crown Prosecution Service: Guidelines on Prosecuting Cases of Child Sexual Abuse
http://www.cps.gov.uk/legal/a_to_c/child_sexual_abuse/#a21

Samaritans - Suicide statistics report 2017
https://www.samaritans.org/sites/default/files/kcfinder/files/Suicide_statistics_report_2017_Final.pdf

The Therapeutic Care Journal - The Underwood Report :Chaired by J.E.A. Underwood
http://www.thetcj.org/child-care-history-policy/the-underwood-report-chaired-by-jea-underwood

The Telegraph - 76 politicians, 178 celebrities and 7 sports stars: the scale of VIP child sex abuse inquiry
http://www.telegraph.co.uk/news/uknews/law-and-order/11617789/Scale-of-child-sex-abuse-revealed-in-new-police-figures.html

Appendix G: Boarding School Syndrome #1

Shed a Tear for Britain's Messed Up Boarding School Kids

https://www.vice.com/en_uk/article/ex9ggz/boarding-school-syndrome

KATIE ENGELHART

Sep 24 2013, 8:00am

Illustration by Cei Willis

Nick Duffell, a London-based psychotherapist, says he can usually spot an ex-boarding school student on first glance. The giveaway won't be the "good breeding" and blue-blooded lilt to the voice. It will be something more equivocal: "A kind of wounded quality." One might even call it a syndrome: "Boarding School Syndrome."

Today, Duffell and a small coterie of British therapists want to see "Boarding School Syndrome" (BSS) recognised as a legit medical condition. The idea is simple: that boarding school – long a bastion of Englishness, now a nugget of colonial nostalgia – is, today, an avenue to lasting psychological trauma. It's also an idea that's catching on. Today, ex-boarders flock to therapists in droves; attending weekend healing workshops and congregating in online support groups.

Meanwhile, Britain's Boarding School Association (BSA) is steeling itself: stressing that the Dickensian reformatories of yore have given way to far more nurturing schools – and that the science behind BSS remains pretty sketchy.

Illustration by Cei Willis

Boarding School Syndrome "is a British problem", Duffell sighs. And it has history: its roots stretch back to long-ago Imperial days, when boarding schools were meant to build character and shape sons of Empire. Is it time for a pedagogical reckoning?

Last Spring, Dr Joy Schaverien gave a lecture on BSS to London's Society of Analytical Psychology. Her talk described the developmental trauma that young borders purportedly endure – and the way this trauma manifests as adult dysfunction.

For Schaverien, it was the sum of a two-year media blitz, which began in 2011 when she coined the term "Boarding School Syndrome" in The British Journal of Psychotherapy. Then, Schaverien defined BSS as a "cluster of learned behaviours and discontents that... revolve around problems with intimacy".

The British press pounced. "The British boarding school remains a bastion of cruelty," the Guardian cried, the article's writer George Monbiot musing elsewhere about how "Britain's most overt form of child abuse is mysteriously ignored". "Does 'brusque' and 'rude' David Cameron suffer from Boarding School Syndrome?" the Telegraph wondered aloud. One Daily Mail column was titled: "How boarding school was great preparation for life… nothing will ever be so ghastly."

This was bad news for boarding schools. For the last few decades, boarding school enrolment has been falling fast: from about 120,000 in 1981, to 66,776 in 2013 (37,171 boys compared to 29,605 girls). Today – at a time when the average boarding school costs over £25,000 per year, and many students board just an hour or so from home (really) – the industry is fighting to prove its relevance.

But long before there was BSS the catchphrase, there was BSS the trauma. Nick Duffell has been treating BSS for decades. "In 1989, I was working in men's groups. This was the time of the so-called Men's Movement, which was really an offshoot of feminism. And I realised that there was a specific category of men for which our work didn't quite fit. They all had something in common…" They had been to boarding school. In 1990, Duffell founded Boarding School Survivors, which he followed with a book, The Making of Them: The British Attitude to Children and the Boarding School System.

Duffell, 64, was intimately acquainted with his subject. He boarded as a child. After undergrad at Oxford, where he studied Sanskrit and Indian philosophy, he even taught at a girl's boarding school in India. "I was an absolutely hopeless teacher, crikey! But it was India; they didn't have the same harsh regime that British schools had. They're more used to loving their children than the Brits."

Boarding Concern is a support group for ex-boarders. It was started in 2001 by James Foucar, who was emotionally scarred at St Aubyns (which he attended from age eight) and Millfield (which he left, exasperated, at 16). I met Foucar (who boasts, on his personal website, of "an IQ that puts him above 99.6 percent of the population") in a glass-windowed conference room at the large insurance firm where he worked – with an expansive view of the City and London's heady urban shuffle.

For his part, Foucar did not initially experience boarding school as traumatic. His first stop was "a very traditional, authoritarian, prudish prep school", where "I spent a lot of time being caned… because I was naughty". Later, he attended Millfield: "It was a very progressive school… When I arrived, the sixth form girls were wearing hot pants!" There, he saw darker days. Foucar claims that he experienced "grooming" by a male teacher – though it never extended to sexual assault. "I had a nervous breakdown at age 12 over the way that this teacher was behaving towards me… I was aware that things were happening to other boys."

Twelve years after its founding, Boarding Concern has "a good group of core supporters", an annual conference and a newsletter – and a website featuring an image of a melancholy young boy, glowering at the camera through a chain-linked fence. It also has an advocacy wing, which argues against so-called "early boarding" of very young children. Activists argue that boarding school "offends no fewer than 11 articles of the UN Convention on the Rights of the Child".

Illustration by Cei Willis

To illustrate how very dangerous early boarding is, ex-boarders often refer to the popular 1994 documentary The Making of Them – whose dramatic climax is a young father chuckling to himself, shortly after sending off his eight-year-old: "A friend of ours used to have to be heavily sedated in order to go to school. Perfectly normal chap now!"

So-called Boarding School Syndrome is a cluster of behaviours and opinions that typify the adult ex-boarder. Take it away, Schaverien:

Even when not mistreated, being left in the care of strangers is traumatic... A shell is formed to protect the vulnerable self from emotion that cannot be processed. Whilst appearing to conform to the system, a form of unconscious splitting is acquired as a means of keeping the true self hidden... The child then makes no emotional demands but also no longer recognises the need for intimacy. The self begins to become inaccessible; 'Boarding School Syndrome' develops.

The syndrome starts to fester on Day 1; there is loneliness, dejection. But boarders learn to be stoic: they pull themselves up by their bootstraps and take it all on the chin.

More potent BSS symptoms appear decades later, when strategies once adopted to survive boarding school become maladaptive. BSS sufferers have "problems with relationships, problems with intimacy, depression", Schaverien explains. "The men especially are often very closed-off emotionally... They get on with the job, and so on. But they never talk about their feelings."

Forgive me for remarking that this sounds rather... British?

"It is associated in Britain with a kind of national characteristic... the bumbling Hugh Grant character," Nick Duffell concedes. "What Hugh Grant portrays in an immature boyishness. That's our endearing national character. We're rather fond of that sort of thing. We don't think of it as a pathology."

There's much to criticise in this diagnosis. BSS is not a recognised medical ailment – the kind, say, that would be codified in diagnostic manuals. The academic work on BSS is largely qualitative and anecdotal – and a lot of it is conducted by ex-boarders. "We can't really do a double-blind [test] with this," Schaverien insists. "You can't have the same person have two experiences: be traumatised by going away at six and not be traumatised by going away at six." True. But you can do quantitative studies of students, boarders and non-boarders, over time – with an eye for variations in behaviour and measures of sanity.

Still, psychotherapists across the UK are advertising their expertise in BSS treatment. Nick Duffell's weekend therapy workshops are a model: "In the first session, we are allowing people to tell stories that perhaps they've never told about what it was like... The second week, we devote to: How did you survive?" One activity involves role-playing; ex-boarders are asked to "play" their parents – to discover what it might have been like to send a young child away.

Perhaps they felt conflicted? Emotionally torn asunder? Or perhaps they were just part of what Schaverien calls "the privileged elite, who of course send their children to boarding school because it's what you do, dahling".

The thing is, most of Britain is run by (mostly) men who hail from the "it's what you do" clan: men who were sent away before the boarding school reforms of the last few decades. BSS, its sufferers insist, is thus a political malady, as much as a mental one.

Illustration by Cei Willis

Left-minded British political hacks like nothing more than to observe how many current Cabinet members went to boarding school: and particularly, Eton. David Cameron is an Old Etonian. And according to the Telegraph, he "has more boys from his school around him than any PM since Harold MacMillan". His Chief of Staff, Chip Whip, Cabinet Office Minister, Head of the Number 10 Policy Unit, Minister of State for the Foreign Office and Chief Economic Adviser are all Old Etonians. (As are, for the record, Princes William and Harry, the Mayor of London and the Archbishop of Canterbury.) But a great swathe of boarding schools is represented at the highest echelons.

Indeed, Cameron lived the quintessential boarding school experience, as described by older "survivors". A few years ago, he admitted that at prep school, he was beaten several times with the hard end of a clothes brush – once, after stealing from the headmaster's wife.

Some speculate that old boarding school habits die hard. Cameron's governing style has been compared to that of a cocksure school prefect. His alleged tactlessness and viciousness with junior MPs has reportedly been dubbed "The Flashman Tendency", a reference to the bully character in Tom Brown's popular School Days novel (set at boarding school). When MP Sarah Wollaston received a talking-down by the PM's office, the Daily Mail explained, "she was Flashmaned".

"It is a system," Nick Duffel bemoans. The psychotherapist insists that BSS research has been held back – that the diagnosis has escaped the interest of the British public – because boarding school "is built into society". Thus, the diagnosis "has political implications. It's rather unusual that a psychological syndrome should have political implication.... [But] the current leaders, they don't have empathy. It's very bizarre!" In Therapy Today, Duffell observes that:

The majority [of British leaders] have boarded at our famous public schools and embody a recognisable veneer of confidence, linked with the ability to suggest sincerity while disregarding feelings and bullying others at work.

Is this Conservative dirtbaggery, or the manifestation of early childhood trauma? BSS champions are hoping to make the point stick: that for political reasons, BSS is deserving of broad national attention.

In 1693, philosopher John Locke opined that boarding schools made pupils "bolder and better able to bustle and shift among boys". But he sensed that when you send little boys away, all kinds of corruption await them. Parents who do so, he rued, "think it worthwhile to hazard [their] son's innocence and virtue for a little Greek and Latin".

By then, British boarding schools were national institutions. In the 14th and 15th centuries, boarding schools were monastic training grounds, run by clergymen. They were reborn as scholarly hubs at the height of Empire, when they housed the tots of colonial administrators sent abroad. Only under Queen Victoria did middle classes begin to see boarding schools as places where a young man might imbibe character and social standing.

The interwar period brought an industry lull. Critics lambasted boarding schools for their war-like preoccupation with sport and physical prowess (the "tyranny of games"). After WWII, more schools closed. Those that survived were not known for their creature comforts. Just asked Prince Charles: the first direct heir to the throne to be schooled away from home. In the 60s, Charles studied at Gordonstoun School, in Scotland. There, he was roused from bed at the crack of dawn for a brisk run and a cold shower. He later described his education as a "prison sentence".

After it all, the cultural legacy of the boarding school is mixed. There are hordes of Enid Blyton and Enid Blyton-esque volumes: books in which rosy-cheeked boarders pass their days in endless fits of practical jokery. But there is also Charles Dickens' Dotheboys Hall for unwanted children. Today, there is Harry Potter, whose merry days at Hogwarts have reportedly inspired a new rush of boarding school enthusiasts. "Children of this generation," remarks Hilary Moriarty, national director of the UK's Boarding Schools' Association, "have seen people like Harry Potter going to a boarding school and having a great time! Mind you, Hogwarts would not pass the National Minimum Standards, never mind talking pictures and so on..."

Critics of the Boarding School Syndrome hypothesis stress that Britain's boarding schools have changed for the better. They're right.

A few weeks ago, I met Sam Roots, 26, for lunch in London's Spitalfields Market. Over a fish finger sandwich, Roots – a slight, quick-witted renewable energy consultant – recalled his boyhood days at Winchester, which claims to be longest continuously

Illustration by Cei Willis

operating boarding school in the world. (Founded: 1382. Slogan: Manners makyth man.)

I listed the symptoms of BSS aloud, trying to spot a flinch or an emotion-laden sigh. Bullying? "Sometimes after lights out, there would be a dorm raid with pillow fighting…" Homophobia? Nope. A shattered home? "No, I would hazard to say that I'm closer with my family for having gone to boarding school – because it meant that I rebelled against the school, instead of against them."

Roots' memories are mostly fond. He passed many an afternoon studying music – eventually becoming an accomplished singer and pianist. During free time, he often reserved spots along the nearby river, where he would go to fish in calm solitude. And he usually went home on Sundays. During schooldays, Roots was challenged by good teachers, many of whom had PhDs and were passionate scholars. "There was a maths teacher who was really into illuminated manuscripts," he recalls. "He ran an illuminated manuscript club. And he inspired some people to study Medieval English.

Today, even students at less swank academies will have dozens of rules and regulations and independent inspectors safeguarding their good times. In recent decades, the Boarding School Association tightened its reigns – as evidenced by its latest "Minimum Standards," which governs everything from security (CCTV cameras may not "intrude unreasonably on children's privacy") to decorations (students may have "suitable posters") to mental health services. BSA also hosts professional workshops, on subjects like: "Understanding & supporting children who self-harm" and "Developing Resilience in Pupils." There is much talk of "pastoral care".

There are broader changes. Early boarding is on the steep decline. As of last year, there were only 123 seven-year-old boarders in Britain. In her book Harry Potter and History, Nancy Reagin, a history professor at Pace University in New York, argues that early boarding has become sufficiently "unfashionable" that it led some publishers to turn down JK Rowling's first draft of Harry Potter. Boarding schools have also become adjustable. More students are "weekly boarders", who spend weekends at home, or "flexi-boarders", who board on a day-by-day basis.

And the boarding experience is oh-so-slowly being extended to the less-than-moneyed. There are currently 35 state-funded boarding schools – and the Department of Education hopes to open more. Earlier this year, Eton College announced that it would open its own state-funded boarding school in Berkshire.

Despite all this, BSA's Hilary Moriarty anticipates a slide backwards: "I half expect that there will be a resurgence in junior boarding in six or seven years' time." Today's babes, Moriarty argues, are ferried from daycare to school to babysitter to bed – passing only scant minutes with busy, career-driven parents. A parent might just say: "How about a boarding school at seven? I'll make her a weekly boarder and I'll actually see as much of her as I do now."

On that note: perhaps, as boarding schools become more pleasant, attention will shift to parents, potentially traumatised by the act of potentially traumatising their children? Anybody for an Empty Nest Syndrome? **Katie Engelhart**

Copyright © Vice.com/Katie Engelhart

Appendix H: John Downing

John Downing

Credit: Irving of Exeter

Devon Live: Ex Devon teacher facing new boarding school abuse charges
http://www.devonlive.com/ex-devon-teacher-facing-new-boarding-school-abuse/story-26124909-detail/story.html

Devon Live: Devon boarding school housemaster denies abusing boys at school
http://www.devonlive.com/devon-boarding-school-housemaster-denies-abusing/story-21207967-detail/story.html

Ipswich Star: Kesgrave/Devon: Teacher accused of child sex offences at school linked to Kesgrave Hall
http://www.ipswichstar.co.uk/news/kesgrave-devon-teacher-accused-of-child-sex-offences-at-school-linked-to-kesgrave-hall-1-3063473

The UK & Ireland Database:
https://theukdatabase.com/2015/04/10/john-downing-torrington/

Devon Live: Former Devon headmaster and organist jailed for "cruel and shocking" abuse regime on vulnerable school boys
http://www.devonlive.com/devon-headmaster-organist-jailed-cruel-shocking/story-26320051-detail/story.html

ITV: Former North Devon teacher jailed for sexually abusing pupils
http://www.itv.com/news/westcountry/update/2015-04-10/former-north-devon-teacher-jailed-for-sexually-abusing-pupils/

As of 25th August 2017, all DevonLive links and stories regarding John Downing, his trials and subsequent jailing, etc have been removed. This includes all reports and stories published in Express & Echo, the Torquay Herald Express, the Mid Devon Gazette and the North Devon Journal. As the primary reporting source for the Heanton School investigation and subsequent arrest and jailing of John Downing, this is disgraceful. Two years on from a huge public story and milestone court ruling and custodial sentence of 21 years, I cannot help but be suspicious of this and wonder if this move is supporting someone else's agenda. I contacted DevonLive of 25.08.17 and enquired why all media and references to John Downing (Heanton School) had been pulled. There reason is due to a Website restructure. There has been some editorial decision here on what goes and what remains. They are after all in the business of reporting news and informing people of what's been happening in their community. I hope that the numerous stories that were available online, in respect of John Downing are reinstated soon.

John Downing – as Choir Master at St Michael & All Angels Church, Great Torrington, before he was exposed as a predatory paedophile.

PIC Credit: St Michael & All Angels Church, Great Torrington

Former Devon headmaster and organist jailed for "cruel and shocking" abuse regime on vulnerable school boys
By Exeter Express and Echo 4/12/15

A boarding school teacher has been jailed for 21 years after being found guilty of inflicting a reign of terror over vulnerable boys for two decades.

John Downing took advantage of the children by sexually abusing them after they were sent away to a boarding school in North Devon where he was a teacher and deputy headmaster.

He preyed on boys by sexually abusing them in the classroom, wash rooms, on beach outings and during midnight feasts which he arranged for a select group who he called his 'Good Boys'.

Downing imposed a regime of fear in which he regularly beat boys with a slipper or wooden coat hanger.

He punished boys who talked after lights out by making them parade naked in the corridor outside their dormitory and encouraged boys on beach trips to walk around in the nude.

Downing, now aged 74, was a teacher and deputy headmaster of Heanton School, near Braunton, North Devon, from its founding in 1968 to its closure in 1985.

The converted rectory was a privately run boarding school for boys aged six to 12, most of whom were sent there by local authorities because they had problems at home.

This meant they had no-one to turn to when they were sexually and physically abused and their secrets remained hidden for years.

Two of them went to the police in the 1990s but officers decided there was not enough evidence. In the years that followed several got in touch over the internet and fresh complaints were investigated by police….

Downing has been the organist at Torrington church for 50 years during which his activities at the school have remained a secret. He went on to be a teacher at schools all over North and Mid Devon before he retired.

Downing, of Warren Lane, Torrington, denied 39 charges of indecent assault or gross indecency against seven boys aged seven to 12 between 1970 and 1985.

He was jailed for 21 years by Judge Graham Cottle who told him that some of his assaults would now be classified as rape….
http://m.exeterexpressandecho.co.uk/Devon-headmaster-organist-jailed-cruel-shocking/story-26320051-detail/story.html

Copyright ©2015 Local World

Appendix I:

Alan Stancliffe

Ipswich Star: Former teacher accused of sexual abuse
http://www.ipswichstar.co.uk/news/former-teacher-accused-of-sexual-abuse-1-141177

The UK & Ireland Database: Alan Stancliffe – Pontefract/Kesgrave Hall School
https://theukdatabase.com/2013/02/18/alan-stancliffe-pontefractkesgrave-hall-school/

East Anglian Daily Times: Kesgrave: Three-time convicted paedophile teacher Alan Stancliffe dies while on bail facing fourth set of child sex allegations
http://www.eadt.co.uk/news/kesgrave-three-time-convicted-paedophile-teacher-alan-stancliffe-dies-while-on-bail-facing-fourth-set-of-child-sex-allegations-1-3796796

PIC Credit: East Anglian Daily Times

EADT May 6th 1999 - Credit: Archant

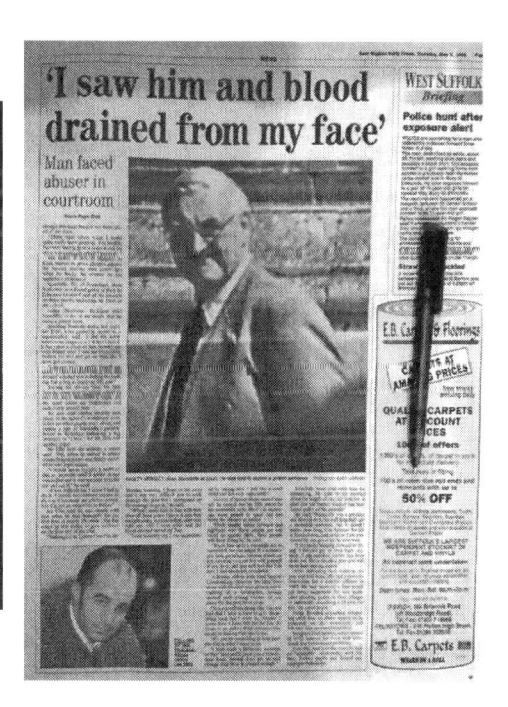

Appendix J:

Media Interviews/Reports
Lee Woolcott-Ellis

PIC Lee Woolcott-Ellis - Credit: The Guardian/Frank Barton

The Guardian: Former pupils call for new investigation into abuse claims at Suffolk school
https://www.theguardian.com/society/2012/dec/14/former-pupils-abuse-claims-suffolk-school

BC Video Interview: Kesgrave Hall School abuse inquiry: Former pupils 'should come forward'
http://www.bbc.co.uk/news/uk-england-suffolk-21162681

The Guardian: Two arrested in Kesgrave Hall boarding school investigation
https://www.theguardian.com/uk-news/2014/apr/11/kesgrave-hall-abuse-inquiry-arrests

East Anglian Daily Times: Suffolk: Police re-open school child abuse inquiry relating to Kesgrave Hall School
http://www.eadt.co.uk/news/suffolk-police-re-open-school-child-abuse-inquiry-relating-to-kesgrave-hall-school-1-1801762

SCHOOL ABUSE PROBE FILES 'NO LONGER EXIST'

MP joins calls for new investigation

Files for school sex abuse investigation 'can't be traced'

MP in call to chief constable to reopen the police inquiry

Teacher was jailed twice

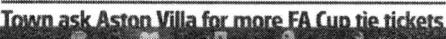

St George's: Fourth man held

Appendix K:

NO MORE SECRETS: The Blogs
Lee Woolcott-Ellis
https://leewe15.wordpress.com/

This blog, and the posts I made to it, were written from February 2015 until June 2015. They provide some valid text. I was exposed at the time of writing these, feeling raw whilst dealing with the police and judiciary. I wrote these whilst battling the system to get Downing back into court. That time frame validtes the posts. Writing these blogs encouraged me to to write this book. It was the genesis of the book project.

You may note that some of the topics covered in the selected blogs, have replecated information in parts of the book. The blogs were a forerunner and I belive the text is equally valid, when read in the original context.

PIC Lee Ellis c.1972 *PIC Lee Woolcott-Ellis c.2012*

INTRODUCTION

My Name is Lee. I am a survivor of historic child sexual abuse, which happened throughout the 1970's when I was in the independent, residential schooling system in the UK. I now write and campaign to support openness and awareness of child sexual abuse and mental health stigma and discrimination. I believe by writing openly and disclosing some details of my past, it will help those that thankfully didn't suffer the same fate as a child, understand better what was happening in the this country only a few decades ago. As horrific as it was, I think the stories need to be told. We cannot truly ensure the safety of children, unless we all understand how paedophiles operate. Predatory paedophiles are intelligent, manipulative individuals who portray as seemingly respectable people.

The other purpose of the blogs will hopefully help other victims come forward and ask for help. Anyone triggered by my writing should initially speak with their GP and there is always the Police.

Talking openly about my mental health has helped me to deal with my issues. Self stigmatizing has been very harmful to me and prolonged the damage that my attackers inflicted on me all those years ago. It is good to talk.

Blogs 1 to 9 below:

Can we trust the media telling us the truth in paedophilia cases?

Posted on February 25, 2015

Over the decades there has been a great mistrust of the media. A general conception is 'The media, like any industry, is driven by profit-making. This is often achieved by creating sensational and attention grabbing news at the price of exaggerating or distorting the truth behind the news stories'. I do not agree with this.

PIC Credit: https://blog.feelter.com/page/media-coverage-on-feelter-2016

I think in every industry, as in any collective of individuals, there will always be a highly competitive people, who will seek to achieve their aims at 'whatever' cost. This includes any profession, not just in the field of journalism.

Is television news really objective? Or are they still trying to entertain us? I think the truth is still there, perhaps with a bit of 'spin' to win over more viewers on occasions – that is their real currency.

In my experience over the past 3 years, where I have given interviews to the BBC, The Guardian Newspaper and independent journalists, in respect of my abusive past, I do have to say I have found the journalists to be professional and sympathetic to the sensitivities of historic abuse cases. After all it has been a two-way road, a mutually agreeable arrangement. I have disclosed a lot of information regarding the institutional abuse I suffered in the 1970's, to support their story and in return I have been able to support numerous police investigations by using the media to appeal for witnesses to come forward. It is evident that following newspaper stories, both national and regional, together with regional news exposure on the BBC, people did make contact with the police. All newspaper articles are also available on the Internet, globally.

I would encourage people to support journalistic pieces on abuse and mental health awareness. This is the best way to get your stories out there. Social media is powerful, but the known media sources are the established routes. Post October 2012, the Savile era, as I like to call it, has seen a huge momentum in public support for police investigations into historic abuse in the UK and quiet rightly too. People are outraged and horrified and want to know what happened? Other common questions are – Why was nothing done about it? And what is being done about it now?

Many victims of historic child abuse have been silent for decades, self-stigmatised and wrongly too ashamed to speak out, but now with so many cases being pursued and gaining convictions, they taken the brave step of speaking up. The media have been very supportive of that to a certain extent, apart from some obvious bias being given to the celebrity cases. It would seem generally, that the momentum to remove the veil of secrecy off child abuse is continuing.

The media as a whole are very careful now in the way they handle historic abuse investigation, only reporting on substantiated facts and making sure allegations are labelled as such. A lot of lessons were learnt in November 2012, when Allister McAlpine was mistakenly implicated in the North Wales child abuse scandal, after the BBC Newsnight programme accused an unnamed "senior Conservative" of abuse. McAlpine was widely rumoured on Twitter and other social media platforms to be the person in question. After The Guardian reported that the accusations were the result of mistaken identity, McAlpine issued a strong denial that he was in any way involved. The accuser, a former care home resident, unreservedly apologised after seeing a photograph of McAlpine and realising that he had been mistaken, leading to a report in The Daily Telegraph that the BBC was "in chaos". The BBC also then apologised.

It is fairly evident that the upper echelons of our society, the hegemonic, have been involved in child sexual abuse for decades and it is only now, post Savile, that the extent of implication and cover-up is becoming known. This is where we need strong, independent investigative journalists and I know of some that are not letting go of those cases unless they are forced to do so. In November, 2012 the Media were 'gagged over bid to report MP Child sex cases'. The Security Services were accused of aiding a Westminster paedophilia cover-up – see the Guardian.

I support media coverage of child abuse cases and trials. I also see the great benefit to be gained from survivors of child abuse speaking out and telling their stories. It is from this that we as a society learn. We cannot truly protect our children unless we know what paedophiles do and how they do it.

https://leewe15.wordpress.com/2015/02/25/can-we-trust-the-media-telling-us-the-truth-in-paedophilia-cases/

I AM NOT MOURNING YOUR DEATH

Posted on February 24, 2015

"Any man's death diminishes me" – John Donne (24 January 1572 – 31 March 1631 / London, England).

I was informed of the death of 4 men last year (2014). All of these men that had died during 2014, had been named by me (and others) in

PIC Credit: http://belkauctionco.com/

police statements. Most of the men had taken their own lives. We had made allegations of indecent assaults and violent physical assaults against these individuals which related to our time together at Kesgrave Hall School, near Ipswich, Suffolk. The allegations were historic and related to the middle to late part of the 1970's. The men had virtually all died quite violently, or certainly unpleasantly. It is this knowledge that created a state of uncertainty as to how I should feel about their passing. At various times throughout 2014, I received police visits or phone calls to tell me of their deaths. After the initial shock of hearing about their deaths, the predicament I faced with that knowledge, was whether I was happy that they had died or not.

It was not just a case of whether I should be celebrating the death of some extremely unpleasant paedophiles and sadists, who had harmed my friends and I greatly, there was the matter of was it right to revel in another man's death?

I am not overly religious, but I consider myself to be a Christian in my morals and values and I certainly support altruistic values. These monsters ideally did not deserve to die, instead they should have been suffering incarceration and solitary conditions for the rest of their lives, so they could contemplate the harm and devastation they have caused to others, through their depraved and destructive actions. In taking their own lives, or in death, not only have their victims been denied justice, the secret of their disgusting behaviour is hidden away from public scrutiny. Consider the injustice of a victim of abuse keeping the harm of the assaults they suffered secret, because of the stigma associated to it – when the perpetrator who undoubtedly has attacked numerous young people, is allowed to fulfil a protected life, due to the silence of the victims.

In looking for positives for the death of these men, there is some satisfaction to be gained in the knowledge that they would no longer be in a position to harm any other young person. It is fairly evident, when you look at the career history of these men, that given the opportunity they would start to groom young people. In whatever they did, they would invariably gravitate towards young people. Although the investigation in Suffolk is still active, I am no longer part of this, due to the untimely death of these individuals. I will therefore name the four men.

Alan Stancliffe – aged 65 – Pontefract, Yorkshire. (Former Teacher/House Parent) He was being questioned (again) by Suffolk Police on allegations of indecent assault/behaviour relating to boys from the age of 11 to 16, in the 1970's at Kesgrave Hall School, Ipswich, Suffolk.

http://www.eadt.co.uk/news/kesgrave_three_time_convicted_paedophile_teacher_alan_stancliffe_dies_while_on_bail_facing_fourth_set_of_child_sex_allegations_1_3796796

Kenneth Scott (Wheatley) – aged 62 – Barnsley, Yorkshire. (Former Teacher/House Parent) Threw himself under a train following his arrest for indecent assault/behaviour relating to boys from the age of 11 to 16, in the 1970's at Kesgrave Hall School, Ipswich, Suffolk. He was also arrested by the National Crime Agency in respect of allegations against him from the North Wales Care Homes (Operation Pallial).

http://www.eadt.co.uk/news/convicted_paedophile_arrested_in_kesgrave_hall_and_north_wales_child_abuse_inquiries_took_his_own_life_two_days_later_inquest_told_1_3899644

David Brockman – aged 59 – Huntingdon, Cambridgeshire. (Former Teacher/House Parent – last known position – Huntingdon Community Radio – Management and Youth Worker) Heart attack following arrest for allegations of indecent assault and physical assault against boys from the age of 11 to 16, in the 1970's at Kesgrave Hall School, Ipswich, Suffolk.

http://www.huntspost.co.uk/news/obituary_huntingdon_radio_stalwart_david_brockman_dies_aged_59_1_3602088

Michael Lafford – aged 67 – Bicester, Oxfordshire. (Former Teacher/House Parent – last known position – Ofsted School Inspector) Took an Overdose prior to arrest for allegations of assault against boys from the age of 11 to 16, in the 1970's at Kesgrave Hall School, Ipswich, Suffolk.

http://www.oxfordmail.co.uk/news/11655764.Ex_teacher_died_after_swallowing_pills_during_police_raid_inquest_told/?ref=mr

It took some time to mentally process the death of these men. It is a great shame that the brave victims of these men were denied justice. The young boys that were affected by them will never truly get over what they did to them. It is right not to celebrate their deaths, but there is no need to mourn their passing. It is my opinion that the world is a better, safer place without them being in it.

https://leewe15.wordpress.com/2015/02/

I DON'T LIKE HEARING ABOUT WHAT HAPPENED TO YOU

Posted on February 19, 2015

Being a victim of child sexual abuse, and the violence and ritual humiliation that goes along with it from the age of 6 until 16 was

PIC: A Label

horrific, as I am sure most people reading this will understand. Living with that inside my head and not telling a living sole (outside of the institution where it occurred for 34 years) created a wide spectrum of mental health related conditions that I have struggled with over the decades.

Today, I am able to talk openly about it, write about it and campaign for more awareness of the discrimination and misconceptions associated with it, because I broke the cycle. I admitted to myself that I needed help. I asked for help and it was granted. Years of psychotherapy being the main route of treatment for me and seeking justice through supporting police investigations and attending Court to give evidence, being another route. The key feature here is the process of 'talking' about what happened. Difficult at first, but if people are willing to listen, it becomes easier with time. The more you talk, the more you want to talk and the greater the benefit to you. I should make it clear that it was in no way easy to deal with what happened to me head on, but I had too. I could never have any quality of life until I put many demons and ghosts to rest. Great respect can be afforded to anyone undertaking such a process. This an extremely brave and courageous act for a former abuse victim to undertake. To go back and face your abuser/s and to relive the horrors is and act that earns my highest respect.

I am very fortunate to have many supportive and understanding friends and family, who want to hear my story and want to help me. I am reminded here of an article I read in the Guardian during May 2014, by Alex Renton (http://www.theguardian.com/society/2014/may/04/abuse-britain-private-schools-personal-memoir). In the article, Alex speaks of why he decided to confront his demons in relation to his time as a boy at the Private School, Ashdown House and the abuse he suffered. This is a recommended read and I applaud Alex for his openness. Alex's experiences were at the other end of the social scale to mine, but then it goes to show that paedophiles and sadists do not conform to class barriers. One phrase Alex writes on talking to people about his abusive past is "These were war stories: they made us feel special."

That is something I can relate to. My ten years of emotional, physical and sexual abuse can easily be contributed to a 'war story'. It was a horrific ordeal that I somehow survived. It is my war story and I feel I have earned the right to talk about it.

Many people find what happened to me inconceivable, when first being told about it. The majority of people, although shocked, are willing to listen to what I have to say. Some are not so willing. It is important for victims of abuse to talk. It is equally important for all of us to listen to someone who is trying to tell us about it. As a society, we cannot truly prevent child abuse happening, unless we learn about the what, who, when and where, including modus operandi, grooming methods and signs of abuse having taken place.

There are a number of factors that come into play here. Child abuse as a subject is very much like mental health illness, surrounded by taboo, misconception and ignorance. Both subjects are linked in that way, in addition to the mental health illness caused by the abuse itself.

People that have suffered or suppressed their own abuse may not be ready or willing to listen to someone talking about abuse. The danger of triggering someone when talking about abuse is something I have always been aware of. I would always say to anyone who is affected by what I say and believe that they were abused, to speak to their GP or the Police.

A lot of people feel ashamed and unable to talk about abuse. They can wrongly think that it shows personal weakness. They think it reflects on them as a failure. If it is their children who have suffered abuse at the hands of others, they think it reflects their failure as parents. This self-inflicted stigma can make it difficult for these people to speak about or abuse and to listen.

Of course, we also do need to understand that some people just do not care about abuse and will be completely closed off to it. 'Burying of the head in the sand' is a human condition after all. It is normally easy to identify these people quite quickly in a conversation.

Encouraging a victim of abuse and helping them talk about it, is a great thing to do. It does not matter how long ago it happened, it is not something a person is likely to get over, ever.

When a victim of abuse starts to talk and tells you about their abuse, you have been placed in a privileged position by that person. The abuse is their deepest, darkest secret and details of which have generally been locked away deeply and rarely spoken of. They would not be talking to you unless they felt they could trust you. Be worthy of that trust.

In return, acknowledgement is all that is needed from you. Sympathy, although well meant, is not going to heal anything. Empathy does count for a lot. It is easier to empathise with a victim, when you have been a victim yourself. Generally, all that the victim is looking for is someone to listen.

I have encountered reactions of people immediately changing the subject, finding excuses to leave or just making jokes of it. Hurtful and very damaging. The worse reaction I experienced was my biological father, the first person I opened up to and properly spoke to about the abuse I suffered. He called me a liar and accused me of just wanting to get some money out of it – Very Hurtful. After that reaction, I did not speak about it again for another 12 years.

Talking about abuse brings it into the open. Removing the taboo and secrecy from abuse is the goal.

https://leewe15.wordpress.com/2015/02/

IT'S OK NOT TO LIKE EVERYONE

Posted on February 16, 2015

Everyone has an opinion, but remember an opinion is 'just an opinion'.

Let's be honest, there are some people who after 5 minutes of meeting that person for the first time, you just know they are 'not your kind of person'. Trust your own initial judgment, in my experience it is generally never wrong. It has taken me too many years to realise that I had wasted so much effort in trying to win people over or to endlessly try to engage with people, who clearly did not like me. The outcome, in most cases did not win them over and left me feeling angry or upset because of the negative influence of all of that wasted time and energy. No one is worth compromising your own mental well-being.

PIC A Label

This is more than just worrying about what people think about you. I used to suffer from that strain of false correctness, but thankfully nearly not as much today. We really should not give a monkeys' what people think about us, but of course some of us do. It is in our nature to always want to be seen to be doing the right thing and do actually care about that. Others of course do not. For those that do, it is about learning how to compromise that part of our makeup and just 'let it go' (I can picture you singing that now!!).

For many years, following a career of police and security training, I have always relied on snap judgement. When approaching a situation or people, I was trained to undertake a 'dynamic risk assessment' to quickly gauge all factors influencing the situation and to identify dangers. This is a process I try to employ when dealing with people also. It sadly doesn't always work, but then we cannot always factor in influences external to our control. Generally, though it is normally spot on. Even with a clearly defined, operational internal radar, set to identify those caustic to me, I still allow some into my influence circle.

Why?

Intimate space – ranges from touching to about 18 inches (46 cm) apart, and is reserved for lovers, children, close family members, close friends, and pet animals. If any of these people were destructive to us and we really did not like them, it is unlikely that they would have progressed to that level.

Personal distance begins about an arm's length away; starting around 18 inches (46 cm) from the person and ending about 4 feet (122 cm) away. This space is used in conversations with friends, some family members, colleagues, and people in group discussions. For me, I think this is the zone in which we can compromise ourselves and allow a destructive force into our heads. The rules of engagement are slightly different when we are at work. Others are forced into our personal zone through our employment, whether we want them there or not. Very often we are thrust into regularly daily contact with people who clearly do not like us. We should of course have decided that we do not like them either, but we do not always readily arrive that (maybe we do on some occasions). For some considerable time, we may try different approaches to attempt to win that person over. The difficulty remaining, is the need for us to remain professional and to be able to fulfil the conditions of our employment contracts. Keep it professional and do not divulge any personal information. Sometimes this dynamic can change, but in my experience – always trust your initial judgement. This is a privileged zone and we expect all people in this zone to be nice and be supportive.

Social distance ranges from 4 to 8 feet (1.2 m – 2.4 m) away from the person and is reserved for strangers, newly formed groups, and new acquaintances. There is minimal emotional commitment in this zone, so if you don't really like someone and vice-versa, you have no real need to engage with them regularly or again.

Public distance includes anything more than 8 feet (2.4 m) away, and is used for speeches, lectures, and theatre. Public distance is essentially that range reserved for larger audience.

> Change the game, don't let the game change you.
>
> - Macklemore

PIC A Quote

Negative people like any negative influence should be avoided at all times. When that is not possible, keep engagement short, sharp and on a business level and do not divulge any personal information, to better protect yourself. Look after your mental state and don't let others drag you down.

https://leewe15.wordpress.com/2015/02/

The Journey from Victim to Survivor

Posted on March 9, 2015

> The enemy doesn't stand a chance when the victim decides to survive.
> - Rae Smith
>
> *PIC A Quote*

I have created the following flow chart to show how a victim of historic child abuse can truly become a survivor. This is based on my own healing journey. I hope that any victim of historic child sexual abuse who has been triggered, or reads this blog, will be inspired by this and chooses to help themselves and expose their abusers.

For me, I was unable to move on until I had done everything possible to get justice and for the truth to be told. The outcome for me was more important than the outcome of the cases. I knew that I could not have done anything else. I was also fortunate to get the support of an excellent psychologist who structured the therapy for me. This was achieved by referral from my doctor (General Practitioner).

In my experience, exposing the abusers from my past was the driving force for my healing journey. I wanted justice and I wanted the truth to be told. I was also shocked to find out through my own enquiries, that many of the men who sexually abused me and my peer group in the 1970's, were still working with or were involved with children in a voluntary capacity, from the year 2000 to 2012. I felt like I had to expose them.

It is very important to acknowledge that any historic police investigation, especially assaults and indecent assaults, etc., are unlikely to be supported by the [CPS] Crown Prosecution Service (i.e. charges being made against the assailants) unless there is clear, corroborating evidence. Due to the time scales involved, this is generally achieved by other witnesses coming forward and their evidence supporting yours.

Victims of historic child sexual abuse are not going to be able to ever forget what happened to them. There will always be trust issues for them and other associated traits. They will not be able to forgive the abusers and those who collaborated with them, but with support they can learn how to live with it.

It is very important for any victim of child sexual abuse to get some professional support. I cannot stress this enough. It is easy to think to yourself 'I can cope', but take it from me – it is ok to ask for help. You deserve that, you have earned the right.

It is this 'learning to live with it' that allows the victim to become a survivor. All victims of abuse deserve a peaceful life, with their demons silenced. I discovered that there was only one way to achieve that. I went back and faced my demons and I fought hard for my future.

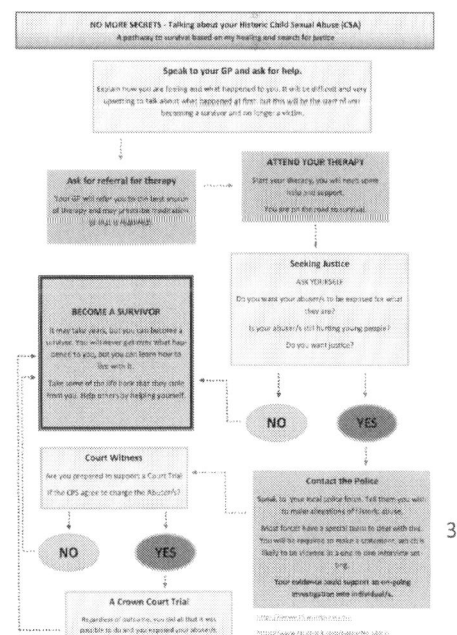

To move on from Survivor to Thriver, I believe it is important that nothing is left unchallenged. To stop looking back, you need to ensure there is nothing to look back on. I am entering the final stages now and I what to share this with other victims of child sexual abuse.

PIC Speaking-Out-Journey

This is the path I followed and it worked for me. This is based on the UK medical and legal system.

Further reading:

CPS Guidelines on prosecuting cases of child sexual abuse

https://leewe15.wordpress.com/2015/03/

Changing the Culture of Child Abuse
Posted on March 3, 2015

In my experience and to my knowledge many of the boys I knew, who were victims of the institutional violence and sexual abuse throughout the 1970's, had at some stage attempted to tell someone about the abuse they were suffering. All cries for help fell on deaf ears or more importantly were ignored by the recipient/s who were either involved in the abuse themselves or held some distorted loyalty towards the system they were protecting. It is welcomed to hear that Prime Minister, David Cameron has announced today (3.3.2015) that Teachers, Councillors and social workers in England and Wales who fail to protect children could face up to five years in jail under new proposals.

I truly hope this is not just electioneering by the Government, with the general election only 2 months away and it is a start to them taking some first 'firm' steps to helping eradicate child abuse (CA) and child sexual abuse (CSA) in the UK. This form of neglect needs to be put into statute and acted upon. There is a culture of ignorance in this Country to child abuse that has harmed 1000's of children for over decades. Health workers, Teachers, Social Workers and Police Officers are all equally implicated in this. Any person who refuses to investigate or fails to act upon any possibility of child abuse is as guilty as the person committing the abuse.

We hear all too often from the amount of historic CSA allegations flooding the media today that in most cases people had been told about what was happening, but they failed to take the allegations seriously, or just failed to act upon them. Any person, professional or otherwise who is found guilty of failing to act upon the report of a child being abused, is in my view, culpable in the act and should be facing charges relating to that.

At the age of 13 years old, I had been in the independent, residential schooling system for 7 years and had been subjected to violence and indecent assaults for the majority of that time. I saw an opportunity and wrote a detailed letter to my mother, telling her about what was happening and who was responsible for it. Because all mail in and out of the school was opened and 'censored' by staff, I sealed my letter in an envelope and asked the school laundry lady to post it for me. I had saved my pocket money and gave that to her to pay for the stamp. I remember feeling somewhat relieved that I had spoken about was happening to me at the school.

A few days later, I was summoned to the headmaster office. He had in front of him the letter I had written to my mother. It had been opened and sat next to the torn envelope. From behind his desk, he told me in a calm voice that he could not understand why I would want to say such things and told me that it was complete nonsense. Walking around to the front of the desk, he pulled me by my arm and stood me on the white line and then proceeded to punch me many times, bouncing me off of the office wall. I did not speak or write about the abuse again, as a child.

Let me explain here what the white line was. The white line was a line marked on the floor in his office parallel to a blank wall. I believe it was white insulating tape. When being punished by the headmaster, we were made to stand behind the white line, with the front of our shoes touching the line. This was designed that when we were punched in the chest, we would hit the wall behind and bounce straight back. Refusing to stand on the white line or faltering during the punishment attracted a harsher punishment, normally six lashes of the bamboo cane across the hand.

I have often wondered what drove the laundry lady to betray me that day. She was a casual worker at the school, who lived in the village. Middle aged and most probably a mother herself.

There were other boys who had reported incidents of violence or indecent acts to staff members. The staff members had then either mysteriously disappeared from the school/s, never to return or they just simply refused to act upon it. I recall over my school years, seeing the police arrive at the school a few times, following allegations made by boys or staff. There was never any action taken as a result of a police visit.

It has also become known, that some boys had complained to their parents or family during the school holidays and they were subsequently removed from the school by their parents, via their local authorities. The striking concern here is that teachers, parents, social workers and the police at various stages between 1969 and 1992 (when both boarding schools I attended were running and numerous boys were beaten and indecently assaulted) had failed to ensure action was taken to protect all of the boys at the schools.

This should not be allowed to happen ever again. Any person harming a child should be stooped, publicly ousted and locked away. We all have a duty to support this. With a surge of public support now, I hope this is a turning point in 'changing the culture of abuse'.

https://leewe15.wordpress.com/2015/03/

Supporting information/Links:

http://www.bbc.co.uk/news/uk-31691061

http://www.bbc.co.uk/news/uk-england-oxfordshire-31643791

http://www.bbc.co.uk/news/uk-28194271

The historic misuse of the word 'Maladjusted'

Posted on March 2, 2015

A dictionary definition of maladjusted 'A maladjusted person, usually a child, has been raised in a way that does not prepare them well for the demands of life, which often leads to problems with behaviour in the future'.

Having been wrongly identified as maladjusted in the past, I feel I have earned the right to state that in my opinion that word has no real place in the English language – or certainly should never be used by clinicians or mental health workers. This is a nonsense word that fails to describe adequately as both a noun and a verb.

PIC bodhidharma quote

I think sometimes it is seen as a term rather than a word that may be used as an instrument, to label. As a child, I was labelled as maladjusted and in doing so the local education authority were then able to deal with me in such a way that would have been difficult to have done otherwise. Their decision-making process apart from being wrong, was criminal and badly flawed.

Hindsight – It is easy for me to look back at my early days now and analyse what had actually happened. My historic investigation indicated that as a child, I reacted badly to the home environment and as an intelligent boy, it would appear that the 2 schools that I attended in Margate had failed to challenge me, academically. A paediatric psychologist had reported that I was 'normal' and in communications to the Educational Department at Springfield, Maidstone suggested that I would undoubtedly come to more harm, by being kept in the home environment. I had been excluded from the local schools by then. By using the label 'maladjusted', I was removed from my home by the County Council and sent 277 miles away to a residential school for disturbed and maladjusted children (as the paperwork reflects). An interesting note here was after 5 years at that school, I was transferred to their sister school, still 133.7 miles away from home and told that I was going their because I was highly intelligent.

The reality of the expert's decision back then in 1969, was I would not effectively be returned to the home environment, until they reached the age of 16 years (1980) (post compulsory educational age). The decade I spent away saw me thrust into the hands of a paedophile ring, who were operating in the independent residential school system in the UK during the 1970's, 1980's and 1990's.

This is a process that still is operated in the UK today sadly. Incredibly, with all the historical investigations into institutional child sexual abuse, you would think that the authorities have understood the inherent dangers of this system. Residential schooling itself is abusive and I would highly recommend anyone with an interest in this subject to read – Joy Schaverien (Boarding School Syndrome).

Another disgusting use of the word maladjusted featured in a Crown Court Trial over the past couple of years, where I was appearing as a witness in an historic child sexual abuse trial. The accused being a former teacher/carer from my residential school days. The barrister defending the former teacher, openly accused me of lying (which was to be expected) but then he also suggested that it was no wonder that I had to be treated firmly by the carers, as I was after all maladjusted. His comments were hurtful, harmful and completely inaccurate.

I would place the word Maladjusted into Room 101, if I had the opportunity of appearing on that show.

https://leewe15.wordpress.com/2015/03/

I live with mental illness

Posted on April 7, 2015

#ILiveWithMentalillness #CSA #NoMoreSecrets

I live with mental illness and I have done so for over 40 years. One of the best things I ever did for myself a few years back was admitting that I had mental illness and then dealing with it. That has been life changing for me. The difference today is that I have learned how to live with and how to control my mental health better, rather than the other way around. For much of my childhood, the informative years, I had learned that I was very much alone in the world and there was no one around to protect me. From the age of 7 years old, I had to look out for myself. Taken from the family home, I was placed into residential schooling/care. I had to protect myself and adapt to learn how to deal with the violence and sexual abuse that was to become a major part of my daily life for an entire decade.

The shame that surrounds mental health caused me to self-stigmatise for many years. I kept it very quiet and felt ashamed that I was not in control of myself. I had deeply locked away the memories of the sexual abuse and violence I suffered from the age of 6 to 16 years. All that trauma was locked away in the sub-conscious mind and it was this naturally that had created the mental health issues I had.

I speak to people about my life experiences and I get a variety of responses. Some people are quite rightly horrified about the abuse I suffered; some people are interested to learn how I faced the challenges of my mental health issues. Some people make it quite clear that they have no interest in what I have to say and some people, family and colleagues included quickly change the subject to avoid engaging with me regarding it. It should be noted from similar reactions I have had that child sexual abuse (CSA) has attracted a similar taboo as mental health. Both these subjects are misguidedly damaging in their mistaken belief.

I think it fair to say under my circumstance, that it was no wonder that my mental health was not as stable as it should have been. At 50 years of age, I see myself as a reasonably intelligent, professional person and I have enjoyed a varied career thus far. Academically I have taken my education to an honours degree level and I still enjoy the challenge of learning new subjects. I do not have social friends as such and I do not socialise, preferring the comfort of my own home and the company of my immediate family. I do not enjoy large groups of people and only function well in those if engaged professionally. I believe this is a symptom of my mental illness.

I have suffered from depression; I have suffered from anxiety, and I have had OCD for as long as I can remember. The severity of that has varied over the years and although always present, it generally has no effect on my ability to live or operate normally. The OCD has been my way of gaining control of factors affecting my life, something that would have been difficult as a young child. I think it would be fair to say that illness has been more compulsion than obsession.

I have attempted to take my own life, in the past and I have self-harmed through a previous compulsion to punch heavy, static objects like brick walls. This frequently caused damage to my hands, primarily the right one. I recently relived this in Court, when giving evidence as a witness to my own suffered child abuse; the defence barrister questioned my ability to recollect events properly. I explained to the Court that when the 'recollections' flood back regarding the beatings and the unwanted sexual activity I was forced into as a child at the hands of male members of staff at Heanton and Kesgrave Hall Boarding Schools (1970's) these generally manifested as nightmares and living horrors that were equally as traumatic as their origins. One way I found to silent the voices screaming in my head was to cause immediate, physical pain to myself, hence the punching of walls, etc.

I did not always recognise that I had mental illness because I felt I was just a loner; in reality, I had withdrawn myself from everyone for decades, rarely attending social gatherings and forging only a few select friendships as previously stated. That is how I liked it to be. I found relationships difficult, people could not be trusted and when I did open up and trust I had failed to recognise that I had entered into abusive relationships on numerous occasions. That took its toll on me also. I have had two failed marriages prior to meeting my partner of 15 years Mandy. She has stuck by me and supported me through the many difficult years of coming to terms with my violent and abusive childhood. I am so grateful to have such a beautiful person in my life, my saviour in many ways. I think it is important to recognise that the partners of adult survivors of child sexual abuse (CSA) deserve high praise indeed. Living with and supporting someone struggling to fight off the demons of their past, without any support themselves, is above and beyond the realms of normality and duty expected of them. All I can say is that Mandy is a wonderful, loving person that has saved my life and given me a life. She is in essence my life.

I would also like to recognise here Tom, a Psychologist in East Kent (UK), who has worked with me and supported me over the past few years. Tom skilfully helped me onto a path of healing and self-awareness that has enabled me to know so much about myself and how I react to life's challenges. Tom has been the best friend any man could ask for. My family and work colleagues live with my mental illness, because they spend time with me. Most people would not know I have mental illness; it is only when I tell them that I have suffered from mental illness that they become aware.

My mental illness is not as debilitating as it was and I am able to recognise changes and deal with them so much better these days. The relationship I have with the majority of people who are told of my mental illness history does not change in any way. There are some people however who see my mental illness as a problem. I think the problem lies solely with them though!!

Today I am not ashamed to tell people that I was sexually abused as a child and that I have suffered from mental health illness. It has been the talking openly about it that has helped things improve for me. The taboo and stigma that surrounds both subjects still very much exist in all walks of our society, but there are signs that this is improving. The media and other national initiatives such as '#TimeToChange' are turning the tide with mental health stigma and discrimination awareness together with the media exposure of historic abuse cases, has helped to create awareness of CSA cases and associated issues. There is a vast Internet community that is also creating awareness and providing support for survivors of CSA.

I self-disclose and write about my experiences with the desire to help and inform others. If you are affected or triggered by my writing, please seek medical support.

https://leewe15.wordpress.com/2015/04/

Why did you not say anything?

Posted on April 8, 2015 by lwe1964

A frequent response from anyone learning first hand of historic child sexual abuse is to ask the question 'why did you not say anything?' I responded to such a question again recently and through this also discovered how manipulative and evil the paedophile ring was at Heanton and Kesgrave Hall Schools in the 1970's. More so than even I imagined.

I would like to discuss the question of "why did you not say anything?" Having recently given evidence in a Crown Court in respect of the abuse I suffered as a child in the independent residential schooling system in the UK (1970's), I was asked this question by my stepfather. I guess it is understandable why anyone outside of historic child sexual abuse would ask that question. Anyone with little or no exposure to it or a victim of it will have some difficulty understanding it. It is abhorrent, unnatural and disgusting. It is against everything that most people would consider to be 'normal' and decent.

After briefly explaining that as a very young child I was frightened and terrified with what was happening to me and I was also living in fear of reprisals for refusing to comply with advances, let alone telling others about it. I did explain to my stepfather that whilst I was at Kesgrave Hall School, Ipswich, I had actually written a letter to my mother during the year of 1976 (I was aged between 11 and 12 years) to explained in the letter that I was unhappy at the school and what had been happening to me for the past 6 years and who was responsible. I wrote about the severe beatings I had received, the constant sexual assaults, the other indecent acts and the general daily violence and humiliation I was subjected to. I recalled that I had asked the school laundry lady to post the letter for me, so as to bypass the open envelope (censorship) process that was operated at the school. I knew that this letter was never going to get past the censor and as such, I had to rely on the goodwill of the lady from the village who came in daily to do the washing at the school.

What happened next with this letter I had entrusted to the laundry lady did was catastrophic for me. She had taken the letter and the money I had saved from my allowance for a stamp and given the letter to the headmaster. It was not long before I was summoned to the headmaster's office (Mr Shepherd), probably a day or so later and I received a severe beating, after being told that the letter was full of lies and fabrication and was never to be repeated. The beating would have consisted of trashes across the lower back with a bamboo cane, whilst bent forward and across the knuckles if any attempt were made to evade the punishment by moving. Mr Shepherd also had a process of standing you near a blank wall in his office and he would punch you in the chest, bouncing you off the wall whilst shouting at you.

This was the first time I had amassed any courage to speak up about the abuse at the school and the last time until 1996. I did not attempt anything like that again whilst at Kesgrave Hall School and I think it should explain adequately why I chose not to speak up. Another implication of a failed attempt to expose the paedophiles and sadists was that of reprisal. It was not worth the risk.

All letters written by us to our parents, etc., where handed to a teacher unsealed and following a censorship process, they were either re-written or accepted for postage and taken. We had no proof that the letters were ever sent out. In the same vein, the letters we received from home where given to us opened. All incoming mail was also censored prior to us reading it.

The 'letter to laundry lady' recollection brought a number of matters to mind. Firstly, the beating I received from Mr Shepherd involved numerous punches to the chest, being buffeted into a wall in his office, to receive further punches on the rebound, a bit like a punch bag, followed by lashes of the cane across the lower back/backside whilst being forcibly held down in a forward bend position. The punches being significant enough to take the wind out of my lungs and the cane leaving a burning sensation and welt marks to be later discovered on removing clothing. This beating was equally memorable as the excessive beatings I received from Mr Lafford (Mike), Mr Leonard (?), Mr Brockman (David), Mr Downing (John) and others, with each member of staff favouring their own particular method of delivery. One beating from Mr Lafford at Kesgrave Hall School put me in the school infirmary for a few days.

Recently (December 2014) I had a back-MRI scan undertaken at QEQM Hospital, Margate following some excessive lower back pain. The MRI was able to successfully signify that the pain had been caused by a lower back muscle spasm. The MRI did however show an injury to the upper spine. An historic compound fracture to the upper spine was clearly visible on the scan. The double fracture has fused together and the broken vertebra was significantly smaller than the healthy ones. I spoke with Mr Casha, a Consultant Orthopaedic Surgeon in East Kent and asked his opinion regarding this. Mr Casha viewed the MRI images and it was in his opinion that the fractured vertebra was historically damaged through an extreme trauma and he was minded to believe that there was a high possibility that this could have happened during my adolescent years (Kesgrave Hall School 1975 to 1980).

Another revelation that unfolded recently, when relaying this story to my mother and stepfather she was about the letters writing. I asked her if she had received my 'normal' censored letters and she said these were received infrequently. I would have written every week, or certainly every other week home and generally wrote to my grandmother on the opposite week.

I told her that in the entire 10 years of boarding school (Heanton and Kesgrave Hall) I had not received regular letters from her, only those from my Grandmother. She was very surprised to hear this and explained that she had written to me constantly, virtually weekly. I told her that I certainly had not received the letters.

This then brought to mind an incident from May 1999, when I was giving evidence in Ipswich Crown Court, as a witness in the Alan Stancliffe abuse trial (Kesgrave Hall, indecent assaults). During my cross examination, the defence barrister produced as exhibits, letters from my mother to me whilst I was at Kesgrave Hall School during the late 1970's. I confirmed that these were letters seemingly written by mother to me, whilst I was at that school. The purpose being that there were no contents or indications in the letters signifying that there were any problems, issues or concerns. Until now, I had missed the importance of these letters being produced by Stancliffe's defence. I had not provided these to the Court, because I had never been in receipt of them. The letters were obviously retained by the school and had never been passed on to me. Furthermore, the letters must have been retained by Vivian Davies, a director of Kesgrave Hall School (Records Custodian) and former headmaster of Heanton School in May 1999, for them to have been produced by Stancliffe's defence team to establish some angle for defence and be used as such some 20 years later. Highly suspicious and indicative of manipulative minds having the forethought of dealing with future scenarios arising from complaints against the school or staff within.

Going back to the original topic of 'why did you not say anything?' When a victim of childhood sexual abuse comes forward and does speak out, it has taken immeasurable courage for that person to do so. It is probably one of the bravest things that person has done. They will undoubtedly feel frightened and vulnerable because of their actions, but they will have taken this course of action because they want their abuser/s to be exposed. If you ask that person initially – why did you not say something before? They will say, "because I couldn't". Initially that will be all you will get from them. The real reasons will come out later in the healing process.

Many of the boys who went through the schools I did, like me they would have experienced abuse and violence at a very young age (7+). We were in effect extremely vulnerable and alone. There were no regular inspections or audits of these schools that we knew of. I never recall any inspections of the schools or being asked any questions about the school or my time there. For us institutional abuse was a way of life, it was our life. We grew up in it and knew no different. This was normal everyday (and night time) activity that demanded total submission from us. Any attempt made to subvert or refuse advances from the staff was met with violence and brute force. It soon became very clear that fighting against them was totally counterproductive.

I can state that I was left feeling highly ashamed of what had happened to me. The attackers were very skilful in transferring the guilt on to you. They were indecently assaulting us and forcing us to touch them and to engage in sexual activity with them. After all you can only pretend to be asleep for part of time. You think that no one will believe you and if you talk it about it, you will be ridiculed or hurt further. It was a dirty secret that you had to keep quiet about.

A victim of abuse may feel if they tell someone, they will be blamed for what had happened or be accused of lying about it. My biological father accused me of lying, when I told him in 1996 that I had been abused as a child and I was speaking to the police about it. He was one of the first people I told and one of the last for another 17 years.

Many victims of abuse are told to keep it a secret and sadly most do keep it a secret and keep it locked away deep inside for a very long time. It is very difficult having to think about it, even more so trying to talk about it and for some, they will be fearful of mentioning it, in case it is not accepted or listened to. I know from my experience, the actual act of talking about it to someone else was extremely difficult and it took a few years to get past that. The conditioned instinct of not talking about it meant I had to physically force the words out. This does improve with time.

Many abusers will threaten the victim that if they tell, they might kill someone in their family or threaten that the authorities will come in and break up their family. Many victims of abuse dissociate when memories of their own abuse surfaces, to distance themselves from the pain or to protect their loved ones from the pain. Some victims will only be able to speak out once their abuser is dead; not that speaking about it becomes any easier for them.

It is easy and natural for any caring, compassionate person to say to a victim/survivor of historic child sexual abuse 'why did you not say anything?' And hopefully they will in time understand the reasons why that would never have been possible.

I applaud the bravery of any victim of historic CSA who speaks up and exposes their attacker/s. Sadly, there is a battle still getting the system to believe you but stand your ground, the truth will always win. Justice is the ultimate goal, but uncovering the abuser/s serves a purpose too. They can no longer hide behind a veil of respectability. They will be exposed. They will never hurt anyone again.

In my experience, once I had exposed paedophiles from my past, normally through the regional and national media, other victims came forward and reported allegations against them. Other investigations were undertaken and other trials ensued. Although these individuals will ultimately face their final judgment for what they have done, there is some personal benefit to be gained from having 'your day in Court'.

https://leewe15.wordpress.com/2015/04/08/why-did-you-not-say-anything/

Someone's Therapist Knows all about You

Posted on June 3, 2015 by lwe1964

The police investigation into abuse allegations at Heanton School, by Devon & Cornwall Constabulary concluded in April 2015. The Police investigation into Kesgrave Hall School (part of Operation Garford) is currently being wound down (May 2015).

Life Begins at 50.

We frequently hear or are told "forget the past and enjoy the future" or some derivatives of that saying. It is true that some merit can be attributed to this for some situations. I would argue, from my experience, that you cannot create a better future yourself by burying issues from your past. My childhood years, or more precisely the injuries inflicted on me as a developing child, although repressed by me for decades, have caused me and those associated with me great harm. My denial and refusal to challenge the ghosts of the past have been a destructive influence on my adult life. The only way I found to lessen the impact of this damaging influence was to face up to those elements from my past, challenge them directly and then lay them to rest. It is true that anyone who has suffered great trauma in their life will undoubtedly never truly get over what happened to them, but you can at least learn how to live with it. That is the true definition of a survivor.

I have had to live with the consequences of sexual, physical and mental abuse inflicted upon me as a child, for past 44 years. This systemic abuse was prevalent in the institutions I was forced to attend from the age of 6 to 16 years of age. Heanton School, North Devon and Kesgrave Hall School, Suffolk were residential, private organisations I attended as a boarder. These schools were owned and run by the same group of directors. Spending 5 years at each school during the 1970's was to have a far-reaching impact on my adult life and affect every facet of my social and professional interactions.

With hindsight, I can now say without any argument that the best thing I ever did for myself, was to speak to someone about what happened to me all those years ago. Talking about the abuse I suffered was painful and difficult at first, but in doing so it changed everything. Today, all these years later, I am in a better place and it is some comfort to know that so is a particularly nasty abuser, John Downing, who thought he had got away with all he had done. He is now in prison and at the age of 74, I have no doubt he is feeling as frightened and vulnerable as the other boys and I did when I was 6 years of age.

Picture (see featured Image): Highlighted is John Downing, Choir Master – Induction and Institution Service (5th September 2011) St Michael & All Angels Church, Great Torrington, Devon –

PIC Credit: St Michaels & All Angels Church

http://www.stmichaelstorrington.org.uk/gallery.html {*All images featuring Downing appear to have been removed by St Michael & All Angels Church from their Website galleries – and are no longer available. You cannot blame them for wanting to distance themselves from John Downing*}

When I saw this picture of John Downing tucked away inside St Michael & All Angels Church – Great Torrington, Devon back in 2012, seemingly hiding behind a Bishop, I knew that this would not do. This seemingly respectable member of the choir, at that church, presented as an insult to all the victims that had suffered at Downing's hands between 1968 and 1985. This man is a monster. A predatory and debased paedophile and sadist who used his position of trust to satisfy his disgusting sexual appetite. I was horrified to learn that he was still associated with young boy's way and I had to speak to the police about him. That image was the main driving force for me to make my allegations to the Devon & Cornwall Police regarding John Downing.

For me life really did begin at 50. I write this on the other side of a two-week trial at Exeter Crown Court, which finished on Friday 10th April 2015. The former Heanton School teacher John Downing was found guilty of 39 counts of gross indecency and indecent assaults on 6 boys, from the former Heanton School, North Devon. These offences were committed between 1968 and 1985. I was at Heanton School from 1970 to 1975. John Downing was sentenced to 21 years in prison and he was taken away from Court on the afternoon of 10th April.

The judges' comments on sentencing John Downing on 10th April 2015 were insightful, accurate and extremely comforting. It was as though he could read the victim's minds:

Judge Graham Cottle who told him that some of his assaults would now be classified as rape.

He told Downing: "It is many years since these crimes were committed but you must now answer for the catalogue of sexual abuse that you perpetrated on the seven complainants.

"I strongly suspect this case has no more than scratched the surface of the extent of the abuse of children at Heanton School for which you were responsible, but I only sentence you for the offences of which you were convicted.

"These boys came from unfortunate and disadvantaged backgrounds from which they were plucked when they were six or seven and taken to this school in North Devon.

"They arrived no doubt as bewildered, frightened and abandoned children. On any view, they were exceptionally vulnerable. They were introduced to a regime that was at best inappropriate and at worst cruel and shocking.

"Excessive punishment of boys was routine and in that climate, you, as deputy head, took the opportunity to regularly, repeatedly and over many years abuse small boys as and when you pleased

"The level and type of abuse was to right minded people truly horrendous and the victims have been scarred for life as a result. They were all required to relive their experiences by your denial.

"They were exposed to humiliating and embarrassing ordeal of having to tell their experiences to a room full of strangers. Nobody could fail to be moved by seeing them struggling to cope with that ordeal.

"They were demonstrably truthful but they had to contend with accusations of lying and fabrication.

"As a teacher and deputy head you subjected them to very serious sexual abuse. The regime at the school gave you licence to do whatever you wanted to these vulnerable and defenceless children and that is precisely what you did.

"For years you abused one boy after another after another. Apart from anal penetration you committed every form of sexual assault on one or more of them. One act of indecency would now be charged as rape.

"You made boys engage in sexual activity with each other for your sexual gratification and entertainment.

"At this trial, you have maintained an arrogant and defiant stance in the face of overwhelming evidence. I have to arrive at a total sentence that reflects the enormity of these crimes against vulnerable young children over many years.

"Your victims have tried to make something of their lives but drugs, alcohol, depression and imprisonment are common features. They are deeply scarred by and the majority of the blame for that can be lain at your door."

http://www.northdevonjournal.co.uk/North-Devon-teacher-jailed-21-years-boarding/story-26314113-detail/story.html

Anyone who has suffered from historic child sexual abuse has suffered from the stigma associated with that. That stigma is lifting, society is willing to listen to you now. Do not continue to self-stigmatise. Mental health and child sexual abuse naturally is closely linked with each other. In my journey, it became evident to me that misconceptions about mental health conditions are still sadly present in our society today. A general reluctance to discuss mental health is something I experience daily, although I have seen some change in that over the past 12 months. Campaigns such as 'Time to Change' are helping to combat stigma and discrimination with mental health.

http://www.time-to-change.org.uk/talking-about-mental-health

I am willing to share information about my mental health. Talking about it makes me feel empowered and justified. It is a great shame that not everyone I occasion is just as willing to listen to me talking about it.

I am at the end of a very long journey, which started in 1969. On the 10th April 2015, I completed the journey which saw the truth being known about what had happened at Heanton School, Devon and Kesgrave Hall School, Suffolk from 1968 to the early 1990's. More so the truth is now known about the people responsible for the violence and depraved actions they perpetrated against defenceless young boys who were in need of care, guidance and support. I saw the last of the monsters from my past being locked away. I have since discharged myself from psychotherapy support and I now consider myself to be a true survivor.

I appeal for any other victim of historic abuse to follow the path I took. You cannot truly get over what happened to you, but you can learn how to live with it. You cannot learn how to live with your past unless you face it and deal with it. You can achieve whatever you want when you put your mind to it. Persistence is the key to success and always remember it only takes 20 seconds of bravery to effect some positive change in your life.

Child sexual abuse is disgusting and is more prevalent in the UK than a lot of people realise. It was perpetrated openly and covered up widely during the 1970's, 1980's and 1990's, although it has always been there and is still happening today sadly. I encourage victims of abuse to speak out to prevent the shroud of secrecy being pulled over this abhorrent plague again.

To close – It is ok to talk about what happened to you, in fact it is very healthy to do so. You will destroy the secrecy that your abuser/s have created to protect themselves. You will expose them and not yourselves. We all need some support at times throughout our lives and it is there for you. You just need to ask. You GP should be a good vehicle for support.

A great comment I picked up from social media last week – 'Someone's therapist knows all about you'. I think that explains a lot.

https://leewe15.wordpress.com/

https://twitter.com/lwe5

I also run a Facebook awareness page:

https://www.facebook.com/pages/No-More-Secrets/809446972476085?fref=ts

#NoMoreSecrets

Anyone triggered by this page should initially speak with their GP or a close family member or friend. Allegations of historic abuse can be made to any Police force.

https://leewe15.wordpress.com/2015/06/03/someones-therapist-knows-all-about-you/

Appendix L: Boarding School Syndrome #2

The truth about 'boarding school syndrome'

By Wendy Leigh – The Telegraph

http://www.telegraph.co.uk/education/secondaryeducation/11662001/The-truth-about-boarding-school-syndrome.html

The nightmares come more often these days, but lose nothing of their intricacy for their increase in frequency.

They all begin on a cold morning in 1968, when I am 12 years old and standing on the platform at Charing Cross Station, surrounded by a gaggle of girls dressed, as I am, in navy blue uniform.

Pic The Author at School (photo: Wendy Leigh)

In the near distance, my mother's image is already fading – I've long since learned that the last thing I need is to draw any more attention to the tears beginning to brim than having her taking me right up to the carriage before she leaves.

Even when I wake at 4am in a cold sweat in my flat overlooking the Thames, my home for the past ten years, I still can't shake the smell, noise and desolation of my nightmare's destination: St Margaret's, Folkestone, the boarding school where I was incarcerated for four years of my life.

I don't use the word "incarcerated" lightly; even (perhaps, especially) as a child, it always seemed more akin to Wandsworth Prison than an educational establishment for the upper classes. But it is one that seems all the more fitting now I have read Boarding School Syndrome: The Psychological Drama of the 'Privileged Child', a newly published study of former boarders like me, by Professor Joy Scheverin.

A Jungian psychoanalyst, Schaverien first coined the term "boarding school syndrome" a decade ago, after seeing a multitude of former pupils among her patients – characterised by problems with anger, depression, anxiety, a failure to sustain relationships, fear of abandonment, substance abuse, and so forth. She, herself, was following in the footsteps of Nick Duffell, a psychotherapist and author of influential study, The Making of Them, about the wounds such schooling can inflict. Duffell defines ex-pupils, and indeed himself, as "boarding school survivors" – a term that resonates strongly with me, given I still feel scarred by the six formative years I spent attending two of the (minor) cornerstones of the British establishment.

PIC Wendy Leigh as a child (Photo: Jeff Gilbert)

Before St Margaret's, I was sent to Hookstead, Crowborough, when I was 10; ostensibly because my parents had just divorced, and also because my mother, a teacher, was certain that boarding school would provide me with the best and most gilded start in life.

I was keen it wouldn't disappoint her, and initially, given I had been steeped in Enid Blyton's St. Clare series – bracing books about boarding schools, populated by top drawer, kind and jolly girls, each one a brick – I was happy to be going.

- Could boarding school be the best thing for your child?

- Inside the most expensive boarding school in the world

But nothing could have prepared me for the pain of being far from home, and the mother I adored. A sensitive loner of a child, I struggled with the lack of privacy by isolating myself from the other girls – an odd and ungainly peg rammed into an ill-fitting hole. The only consolation was that I could spend every weekend at home with my mother – the only moments of love and happiness punctuating long weeks of cold baths, regulation knickers and barebones dinners of baked beans and bread.

Much, I know, has changed for today's pupils, which Schaverien readily acknowledges. But however warm and cuddly modern boarding schools may be in comparison to mine, she insists children sent away to school – no matter how well they are looked after – will still suffer trauma at being separated from those who love them best.

My two years at Hookstead were a holiday camp compared to the four years I spent at St Margaret's, from which I was only allowed to escape three times a term. These rare weekends at home compensated somewhat for my increasing unhappiness at school – my mother made sure each was akin to a party, filled with my favourite food on hand, a trip to see any movie I wanted (even the musicals she hated). But however, pampered I was, I could never forget each tick of the clock brought me closer to the moment we would have to part again at Paddock Wood Station in Kent.

Somehow these partings never got easier. Although I was outwardly stoic and careful never to cry in front of her, the jaunty carefree air I managed to maintain up to the carriage would turn to flood of tears as soon as we pulled out of the station – and then I would hate myself for my babyishness as much as I hated the return to my nightmare ahead.

I never told my mother that I loathed school with every fibre of my being, or begged her not to send me back; even then, I understood her subconscious motives for dispatching me, her cherished only child. I knew she was doing everything she could to give me what she thought was a superior education. And that, never mind money, it had cost even more pride to get her to convince my father – who was dead set against the idea of wasting money on my education – to foot the bill.

It was only many years later, when I was 28, and my maternal grandmother's death overwhelmed me with enough grief to seek therapy, that distinguished psychoanalyst Dr Erika Padan Freeman helped me join up more dots.

My mother, Marion, had been traumatised as a child herself when, at the age of 11, in July 1939, she was sent out of Germany on the Kindertransport, which spirited her and 10,000 other children to safety in England. The train, of course, left from the railway station, where little Marion was forced to part from her father on the platform, never to see him again.

As Dr Freeman explained, in sending me away at a similar age, and continually re-enacting that heartrending scene on the railway station, my mother was unconsciously repeating the pattern of her past. Putting me on the train, separating from me and unconsciously hoping that I wouldn't be hurt like she was, I wouldn't suffer, and that, this time, the story would end happily.

Of course, it didn't. Instead, just as Schaverien posits, it forged a kind of dual identity within me. She explains: "One of the characteristics of the child coping with leaving home and living without love is that they form a psychological split into two aspects of personality, which I call the 'home self' and the 'boarding school self'."

So, there was the fragile Wendy, beset by separation anxiety, crying late at night under her counterpane. And there was tough Wendy, who developed a thread of steel in her soul, and knew she needed to protect herself from this pain as much as her mother.

Uncannily enough, both those sides of me are currently merging, as my mother, now 87, has been diagnosed with terminal non-Hodgkin's lymphoma. She has been in hospital since April, and may have very little time left.

While my softer self is reliving the trauma and heartbreak of that first enforced separation, at just 10 years old, my tough boarding school self would still die before crying in front of her when I visit each day – determined to bring nothing but love and cheer to her bedside. Instead I busy myself, when tears threaten, with the pragmatic details of palliative care.

Here, at least, I am able to see one boon to being a boarding school survivor: however tough it may be when my mother leaves me again, for good, I know that I have already forged the strength I'll need to endure it.

- Boarding School Syndrome by Joy Schaverien is published by Routledge, £27.99

- Buy Boarding School Syndrome by Joy Schaverien from Telegraph Books

Appendix M: Jimmy Savile: timeline of his sexual abuse and its uncovering

Jimmy Savile: timeline of his sexual abuse and its uncovering
The Guardian: First published on Thursday 26 June 2014 11.38 BST
Josh Halliday
https://www.theguardian.com/media/2014/jun/26/jimmy-savile-sexual-abuse-timeline

Investigators now believe the late Top of the Pops host preyed on around 500 vulnerable victims as young as two years old

Jimmy Savile's most prolific period of sexual abuse was in the late 1960s and early 70s, according to police. Photograph: John Redman/AP

Thursday 26 June 2014 11.38 BST First published on Thursday 26 June 2014 11.38 BST

It is now known that Jimmy Savile sexually abused hundreds of children and women at the height of his fame.

Investigators believe the late Top of the Pops host preyed on around 500 vulnerable victims as young as two years old at institutions including the BBC's broadcasting studios, 14 hospitals and 20 children's hospitals across England.

Since his death in October 2011, a string of official inquiries have been launched into his offending at hospitals, schools and the BBC.

Today an independent inquiry found that Savile abused 60 people, including at least 33 patients aged from five to 75, at Leeds general infirmary. Other hospitals have also released the results of their Savile investigations.

31 October 1926: Savile is born in Leeds, the youngest of seven children.

1955: The earliest incident of abuse recorded by the police. It took place in Manchester, where at the time he managed a dance hall.

1960: In one of a handful of example cases given by the police, a 10-year-old boy asked Savile for his autograph outside a hotel. Savile took the boy inside and seriously sexually assaulted him.

1 January 1964: Savile presents the first ever Top of the Pops for the BBC. He had previously been a DJ at Radio Luxembourg in 1958.

1965: Records show abuse started at the BBC, at Leeds general infirmary, where Savile was a long-term volunteer porter, and at Stoke Mandeville hospital, where he also volunteered.

1966: This was the start of what police have identified as Savile's peak period for abuse, which lasted a decade.

1970: Records show Savile started to abuse girls at Duncroft girls' school near Staines, Surrey, where he was a regular visitor.

1972: In another example of Savile's offences listed by police, he is recorded as groping a 12-year-old boy and his two female friends who were attending a recording of Top of the Pops.

1980s: At some point in the decade, a female victim is believed to have told the Metropolitan police she was assaulted in Savile's campervan in a BBC car park. The police file cannot be located and the investigating officer is now dead.

1990: Savile is knighted, also receiving a papal knighthood.

April 2000: In a TV documentary presented by Louis Theroux, Savile acknowledges the rumours about him being a paedophile, but denies it.

26 July 2006: Savile co-presents the final Top of the Pops, an occasion that gave rise to one of the allegations made to police.

March 2008: Savile begins legal proceedings against a newspaper that linked him to abuse at the Jersey children's home Haut de la Garenne.

2009: Savile is interviewed under caution by Surrey police investigating an alleged indecent assault at Duncroft school. The CPS advised there was insufficient evidence to take any further action. This was the year of the last offence recorded by the current investigation.

Police have given another example offence dating from this year in which a 43-year-old woman was sexually assaulted by Savile on a train journey between Leeds and London.

2011: the scandal breaks

29 October: Jimmy Savile dies.

Early November: A Newsnight investigation into Savile begins. Reporter Liz Mackean and researcher Hannah Livingston make contact with former Duncroft pupils.

11 November: A BBC tribute programme is aired on BBC1 called Jimmy Savile: As It Happened.

1 December: The Newsnight editor Peter Rippon emails reporter Meirion Jones telling him to stop working on other elements of the investigation because it is not strong enough without confirmation of the CPS angle and saying that he (Rippon) will pull the editing.

Jones emails himself the "red flag email" in which he sets out what he sees as the consequences for the BBC if the story does not run.

5 December: Surrey police confirm that they investigated "a historic allegation of indecent assault ... alleged to have occurred at a children's home in Staines in the 1970s" and that they referred this to the CPS.

9 December: The CPS informs Jones it decided not to prosecute Savile because of lack of evidence and not because he was old or infirm.

Rippon and Jones meet and Jones tells Rippon that he accepts the decision that he is not to pursue the story any more.

2012

8 January: The Sunday Mirror reports that the Newsnight investigation was axed and refers to a clash with the Fix It tribute show.

9 February: Miles Goslett reports in the Oldie that Newsnight's Savile investigation was pulled because of the tribute programmes and that allegations were made about abuse on BBC premises. The article alleges that the BBC had information the police did not and that Mark Thompson knew of the report. Further stories follow in the Daily Telegraph and the Daily Mail.

7 September: The BBC receives a letter from ITV giving notice of the Exposure documentary on the Savile sex abuse allegations and posing questions.

3 October: The ITV Exposure programme on Savile is broadcast.

8 October: The BBC director-general George Entwistle appears on the Today programme. Mackean emails Entwistle to share her "disquiet" with "the handling of the Newsnight Savile story" and pointing out inaccuracy in an all-staff email.

Entwistle asks Ken MacQuarrie, BBC Scotland director, to investigate the circumstances in which the Newsnight investigation was dropped.

22 October: The Panorama special on the BBC and Savile is broadcast.

23 October: Entwistle appears before the Commons culture, media and sport select committee.

George Entwistle after giving evidence to a Commons select committee over the Jimmy Savile scandal

October: BBC asks Dame Janet Smith to investigate the culture and practices of the BBC in the decades that Savile worked there.

10 November: Entwistle resigns as director-general of the BBC.

BBC director-general George Entwistle leaves Portcullis House after giving evidence to MPs. Photograph: Peter Macdiarmid/Getty Images

2013

11 January: Scotland Yard labels Savile a "prolific, predatory" sex offender after its investigation reveals 214 criminal offences across 28 police forces, between 1955 and 2009. Its report, Giving Victims a Voice, found that 73% of his victims were children, and the allegations of abuse span 14 medical establishments.

2014

2 June: NSPCC research for BBC Panorama confirms there have been at least 500 reports of abuse by Savile.

26 June: Department of Health publishes the results of investigations by 28 medical establishments, including Leeds General infirmary and Broadmoor hospital. In Leeds, Savile abused 60 people including at least 33 patients aged from five to 75. At high-security Broadmoor hospital, the broadcaster abused at least five individuals, including two patients who were subjected to repeated assaults.

• Anyone needing support should contact the National Association for People Abused in Childhood (NAPAC) on 0808 801 0331

Copyright © The Guardian/Josh Halliday

Other Guardian links:

https://www.theguardian.com/media/2014/jun/26/savile-bodies-sex-acts-corpses-glass-eyes-mortuary

https://www.theguardian.com/uk-news/2014/jun/26/edwina-currie-shocked-jimmy-savile-role

https://www.theguardian.com/uk-news/2014/jun/26/jimmy-savile-institutions-victims-abuse

https://www.theguardian.com/media/2014/jun/26/former-child-patients-recount-jimmy-savile-abuse-leeds-hospital

https://www.theguardian.com/media/2014/nov/06/jimmy-savile-inquiry-extends-41-hospitals

https://www.theguardian.com/media/2014/dec/18/jimmy-savile-victims-apology-police-north-yorkshire

https://www.theguardian.com/media/2014/dec/16/jimmy-savile-appeal-court-compensation-scheme

Appendix N: The Dame Janet Smith Review (Jimmy Savile)

25 February 2016

The BBC published Dame Janet Smith's Report (which includes Dame Linda Dobbs' Report into the activities of Stuart Hall) on 25 February 2016. The Report is available in full at www.bbc.co.uk/bbctrust/dame_janet_smith.

Click here to download Dame Janet Smith's Opening Statement.

All media enquiries concerning the Review should be addressed to Melanie Riley, Bell Yard Communications; BellYard@bell-yard.com

O: 020 7936 2021   M: 07775 591244.

Introduction

The Dame Janet Smith Review was established in October 2012 by the BBC to conduct an impartial, thorough and independent review of the culture and practices of the BBC during the years that Jimmy Savile worked there. In respect of Jimmy Savile, the Review has received evidence from those who were the subject of inappropriate sexual conduct by Jimmy Savile in connection with his work for the BBC and from others who had raised concerns about his conduct with the BBC. The Review is chaired by the former Court of Appeal Judge, Dame Janet Smith DBE.

On 14 May 2013, Stuart Hall pleaded guilty to 14 charges of indecent assault. Shortly afterwards, the BBC announced that a further investigation would be undertaken into the conduct of Stuart Hall. As Dame Janet Smith had a potential conflict of interest, the Stuart Hall investigation was chaired by the former High Court judge, Dame Linda Dobbs DBE.

Terms of reference for the Jimmy Savile investigation and the Stuart Hall investigation are accessed through the tabs above. In addition, there is a further explanatory note to the Stuart Hall investigation, which is also accessed above.

Copyright © The Dame Janet Smith Review 2017

Appendix O: Westminster Abuse Scandal

The Westminster child abuse 'coverup': how much did MPs know?
The Guardian
Michael White - Tuesday 17 March 2015 18.40 GMT

https://www.theguardian.com/politics/2015/mar/17/westminster-child-abuse-paedophile-ring-failure

Dolphin Square, Westminster, home to politicians and at the centre of allegations of historical sexual abuse by establishment figures. Photograph: Suzanne Plunkett/Reuters

Claims that the establishment covered up a paedophile ring at the heart of Westminster are finally being investigated, decades after rumours first surfaced. Michael White, who was a parliamentary reporter at the time, asks veteran politicians why no one wanted to believe the worst

Another day, another set of shocking headlines about allegations of historical child abuse and high-level coverups, this time a dossier being handed over by the Metropolitan police themselves to the Independent Police Complaints Commission to examine 14 allegations of Scotland Yard's own complicity in the alleged coverup of a high-level paedophile ring.

Two weeks ago it emerged that former MP Harvey Proctor's grace-and-favour home in Belvoir Castle had been raided by police investigating historic allegations of child abuse. Proctor has denied any involvement in, or knowledge of, the alleged establishment abuse. Other claims fester. A raid was also made on the home of the former home secretary Leon Brittan.

Conservative politician Harvey Proctor in 1987: the former MP's home has been searched by police investigating historical allegations of child sex abuse. Photograph: PA/PA Archive Images

All have denied charges levelled by alleged victims, some of them in files passed on by current MPs convinced of an extensive establishment coverup that lasted decades. But so did Cyril Smith, who got his knighthood in 1988 despite officials warning Margaret Thatcher of paedophile allegations against him, confirmed only after the former Liberal MP was dead. Freedom of Information (FoI) papers filled in fresh details this month. Smith is again central to today's claims.

The allegations centering on Dolphin Square, a 7.5-acre, 1,250-flat complex by the Thames, include claims that boys in nearby Lambeth care homes were recruited as rent boys and ferried to the apartments for violent orgies where VIPs, defence and Whitehall officials, establishment types, as well as Tory MPs (one "cabinet minister"), were said to be participants. The Yard has spoken of "possible homicide" being committed. Historical and more recent allegations have been backed by

154

Labour MP John Mann, who first encountered them as a Lambeth councillor in the 80s, but was told by police contacts that their inquiries had been stopped on orders from superiors.

How could it happen, politicians prominent in the 80s ask themselves? Were some of them mixed up in coverups, voters ask? So, does the media, though it, too, has questions to answer. I was a Westminster political reporter at the time. I have been asking around.

This is a controversy with a long fuse. About 30 years ago, one of Margaret Thatcher's junior ministers took me aside at Westminster and told me of serious allegations against a senior colleague. Since his version of events involved the abuse of other well-placed Tories' children, it sounded pretty implausible to me. It still does, so I will not repeat it here, though both men are now dead and other versions of the same rumour have since surfaced.

With one borderline exception, it was the only such allegation that I heard as a working political journalist in the 1980s that was not also known to a wider public beyond Westminster. In the pre-Twitter era, such stories often surfaced via Private Eye, which picked up all sorts of gossip, some of which it concluded was untrue. Occasionally, a smear might be traced to security sources trying to damage someone, as may have been the case with my junior minister: a willing conduit for malice against a reforming minister who threatened vested interests?

As the Met's Operation Midland ploughs through long-neglected allegations – the IPCC is now formally involved, too – and the New Zealand high court judge Lowell Goddard takes up the onerous chairmanship of the official inquiry, how do surviving politicians of the 70s and 80s react to what they are now reading? To allegations of politically powerful coverups, even of murder linked to Dolphin Square, where MPs have lived on weekdays for decades? Mostly with alarm and surprise, tinged with regret at their own naivety or complacency. Coverups? Perhaps one or two, concede a couple of people I spoke to. Among such sentiments from old stagers – MPs, ex-MPs, some now peers – and other veterans of Whitehall and Westminster, come admissions that they did hear – or read in the Eye – of shocking sexual allegations against some colleagues at the time.

They came to believe claims of a double life made against the then-Liberal leader Jeremy Thorpe. But they did not against some others since named – including Tory Peter Morrison, who was implicated in an abuse scandal centred on North Wales children's homes, and even Cyril Smith. "A peculiar character, living with mum, but no one suggested anything else," admits one avowedly naive Lib Dem colleague of the period.

In contrast to the sex-abuse cases that have rocked TV and showbusiness, no one actually saw anything. Most MPs are less worldly than celebs, Mrs Thatcher among them. A child of provincial Lincolnshire, raised in an austere Methodist household, what did she know about such things? A more clued up figure would not have said, in praise of her deputy, Lord Whitelaw: "Every prime minister needs a Willie."

Among more than a dozen old stagers I interviewed recently – most willing to speak only off the record – none recalls hearing anything about the now-notorious paedophile haunt Elm Guest House in Barnes, let alone about such crimes allegedly being committed at Dolphin Square – also part of the IPCC's new inquiry. Up to 70 MPs lived in Dolphin Square, often without knowing their neighbours, fellow MPs included. "I only realised [a Tory colleague] had been living here for five years when I met him in the lift," one recalls. "I thought it was where rich men parked ex-mistresses, old ladies with dogs," says another former resident.

A common reaction to lurid gossip at the time, among political journalists as well as politicians, was that "It can't be true – or someone would have been arrested." Respectable provincial newspapers routinely protected readers from sordid tales. Tory ex-ministers with security experience also point out that "in those days the police were much more subservient to senior politicians. You did not get chief constables with minds of their own." The police were more corrupt, too, some point out.

But, as in other recently uncovered scandals, the culture was different, too. One Conservative ex-MP recalls once being with Whitelaw, the ultimate old-school insider, when yet another "Tories and prostitutes" sex scandal broke in the Sunday papers. The reaction of the future home secretary and deputy prime minister was immediate. "Why has this been allowed to come out?" Whitelaw is now accused of demanding that police drop an investigation into the Westminster paedophile ring.

But widespread political coverups, even of a murder at Dolphin Square? "I don't see how it would work," says a former Labour chief whip. Whitehall was not wholly out of the loop. Robert Armstrong, Thatcher's cabinet secretary from 1979 to 1987, tells me: "One got to know a certain amount about politicians' sex lives, but I never heard a whisper about paedophilia."

Officials such as Lord Armstrong were not wholly passive. As Edward Heath's civil service adviser during his abortive Lib-Con coalition negotiations after losing the "who governs Britain?" election in 1974, Armstrong says the then-PM knew the rumours about Jeremy Thorpe's private promiscuity. "Thorpe mentioned the possibility [of becoming home secretary in charge of security files], but that's the last thing Heath would have offered him," he now says.

Years later Armstrong gave Thatcher what he calls a "veiled" warning not to sanction Jimmy Savile's knighthood for charitable work. She ignored it, as did David Steel in proposing Smith for a knighthood in 1998 despite known allegations against him by the alternative Rochdale Free Press, repeated in Private Eye. Armstrong's successor, Robin (now Lord) Butler, flagged up concerns about Smith, we now know. So did the political honours scrutiny committee.

Sir Robert Armstrong: gave Thatcher a 'veiled' warning not to sanction Jimmy Savile's knighthood. Photograph: PA/Empics Sports Photo Agency

That Armstrong and Butler at least raised a problem may reassure the prominent Whitehall-watcher Professor Peter Hennessy. Journalist turned academic, now a peer, Hennessy remains astonished that a triple-lock defence line of security services, police special branch and the tax authorities did not tip off No 10 more effectively about dubious recipients of honours. But as a 1970s Westminster political correspondent, Hennessy too admits he shared widespread scepticism towards the Eye's allegations against Smith and others.

Each case is different. Colleagues recall John Wakeham, Margaret Thatcher's "Mr Fixit" and powerful chief whip in the mid-1980s, telling MPs who came to him with concerns about Morrison having cottaging skirmishes with the police: "If someone brings me some evidence I can do something about it, if required." Wakeham would say years later: "I got no evidence at all."

Morrison, scion of a wealthy Tory dynasty and MP for Chester, had powerful friends, including Thatcher, the defence of whose premiership he organised (disastrously) against Michael Heseltine's challenge in 1990. The suspicion persists that, somewhere along the line, he was protected. "It never got out, but people said: 'They'll never be able to do that for Peter again,'" recalls one Tory. Morrison quit the Commons in 1992 and died in 1995, aged just 51.

"He was a very unhappy man and drank himself to death," explains the former Tory cabinet minister and friend, who remembers being equally dismissive of unsavoury rumours about Cyril Smith. "I looked at Smith and thought, what an unlikely figure, that huge bulk and he could hardly walk properly."

Evidence suppressed about Cyril Smith? Wakeham's assumption today remains that the Director of Public Prosecutions (DPP) must have decided the evidence wasn't good enough. This month's FoI revelations confirmed that in 1970 the then-DPP did examine a Lancashire police file and concluded a conviction would be unlikely. Others say the problem was wider. This week's claims on BBC Newsnight that officers were told to suppress their video evidence against Smith and forget it – on the orders of a senior colleague – suggests the critics are right.

Quite apart from the instinct to cover up rumours of abuse, another attitude was widely shared at the time by the press and public, too. "There was a universal desire to ignore it," says another of the retired MPs interviewed. "We just didn't understand it. It wasn't deliberate neglect, more a lack of experience," explains a Labour woman of cabinet rank. "Forty years ago attitudes were more relaxed," explains Labour veteran and Old Etonian Tam Dalyell.

The former Elm guest house near Barnes, south-west London. Photograph: Ray Tang/Rex

There were other significant features of the period. Though divorce was no longer a bar to elected office and homosexual behaviour between adults had been legal since 1967, it didn't always feel that way: voters were less tolerant of MPs following them into the permissive society. Besides, people did not talk openly about private sexual behaviour, as they do now. Some MPs had affairs (women, including Barbara Castle, as well as men) and a few (Labour's Tom Driberg, later Lord Bradwell) chased male members of the Commons staff. Driberg was protected by his old press patron, Lord Beaverbrook (much as Edward VIII's love life had been) and by the security services. Most of it remained mere gossip.

Another factor different from today was solidarity. "There was a feeling at the time that you didn't make trouble for other MPs," recalls Dalyell, one of parliament's great troublemakers for 40 years, but on political, not personal, matters. Dalyell shared the general distaste for Geoffrey Dickens, when the Tory populist made paedophile allegations – now being re-examined by police – in the 80s.

Suspecting Dickens of mere publicity-seeking, perhaps in collusion with a tabloid, he refused his appeal for help. "I'm much more concerned about our economic problems than this mire," he recalls his admired ex-cabinet colleague Joel Barnett, a parliamentary neighbour of both Dickens and Cyril Smith, confiding at the time. Dickens, whose habit of mis-saying "fido-pilia" did not help his cause, was dismissed as a joke, though not all contemporary MPs discount claims that a senior home office official might have destroyed files. "That civil servant is a very bad man with nasty sexual habits," one recalls being warned about one such.

Dickens was proved right in naming diplomat Sir Peter Hayman, later jailed. But suspicion of such boat-rocking MP colleagues lingers on, with eyebrows raised against the likes of Tom Watson, Simon Danczuk or John Mann, who have all campaigned for the investigation of abuse allegations. So does the hunch that some of the claims today by former victims may prove to be fantasy, exaggeration or revenge – "someone getting their own back".

If the Westminster majority understood little about the gay world inhabited by some of their colleagues, paedophilia was a closed one. As the Daily Mail demonstrated in its campaign against Harriet Harman and Patricia Hewitt, two future cabinet ministers who worked at the National Council for Civil Liberties (now Liberty), the "anything goes" 70s tolerated a campaign that openly advocated consenting sexual relationships with children – the Paedophile Information Exchange – to affiliate to the NCCL before being discredited.

"We just didn't understand," ex-MPs now say. Just as women in all walks of life experienced bottom pinching (they knew which male colleagues were "not safe in taxis"), unwelcome advances, and worse, so both sexes were what they call "more relaxed" about male acquaintances with an unhealthy interest in boys, girls or Commons secretaries. Society's default position was to disbelieve complainants to the police. A northern Labour MP, now a peer ("I was so ugly the perverts didn't fancy me"), recalls being spanked on his bare bottom by a teacher. But when his father offered to go to the police, his mother said: "We can't do that, the man's a priest." Denials by those in authority were usually believed – the opposite of today.

Politicians of the day, beset with familiar problems such as economic growth, were fearful of delving into claims often made by those on the margins of society. They were wary of the twin Whitehall elephant traps known as "the can of worms" and "the slippery slope" that leads to who knows where. "Whatever you do, don't go near the Kincora boy's home scandal [in Belfast], it's a can of worms from which you won't escape," one probing MP was warned only last year. He took the advice. But Kincora, too, is back in the headlines.

Ignorance, naivety, complacency and discretion, loyalty too, all are contributory explanations for decades of neglect. As the famous opening sentence of The Go-Between, LP Hartley's novel of sexual intrigue, put it as long ago as 1953: "The past is a foreign country: they do things differently there."

Copyright © The Guardian/Michael White

Appendix P: Operation Pallial - National Crime Agency

Operation Pallial: Update
National Crime Agency
20 July 2016

http://www.nationalcrimeagency.gov.uk/news/891-operation-pallial-update

Operation Pallial, an independent National Crime Agency investigation into recent allegations of past abuse in the care system in North Wales, will not investigate accounts from new victims and survivors received after 31 August 2016.

Operation Pallial began enquiries in November 2012 at the request of North Wales Chief Constable Mark Polin. The investigation has so far resulted in the conviction of eight men, including care home owner John Allen who was sentenced to life in prison in December 2014.

A total of 340 people have made contact with the investigation and 84 complaints are still being actively investigated.

North Wales Police will receive and investigate all new allegations of past abuse received from 1 September 2016 onwards.

Operation Pallial will remain active, completing enquiries into all outstanding lines of enquiry, in addition to supporting victims and survivors through any future trials. One trial is due to take place in September and charging advice in relation to 27 suspects is awaited from the Crown Prosecution Service.

Chief Constable Mark Polin said: "I have full confidence in North Wales Police's current arrangements to listen to victims and deliver effective support, with partner agencies, and to investigate crimes.

"Officers from Operation Pallial will continue to deliver investigative activity for many months as they complete enquiries and assist the Crown Prosecution Service with further court cases, but today is the start of a return to all new crimes reported in North Wales being investigated by local officers and staff.

"North Wales Police has a dedicated team in place for receiving and investigating allegations of sexual abuse. The Amethyst Team, which includes detectives and specially trained officers working alongside colleagues from the local health board, deals solely with victims, seeing them through from reporting to case conclusion. They have a track record of a high level of reporting which shows that victims have the confidence to come forward.

"I would like to thank the NCA for the thorough and professional investigation they have conducted so far."

Operation Pallial continues to work closely with other partners and agencies to deliver advice and support to victims of past abuse. Support services will continue to be coordinated by Conwy County

Borough Council on behalf of all local authorities in North Wales and there is no change in services for those currently receiving support.

Any member of the public wishing to report new allegations of past abuse in the care system in North Wales to the National Crime Agency, rather than North Wales Police, has until 31 August 2016 to do so.

© Crown Copyright

Appendix Q: Operation Garford - Suffolk Police

Kesgrave/Stowmarket: Inquiries into historic child abuse allegations at three former schools

East Anglian Daily Times: PUBLISHED: 14:04 04 February 2013 | UPDATED: 14:04 04 February 2013

Colin Adwent Crime Correspondent
THREE former Suffolk schools are now at the centre of criminal investigations into historic child abuse allegations.
http://www.eadt.co.uk/news/kesgrave-stowmarket-inquiries-into-historic-child-abuse-allegations-at-three-former-schools-1-1857903

Credit: Archant

The accusations, which relate to alleged physical and sexual assaults, are said to have occurred between the late 1970s and run through to the 1990s.

A solicitor representing ex-pupils of one of the schools - Oakwood School in Stowmarket - has said the number of claimants has reached three figures.

Andrew Grove, who is based in Cambridge, said: "We now have 100 complainants on the civil claim relating to Oakwood School."

Last week detectives said they were re-opening the 1992 inquiry into alleged abuse at Kesgrave Hall independent school.

The investigation, codenamed Operation Garford, comes after former students' calls for it to be re-opened were backed by Central Suffolk and North Ipswich MP Dr Dan Poulter.

Responding to the new inquiry, Dr Poulter said: "I am pleased that Suffolk Police are conducting a full and thorough investigation into the alleged child abuse at Kesgrave Hall school, following my intervention.

"A number of people have written to me raising concerns about abuse when they or their family members were pupils at the school, and I would again urge anyone who has been the victim of abuse to come forward and immediately contact Suffolk police."

Four people were suspended in 1992 during the Kesgrave Hall inquiry. No charges were ever brought. The school closed in 1993.

However, a woodwork teacher Alan Stancliffe, was convicted and jailed in 1999 and again in 2007 for indecent assaults on three ex-pupils.

Two other police inquiries involving the former St George's School in Great Finborough, near Stowmarket, and Oakwood School are also continuing.

Operation Racecourse (St George's) has been running since the late 2000s. It has led to the independent school's ex-headmaster Derek Slade being jailed for 21 years in 2010 for sexual and physical abuse against pupils between the late 1970s and early 1980s.

Alan Brigden (aka Morton), 67, who taught maths at St George's, was jailed for five years last year for sexual abuse after being extradited back from Holland despite two suicide attempts.

A third man, music teacher Alan Williams, 59, who lived in Stowmarket, took his own life after being arrested on suspicion of abuse.

A 59-year-old man who taught at St George's is currently on police bail after being arrested on suspicion of sexual abuse.

Operation Oxenton (Oakwood School) is a criminal inquiry involving 95 complainants from the civil case.

There have already been convictions linked to Oakwood School dating back to the late 1980s.

Teacher Keith Hatton was jailed for four years in 1987 for nine sex assaults, while a part-time assistant John Wills, 45, of Stowmarket – who was a teacher in other schools and a foster carer – was jailed for eight months in 1995 for sexually abusing a child.

A Stowmarket clergyman with connections to the school, took his own life in 2003 after being arrested on suspicion of sexual assault

Oakwood School shut in 2000.

Copyright © Archant

Appendix R: Do not jail all paedophiles, says police chief

BBC News 28 February 2017 - From the section UK
http://www.bbc.co.uk/news/uk-39112911

Credit: BBC video image – Chief Constable Bailey

Paedophiles who view indecent images but go no further should not be jailed but rehabilitated, a leading child protection police officer has said.

Police forces "cannot cope" with the "huge" rise in reports, Chief Constable Simon Bailey, of the National Police Chiefs' Council, told the BBC.

Figures show the number of child abuse reports is up by 80% in three years.

The Home Office said, "viewing child abuse images is a terrible crime and should be treated as such".

Chief Constable Bailey, the head of Operation Hydrant, which is investigating multiple allegations of historic sexual abuse across the UK, said he knew his view would cause nervousness and draw headlines.

But he said the numbers of reports of abuse were at "huge proportions" - an NSPCC study in late 2016 used figures which suggested the number of individuals looking at such images could exceed half a million.

'Contact cases' focus

He told BBC Radio 4's Today programme about 400 people were arrested by police in conjunction with the National Crime Agency every month, for looking at indecent images.

"There are undoubtedly tens of thousands of men that are seeking to exploit children online with a view to meeting them, with a view to then raping them and performing the most awful sexual abuse upon them," he said.

"That's where I believe our focus has got to be. They are the individuals that pose the really significant threat."

Offenders who viewed online child abuse images should be placed on the sex offenders register, cautioned and managed in the community undergoing rehabilitation, he said.

Referrals to rehabilitation "increasingly are effective", he said and not using the court system would "speed things up".

He added: "Every time an image is viewed, the victim is being victimised again and there is nothing as abhorrent. But we have to be able to manage the totality."

A Home Office spokesperson said the government had committed £20m to the National Crime Agency for specialist teams to tackle online child sexual exploitation.

Credit: Thinkstock

"Alongside ensuring we have a tough law enforcement response to bring offenders to justice, we are also committed to preventing offending in the first place," they added.

The NSPCC agreed that prison sentences served a vital purpose in terms of public protection, justice, and acting as a deterrent.

But a spokesman added: "We cannot arrest our way out of the situation. If we are to protect more children we must make prevention and rehabilitation a priority."

'Not naive' to offenders

Those working in the area are already stretched.

Lisa Thornhill, is a senior practitioner at the Lucy Faithfull Foundation, which works with people who have sexually harmed or fear they may harm a child.

It offers "non-judgemental support" to help to change people's behaviour - such as a 10-week group programme, its website and Stop It Now confidential helpline. Calls to the helpline are over capacity - about 800 people each month call, but about 2,500 calls are unable to be taken due to demand.

While the organisation was "not naive" to the fact that some sex offenders were solely motivated to access children for abuse, she said, there was "a moral responsibility to help those who want it".

Natcen research on the helpline showed the importance of support, she added.

"Most people who commit these offences have some idea what they are doing is wrong," she said. "We appeal to the brave and responsible part of those people to get in touch with us and stop, and stay stopped."

Chief Constable Bailey's comments came as the Independent Inquiry into Child Sexual Abuse in England and Wales (IICSA) began its full public hearings on Monday with an examination of allegations made by children in care who were sent abroad.

The wide-reaching inquiry will look at child abuse claims against local authorities, religious organisations, the armed forces and public and private institutions - as well as people in the public eye.

Copyright © BBC News

Appendix S: (IICSA) Independent Inquiry into Child Sexual Abuse

Investigating the extent to which institutions have failed to protect children from sexual abuse

https://www.iicsa.org.uk/

This Inquiry will investigate whether public bodies and other non-state institutions in England and Wales have taken seriously their responsibility to protect children from sexual abuse, and make meaningful recommendations for change in the future. In December 2016 the Chair of the Inquiry, Professor Alexis Jay OBE, published the results of her internal review into the Inquiry's ways of working. The report sets out how the Inquiry will carry out its work as swiftly and effectively as possible. The review sharpens the focus of the Inquiry and lays out a detailed schedule of work for 2017.

© Crown copyright

Appendix T: The Doctors Letters

These are the four letters that are stored in my medical records and are referred to in the book text. With the amount of activity that between my Mother, the family GP and the School Health Service, I would have expected more letters. There is a gap in correspondence between 23rd Oct. 1969 and 7th sept. 1970, which I believe suggests some documents have been removed from my medical records at some stage.

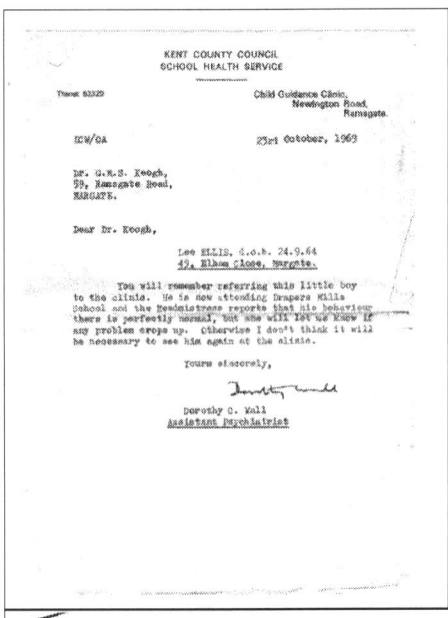

KENT COUNTY COUNCIL
SCHOOL HEALTH SERVICE

Thanet 52329

Child Guidance Clinic,
Newington Road,
Ramsgate.

DCW/OA

23rd October, 1969

Dr. C.R.S. Keogh,
59, Ramsgate Road,
MARGATE.

Dear Dr. Keogh,

      Lee ELLIS, d.o.b. 24.9.64
      49, Elham Close, Margate.

    You will remember referring this little boy to the clinic. He is now attending Drapers Mills School and the Headmistress reports that his behaviour there is perfectly normal, but she will let me know if any problem crops up. Otherwise I don't think it will be necessary to see him again at the clinic.

        Yours sincerely,

        Dorothy C. Wall
        Assistant Psychiatrist

KENT COUNTY COUNCIL
SCHOOL HEALTH SERVICE

Telephone No
Thanet 52329

Child Guidance Clinic,
Newington Road,
Ramsgate.

29th July, 1969.

Dear Dr. Keogh,

      Lee Ellis (24.9.64)
      49, Elham Close, Margate.

    Thank you for referring this child whom I saw for Dr. Fraser. In the play room here he gave no indication of the disturbed behaviour he shows at home. He was very active, but friendly and most amenable.

    He was an unwanted child and the mother has had to cope with the marriage breaking down soon after Lee's birth and bringing up the two children alone.

    I think the basic problem is the mother/child relationship. Difficulties began when Lee was about two, just when he was beginning to assert himself as an individual, and most of his behaviour problems can be considered as ways of annoying his mother.

    If it is possible to fit him into a pre-school play group here during the summer this will be arranged, but in any case he starts school in September and it may well be that with wider outlets and less continuous contact with his mother he may behave quite normally and we shall enquire about his progress in September.

        Yours sincerely,

        Dorothy C. Wall
        Assistant to Dr. Fraser

Dr. C.R.S. Keogh,
59, Ramsgate Road,
Margate.

COPY FOR DR. KEOGH

CHILD GUIDANCE CLINIC
NEWINGTON ROAD,
RAMSGATE.

52329

KMF/GA   14th September, 1970

Dr. A. Elliott,
Principal School Medical Officer,
"Springfield",
MAIDSTONE.

Dear Dr. Elliott,

       Lee ELLIS, d.o.b. 24.9.64
       49, Elham Close, Margate.

   This little boy who was seen by Dr. Wall on my behalf in the middle of last year, is again causing his mother much concern. The list of behaviour difficulties he presents is an impressive one, but I feel that it would be reasonable to take him on for out-patient treatment, with the addition of Mellaril 1mg twice a day.

   Mrs. Ellis, although divorced from her husband who has remarried, is still in some touch with him and has allowed Lee to spend a holiday with his father, which he apparently enjoyed. At the moment I do not recommend that the boy is placed with his father permanently, but will keep this possibility under review. Lee's behaviour seems to me to be purely that of deprivation, and treatment appointments will be offered as soon as possible.

          Yours sincerely,

          K.Z. Fraser
          Consultant Psychiatrist

Copy to:
Dr. Keogh
Dr. E. Thompson

Dr. Fraser
Child Guidance Clinic,
Newington Road,
Ramsgate,
Kent.

              7th September 1970

      Re. Lee Ellis (6)
      49 Elham Close,
      Margate, Kent.

Dear Dr. Fraser,
   You will no doubt remember seeing this child in July 1969. The mother now states that she finds it impossible to cope with him and she states that he now steals, breaks toys, windows etc. He micturates and defaecates on carpets and floors rather than go to the lavatory. He has on one occasion set fire to his clothes.
   At school he does not appear backward but causes much disturbance with the other children and teachers who apparently do not want him in their forms.
   His mother now feels that she might one day hit him so hard (which she has, I think) that she might cause severe bodily harm to Lee.
   Thank you for reviewing his case for me.
       Yours sincerely,

           C.J.E. Keogh.

Appendix U: The British Journal of Psychotherapy

Volume 27, Issue 2
May 2011
Pages 138–155

BOARDING SCHOOL SYNDROME: BROKEN ATTACHMENTS A HIDDEN TRAUMA

Author - Joy Schaverien

First published: 28 March 2011

DOI: 10.1111/j.1752-0118.2011.01229.x

This paper is copyright © 2011 Joy Schaverien
5 The Square, South Luffenham, Rutland LE15 8NS. [joyschaverien@aol.com]

The following pages (-- to --) are scanned copies of the paper published by Joy Schaverien in The British Journal of Psychotherapy - BOARDING SCHOOL SYNDROME: BROKEN ATTACHMENTS A HIDDEN TRAUMA – this paper remains copyright © 2011 Joy Schaverien

See over:

Individual Practice

BOARDING SCHOOL SYNDROME: BROKEN ATTACHMENTS A HIDDEN TRAUMA

Joy Schaverien

ABSTRACT The aim of this paper is to identify a cluster of symptoms and behaviours, which I am proposing be classified as '*Boarding School Syndrome*'. These patterns are observable in many of the adult patients, with a history of early boarding, who come to psychotherapy. Children sent away to school at an early age suffer the sudden and often irrevocable loss of their primary attachments; for many this constitutes a significant trauma. Bullying and sexual abuse, by staff or other children, may follow and so new attachment figures may become unsafe. In order to adapt to the system, a defensive and protective encapsulation of the self may be acquired; the true identity of the person then remains hidden. This pattern distorts intimate relationships and may continue into adult life. The significance of this may go unnoticed in psychotherapy. It is proposed that one reason for this may be that the transference and, especially the breaks in psychotherapy, replay, for the patient, the childhood experience between school and home. Observations from clinical practice are substantiated by published testimonies, including those from established psychoanalysts who were themselves early boarders.

Key words: attachment, boarding school syndrome, child development, trauma, loss, prep schools, public schools, psychotherapy, transference

Introduction

Tom was 6 years old when he arrived in a preparatory boarding school. He was taken there by his parents and his little sister. This was exciting; a very grown-up event for which there had been much preparation. It was confusing because there were teachers and other boys milling around. His parents were with him, and then he suddenly realized that they, and his sister, were back in their car. Uncomprehending, he saw the wheels of the car turning and he realized with horror that they were driving away. The bottom fell out of his world. Now he realized what it meant to be left at school. He felt alone in the world; deserted by his family.

'Tom' is now a man but, in psychotherapy, he recalls this moment as if it were yesterday. We will return to Tom's story later.

This article[1,2] is an analysis of some of the enduring psychological effects of boarding schools on those, like Tom, who attended them. Whilst boarding might be considered to be a privilege, early boarding can cause profound developmental damage. The wisdom of the time-honoured tradition of the British

---

JOY SCHAVERIEN PhD is a Jungian analyst and supervisor in private practice in the East Midlands. She is a Professional Member of the Society of Analytical Psychology (London), a Training Therapist and Supervisor for the British Association of Psychotherapists (Jungian Section) and Visiting Professor at the Northern Programme for Art Psychotherapy, Leeds Metropolitan University. She teaches and supervises internationally and is on the editorial board of the *Journal of Analytical Psychology*. Among her many publications she is author of: *The Revealing Image* (Jessica Kingsley, 1992), *Desire and the Female Therapist* (Routledge, 1995), *The Dying Patient in Psychotherapy* (Palgrave Macmillan, 2002) and editor of *Gender Countertransference and the Erotic Transference* (Routledge, 2006). She conducts Continuing Professional Development training for psychotherapists working with ex-boarders. Address for correspondence: 5 The Square, South Luffenham, Rutland LE15 8NS. [joyschaverien@aol.com]

Establishment, of sending very young children away from home to boarding schools, is therefore questioned. The psychological impact of this socially condoned, early rupture with home has a lasting influence on attachment patterns.

In normal development the 'good enough' family adapts with the child as he or she grows. For the child in boarding school this process is reversed; the child has to adapt to an inflexible system. The consequence is a form of psychological splitting in which the child becomes apparently self-sufficient. This armouring, initially acquired to save the vulnerable child from further insults to its autonomy, may result in a lasting cluster of symptoms and behaviours which I am identifying as *Boarding School Syndrome*. These patterns are observable in many adult psychotherapy patients with a history of early boarding.

I did not myself attend a boarding school; my interest developed from observations from clinical practice. In my private practice, like many of my colleagues, I repeatedly witness the blight this experience has cast on the lives of many of the adults who come for psychotherapy. These adults are from different generations; some were boarders in the 1950s, others in all the decades to the 1990s, and sometimes I see a current boarder.

In previous publications on this topic I have explored clinical issues relating to men who have boarded (Schaverien, 2002, 2004). Traditionally children are sent to prep schools at 6 or 8 years old but it is not unusual to meet those who went as young as 4 or 5. Whilst, historically, the majority of early boarders were boys, a significant number of girls were also sent away early. Therefore this paper includes the experiences of women. Through my clinical practice I have come to realize that a number of people from apparently privileged backgrounds were, in effect, 'looked after children'. The term 'looked after' here has a double meaning. Children whose families break down are sometimes taken into foster care; in the social care system in Britain, these are called 'looked after children'. Such children are often from economically deprived backgrounds and there is little alternative to this intervention. The initial impression would be that there is little comparison with the child from an affluent home. However, a child living in boarding school is also a 'looked after' child. They spend many of their formative years in institutional care and are, in effect, fostered with strangers. The parents of children in the social care system are often reluctant to let their children go (this is evident from the much publicized custody battles in the press, as well as observations from clinical practice). The boarders' parents choose this form of care for their child and pay a great deal of money for it. In both situations the child experiences loss of attachment figures and the distress of being 'looked after' by strangers.

When boarding schools are discussed the parents' and teachers' voices are often heard but not the children's. For many boarders it is only as adults that they can begin to recognize and then articulate their experience and, for some, the first time they do so is when they engage in psychotherapy. The purpose of this paper is to address the impact of early boarding in the light of developmental theory and to consider why the depth of this trauma may, at times, pass unnoticed in psychotherapy. My wider project is to differentiate the psychological impact of boarding on children at different developmental stages. This is beyond the scope of this article so the focus here is on early boarding and the latency child. Latency is the developmental period, from the age of roughly 5 or 6, until the onset of puberty. A further planned publication will address puberty; this is when gender differences become significant and the respective experiences of girls and boys may become more marked.

Boarding School Syndrome

Syndrome is a term usually applied to a collection of symptoms related to disease, but it is also a combination of opinions, emotions or behaviours. The *Oxford English Dictionary* offers the following definitions: *Syndrome*: '1. a group of medical symptoms which consistently occur together. 2. A set of opinions or behaviour that is typical of a particular group of people.'

Although Boarding School Syndrome is not a medical category, it is a cluster of learned behaviours and discontents that follow growing up in a boarding school. The need for theory leads me to seek such a definition but it is not my intention to pathologize all who attended boarding schools. However, people who present for psychotherapy are often those for whom boarding school was an unhappy, if not a traumatic ordeal. It would be a misunderstanding to limit any one person to specific symptoms, as its manifestation in each case is different; it is the *pattern* that is discernable. The aim is to alert practitioners to common, identifiable elements in the psyche of those for whom early boarding ruptured their primary attachments and who had to adapt to growing up in an inflexible system. The *pattern* may replay in a number of subtle ways, including the re-enactment, in the transference, of the boarding school/parent dynamic. Boarding school is rarely the presenting problem as the traumatic nature of this early experience frequently remains unconscious. The ex-boarder might present with a generalized sense of depression – a history of broken relationships, marital or work related problems. They may only gradually become aware that aspects of their distress originate in the losses and broken attachments of their early childhood.

The cluster of learned behaviours and discontents that result in what I am calling Boarding School Syndrome revolve around problems with intimacy. Whilst appearing socially confident, the ex-boarder may find intimate engagement threatening. This is a pattern well known in couples' psychotherapy where one partner, often the man, attended boarding school and is unable to talk about his feelings. The person may make deeply dependent relationships and then suddenly emotionally or, actually, abandon the loved person (Schaverien, 2002). This cutting off from emotional need can be experienced by the partner as a violent attack or abrupt rejection. This often replays in the transference and may lead to the sudden termination of analysis when the rage associated with dependency begins to surface (Schaverien, 1997).

The data on which this article is based is drawn from observations from clinical practice. Since Freud's early findings, case studies have been the evidence on which much psychotherapy research is based (McLeod, 1994, p. 103; Roth & Fonagy, 1996, p. 49). In that tradition I am drawing on more than 20 years of witnessing these patterns in numerous clients who have attended boarding schools. I have also worked with the siblings, usually girls, who stayed at home whilst their brothers went away to school; the effects on sibling relationships are often profoundly disruptive. These observations are substantiated by a wealth of data accumulated by the psychotherapist, Nick Duffell. Over the last 20 years Duffell has conducted workshops for those he calls 'boarding school survivors'. He has identified many common patterns in adults with a history of early boarding (Duffell, 2000).[4]

Traumatic Losses

Early boarding is a traumatic event in the life of many young children and its psychological impact affects the core of the personality. The sudden loss of attachment figures (parents, siblings, pets and toys) causes the child to protect itself. For the first time in their life the child may be in a situation where there is no intimate contact; no love. Even when not mistreated, being left in the care of strangers is traumatic. There are no words to adequately express the feeling state and so a shell is formed to protect the vulnerable self from emotion that cannot be processed. Whilst appearing to conform to the system, a form of unconscious splitting is acquired as a means of keeping the true self hidden. Duffell has identified this as 'the strategic survival personality' (Duffell, 2000, p. 10). The child then makes no emotional demands but also no longer recognizes the need for intimacy. The self begins to become inaccessible; 'Boarding School Syndrome' develops. This may continue as an unconscious pattern into adult life. Psychological splitting is a well-known reaction to trauma (Fonagy, 1991; Kalsched, 1996; Wilkinson, 2006, 2010). In Boarding School Syndrome the memory of the losses and the associated rage are repressed and only surface later, very often within a marriage or subsequently in psychotherapy.

The initial loss is compounded by its *repetition*. As the pattern of term time, at school, and of holidays, at home, becomes established the child is unable to settle in either place. For those whose parents live abroad the child is effectively homeless. For others, during the holidays, there is the return home and school can be temporarily forgotten; but all too soon the packing starts again. Even as adults many ex-boarders find packing very difficult and it may come as a revelation to make the link with this childhood memory. This pattern is inevitably replayed in psychotherapy because the regular breaks evoke a similar pattern of attachment followed by absence. The transference around breaks is a time for particular vigilance (Schaverien, 1997, 2002, 2004).

Developmental Perspectives

Disrupted early attachments may permanently affect the ex-boarder's investment in intimate relationships. The loss of home and family, alongside the social conditioning of school routines, impinge on the relationship between psyche and soma. Many report the longing for their mother and, in her absence, especially in all boys' schools, the need for a female/mother figure. Temporary respite could be found in being ill for a few days and sent to the sanatorium where matron presided. Homesickness is therefore an appropriate term. The child who misses home becomes physically sick. This pattern was noted by Patrick Kaye (2005) in his role as a GP working for 18 years in a major public school. Children presented with various ailments which he established were attributable to homesickness.

There is increasing evidence to demonstrate that the bond with the primary caretaker influences the baby's physical as well as psychological well-being (Gerhardt, 2004; Lanius, Vermetten & Pain, 2010). Bodily functions of the growing child, as well as the baby, are managed by the mother, or primary carer. The too early loss of this intimate connection may distort the development of relatedness and the ability to move confidently into the world at the appropriate time. Moreover, a child who is perpetually vigilant has little space for symbolic play. In boarding school there is little time for reverie and the life of the imagination may therefore suffer.

Bowlby was an important and, for a time, a lone voice in emphasizing the importance of attachment in early life (Bowlby, 1969, 1973, 1980). However, there is now much published research into the importance of the reciprocity of the infant and its environment (Lewin & Trevarthen, 2000; Stern, 1985, 1988; Trevarthen, 2009). Applying systems theory, Beebe and Lachmann (2002) argue that the attachment between a baby and its mother is a bi-directional system; each plays a part in influencing the other. Their approach in psychotherapy with adult patients is informed by this: 'Particularly at the non-verbal level, mother and infant, as well as analyst and patient, participate in a moment-by-moment coordination of the rhythms of behaviour' (Beebe & Lachmann, 2002, p. 25). Their infant research leads them to argue for mutual influence, rather than separation–differentiation, as the prime tasks of analysis. This is relevant for considering the approach to the treatment of ex-boarders as, with them, working with attachment in the analytic present is essential.

Michael Fordham's work is pertinent to the effects of early boarding. Like Beebe and Lachmann his theoretical formulations were founded on infant observation and are applicable to the latency child, as well as to adults in analysis. Fordham developed Jung's concept of the self through infant observation, realizing that there is a nascent self present from the beginning of life. He proposed the terminology 'integration and de-integration' (Fordham, 1967; 1985, pp. 50–63) for his observation that the baby was already: 'integrated – a person distinct from his mother' (Fordham, 1985, p. 50). He noted that, in the waking state, the baby de-integrates; that is, opens out, complains if uncomfortable, smiles, feeds and so evokes a response from the maternal environment. When sufficient stimulation has been obtained, the baby withdraws and returns to rest, reverie or sleep; integrating into the self. If the mother is depressed, or otherwise unavailable, the baby will adapt, making fewer demands, but, if all goes well, the infant gradually develops a sense that he can trust the environment. This is the foundation of the capacity for reverie and imagination.

The baby, and later the child, is an active participant in its emotional growth, mirrored through relationships that continue from infancy and into latency. This is the point; if the latency child is sent away to school before he or she is ready to leave home, psychological development is likely to be distorted. The child in a boarding school is bereft because his or her primary attachments can longer be relied upon; the environment has become unsafe. Later problems arise because, as time passes, the self remains unknown. Therefore, whilst apparently professionally and socially successful, the ex-boarder is troubled without understanding why.

In a family, influence is reciprocal; its members change in response to the needs of the growing child. Integration and de-integration is therefore a process that embraces the wider environment. At boarding school this is reversed; the child has to conform to survive. Inflexibility is threaded throughout school life; lack of privacy extends to eating and sleeping, which take place *en masse* and at times that suit the institution. At night, lights are put out at a designated time, irrespective of what the child is doing. In some schools, in the past, lavatories had no doors and showers were taken communally. The tradition of fagging, in boys' public schools, meant that junior boys were compelled to be available as servants for the older boys – which condoned bullying as a privilege of age.[5] A child, in a strange institution, where the rules are unknown, is tense and on guard. There is little opportunity for reverie or integration, and de-integration is to the institution. Therefore, whilst independent and intellectual thought are encouraged, emotional autonomy is not fostered.

Learning to Conform

There is little published research or psychoanalytic literature about the enduring psychological effects of boarding school, apart from Duffell (2000) and Schaverien (2002, 2004). Several personal accounts have been published in the journal *Attachment*, and one by Simon Partridge (2007) was followed by a theoretical discussion by Annie Power (2007). However, sociological research was conducted in the 1960s by Royston Lambert (1968) and John Wakeford (1969). Vyvyen Brendon (2009), a historian, has traced the history of prep schools across two centuries through the written testimonies of children. There is not space here to do justice to these texts but it is important to acknowledge them. In each, the approach is even-handed and the psychological damage of the system is implicit. It is my project to make it explicit.

Two documentary TV films reveal the psychological suffering of children who board. In 1994 Colin Luke (*The Making of Them*) filmed 8 year-old boys during their first term in preparatory school. The viewer observes the psychological conflict taking place in the mind of each child who, ignoring his intuitive feelings, speaks words he has been told (i.e. that school is good for him). It is evident that their emotional experience contradicts the explanations given by their parents and teachers. The beginning of acculturation is evident in the psychological gymnastics that the child performs in order to believe what he has been told. This film, like the books, witnesses the children our patients once were. It demonstrates the source of the problems which sometimes emerge in psychotherapy. In *Chosen* (Channel 4, November 2008) four men, in their 40s, talked about the sexual abuse to which they were each, individually, subjected by masters to whose care they were entrusted, in the same school. Their lasting sense of injustice, anger and injury is evident; psyche and soma remain profoundly affected. All admit that they could not have disclosed the abuse, nor made the film, whilst their parents were alive. This is the tragedy of exposure to such maltreatment in an institution in which the parents have placed their trust; it is impossible (except in very rare cases) for the child to tell the parent. The child is ashamed, feeling culpable for the humiliating experiences to which they were subjected, and this cannot be articulated, even many years later. Boarding School Syndrome is thus established; the true self remains hidden and the child is unknown to the parents and so is, in effect, lost.

These films give weight to the importance of being alert to this form of psychological suffering in children, as well as in adults, who seek psychotherapy. Although boarding schools are claimed to have improved, many of the same problems including, in some cases, extreme bullying, physical assault and sexual abuse, continue in the so-called 'best schools'.[6] Often these cases are only known about by the few people involved and do not reach the public arena. Psychotherapists may have privileged access to this information.

The First Days at Prep School: The Threshold

The emotional impact of the first days in prep school is often repressed. The memory may return in psychotherapy, as it did with Tom, described earlier. The awe with which a small child approaches such a socially valorized institution may be encapsulated in the image of a formidable entrance (described by Paech, 2009). This is often followed by recalling a first moment of realization; of perceived parental betrayal. Instead of the special place that has been promised, what looms ahead is exile. The loss is so total and the child so unformed that there are no words adequate to convey the feelings. It is only as adults that words can be found to describe this moment of realization. This moment is vividly conveyed by Roald Dahl (1984, p. 79) and Andrew Motion (2006, pp. 93–101). Partridge describes 'the rising tide of feeling' as he relived this, 'the threshold' in one of Duffell's workshops. He became aware that his parents, his sister and 'the familiarity of our farm-life were about to vanish as I crossed, irrevocably, into the domain of my prep school in 1955' (Partridge, 2007, p. 310). This is a man remembering the experience of his 8 year-old self 50 years after the event. This is a familiar story; as psychotherapy begins memories of such events flood back into consciousness. In order to survive the pain of this moment of loss many shut down, emotionally; this is the genesis of Boarding School Syndrome.

The Unprotected Child: Philippa's Story

The loss and bewilderment are compounded by exposure to danger. In order to convey this, I will give instances of the first days at prep school remembered by two of my psychotherapy clients. The first is 'Philippa'; the second is 'Tom' with whose first day at school the article began. Their stories are very different but each reveals the subtle ways in which the innate capacity, in the young child, for trust may be eroded.

There are those for whom the threshold is not such an extreme experience. For some children there is an excited anticipation of joining the world of older siblings. Very often the imagined thrill is quickly deflated as the realization of the endless stretch of time ahead, before there is contact with family, dawns. Philippa, at first, talked about her school days with humour. She seemed generally to have had a good time at school and she had made lifelong friendships. At 50 Philippa was married with three children, who were nearly grown up. The youngest of four sisters, she was impatient to join her older sisters at school; she had been lonely at home without them. She was well prepared as she knew the school from visiting her sisters. The first day she was excited and remembers arriving and seeing all the other little girls crying. She was 9 and she did not understand why they were crying. This is unusual in that the transition from home to school was apparently gradual. Philippa had always considered that school had been fun and she had not suffered bullying. That was until she started to remember an initiation to which she was subjected:

> As she talked, she realized that she had not previously remembered the first year dormitory, which she shared with 10 other girls. She mentioned, in an off-hand way, an 'initiation' to which she was subjected in that dormitory: she was stripped naked and hit with slippers by the other girls.

Recounted in this way it was quickly told. There was no emotion and Philippa would have left the story at that if I had not asked her to pause and think about what she had just said. As she thought about her 9 year-old self she began to remember how frightening this incident had been. Thinking about her own children, and about how small they were at that age, helped her to have empathy for the child she had been. Her children had attended day schools and she had never considered sending them away; she now began to appreciate why. She recognized that she had completely blocked the memory of that first-year dormitory, remembering instead, her second-year dormitory. This had been much smaller and shared with just two girls whom she liked. Moreover, she was already used to living at school by then.

This is what happens; acceptable words such as 'initiation' are attributed to behaviours which would otherwise be deemed completely unacceptable; a new script is written in which these behaviours are condoned. The law of the mass is accepted and a blind eye turned to it by staff. This child was exposed to the abuse of her peers. This was followed now by another memory; again of an 'initiation':

> Philippa was encouraged to climb a tree and then was tied up in it. The other girls were jeering and laughing at her. She did not understand why.

These incidents were bullying but dignified with a name that made them part of a social norm. To complain about such abuse is to risk the scorn of the group and therefore the potential for increased bullying. If it is endured, with apparent good humour, the person is then considered a 'good sport' and accepted as one of the group: an 'initiate'. This is how Philippa had coped and she had not admitted, even to herself, the shock and humiliation of being treated in this way. Ignoring the pain and shame is a common way of dealing with such incidents but it also has the effect of subtly eroding the person's attitude to themselves. The wounded and vulnerable part of the self remains hidden, safely encapsulated, where its truth is concealed from conscious awareness. This is a common and lasting effect of early trauma (Kalsched, 1996; Wilkinson, 2010). Although glossed over, an incident like this is often traumatic. It is made worse because there is no one to whom it can be recounted so the child has to cope with it alone.

Bullying occurs in day schools too. The difference is that, despite the upsetting nature of such events, the child returns home in the evening and so there is a refuge, a place away from the bully. Even if the child cannot speak of it most parents notice and are concerned if the child is apparently upset. For the boarder there is no respite and no one in whom to confide. The natural instinct may be to tell but there is no one to listen. This may compound the sense of having been abandoned and contribute to a devastating realization of being alone in the world.

Philippa maintained a positive attitude to life and was generally successful. She was good at sport and so she fitted in socially. She used humour and, as she put it, being naughty, to deflect from her loneliness and from potential trouble with her peers.

It was only now, as an adult, that she realized how her relationship to herself had been affected; as, she put it, she spent nine years of her childhood in an environment where she was looked after by adults who did not love her. This encouraged the development of a stance where she seemed, apparently, emotionally unaffected and self-sufficient. In common with many ex-boarders her vulnerability was hidden, even from herself. This is typical of the way the boarding school child comes to deal with such events: and it is how Boarding School Syndrome becomes established.

Philippa's first two analyses had lasted for a number of years but did not address the painful aspects of boarding. It seems that the analysts had been misled by the deflection of the boarding school persona, accepting the superficial version of her school experience. The transference may have replayed the way in which Philippa had glossed over the experience of school with her parents. When she returned home for the vacations she did not recount the incidents of bullying. She had learned to be independent and, along with her older sisters, she gave her parents and herself, at the same time, the happy version of events. Rather unsurprisingly this was replayed in the transference in her first analyses. It was only when she sought a third analysis, for apparently unrelated reasons, that her attention was drawn to the ways in which she deflected from her own suffering. It was persistently pointed out to her when her concern for others masked her own distress; eventually, as she began to notice it, the pain associated with her memories of boarding emerged.

For Philippa boarding had been anticipated as an adventure, and it was only after arriving that the reality of its loneliness dawned. This indicates the problem of the current trend to consider that the child is involved in the decision to choose boarding over day school. Often children as young as 8 or 10 are shown the school by their parents and given the 'choice' to go there or to a day school. However, for small children, until they are left alone in the school, there can be no real understanding of what boarding means.

The Hidden Trauma

In professional papers and case discussions, boarding school is frequently mentioned in passing but, as stated earlier, there is little psychoanalytic theory about its lasting psychological implications. Moreover, the full traumatic impact of early boarding sometimes remains hidden in psychotherapy. This is curious as in my practice, as well as those of some of my colleagues, a high percentage of people presenting for psychotherapy attended these schools.[7] It is possible that analysts and psychotherapists take this damage for granted, as a sort of by-product of a system of privilege in education, which is so familiar that it hardly merits comment. The boarding school child, as we have already seen, learns not to complain.

Whilst there is little psychoanalytic theory, the biographies and autobiographies of well-respected psychoanalysts contribute to understanding of the lasting effects through discussion of their own boarding school experience. Wilfred Bion (1982), writing in the later years of his life, recounts the story of his childhood with wonderful dry humour. He was brought to England, from India, to boarding school at the age of 8 and his family returned to India. He traces the rest of his childhood in this lonely and mysterious world. Bion has the gift of being able to convey the bewilderment of a small boy growing up in a boarding school. With acerbic wit he comments on the absurdity of the situation without being explicitly critical. John Bowlby's (1973) emphasis on the importance of attachment in child development supports our discussion, and it is significant that he was unambiguous in his repudiation of the tradition of sending children under 13 away to boarding school. Bowlby is quoted by Holmes, as describing it as 'merely the traditional first step in *the time-honoured barbarism required to produce English gentlemen*' (Holmes, 1993, p. 17, italics mine). Bowlby, whose own stay in boarding school was relatively short, was not happy boarding (Van Dijken, 1998).

Patrick Casement came from a naval family with the tradition of sending children to boarding school at an early age; he was sent at 8 (Casement, 2006). This is common for those in the armed forces because boarding offers stability when the parents have to move home frequently. Sadly it also distorts the child's developmental needs, as Casement makes clear. It was not until into his adult life that he began to realize how profoundly his early experiences had affected him. In a moving description of his attachment to the buildings of his public school, he shows how, in the absence of family, places are substituted in the imagination of the lonely child (Casement, 2006, p. 29). The attachment to houses, rather than people, is a kind of desperate solution found by the child whose capacity to love is distorted by the absence of human attachment figures (Schaverien, 2002, pp. 32–8). Casement's first psychotherapy did not address the negative transference and therefore the depth of his early experiences of loss (Casement, 2006, pp. 14–15).

There are many other cases where the depth of the pain associated with early boarding has passed unnoticed in psychotherapy. It is rare that boarding school is the presenting problem and the ex-boarder is a master of emotional disguise. The acquired veneer of confidence may contribute to the fact that sometimes the profound significance of this formative experience is missed in psychotherapy. Thus the reality of the lasting distress associated with boarding remains a well-kept secret. Duffell expresses it thus:

> One thing which never seemed to come up in my therapy ... was the effect that my boarding school education had had on me. I sensed that it was one of the things that I was running hardest from, but my psychotherapist never seemed to mention it. I suspected it was either a quite unknown subject or, as I assumed, one not fit for therapeutic enquiry. And I ... was too shy to bring it up ... the critic who lived in my head said I had not yet grown up properly or that I was whingeing on about something which had actually been a privilege. (Duffell, 2000, p. 3)

Duffell blamed himself, fearing that there was something so profoundly wrong with him that it would not be appropriate to raise it. In British society the assumption that boarding school is a privilege is a cultural myth, with some justification. It is partly because of the advantages in material circumstances that the ex-boarder is embarrassed to complain. Duffell (2009, personal communication) was aware that class played a part in this interaction. There are many others whose psychotherapy did not address the extent of this early trauma. Partridge (2007, p. 310) writes that 'deeply disturbing issues' relating to his time at boarding school were not addressed in either of his long-term Kleinian-orientated psychoanalyses.

These are not isolated cases; whilst its extent merits further inquiry this is not uncommon. The published cases, mentioned above, were conducted by experienced practitioners, registered with respected UKCP and BPC organizations. In order to substantiate this I give details. Casement's first analysis was conducted at three times a week over seven years with a psychoanalytic psychotherapist. It was not until his second psychoanalysis, this time conducted at five times a week, that the deficit of the earlier therapy was made good and that he touched the depth of his losses (Casement, 2009, personal communication). Duffell's psychotherapy took place once a week over nine years, with three different psychotherapists, two humanistic and one analytic. He spent three years with each but the significance of his boarding school experiences was not addressed (Duffell, 2010, personal communication). Partridge's first psychoanalysis was conducted at five times a week over nine years and his second, also psychoanalysis, at four times a week over five years. In each case his boarding school trauma was not addressed (Partridge, 2010, personal communication). Philippa's first two analyses were conducted over 10 years: three years at three times a week with a Jungian analyst, one year at once a week with a humanistic psychotherapist, and then she returned to the first analyst for another three years at once a week. It was not until she embarked on a third analysis, some years later, that her positive presentation was challenged and she contacted the trauma of her boarding school experience.

We have seen that the ex-boarder may expertly deflect from their suffering. However, the analysts and psychotherapists in the cases concerned, as I have indicated, were all well trained and were experienced. Therefore I would speculatively suggest that a failure to take up the boarding school experience may have to do with a number of factors which might remain unconscious in the therapeutic dyad. As mentioned above it is possible that class is a factor; but what does this mean? One of the advantages of private boarding school education is that it equips the ex-boarder with a confident presentation that commands respect; this is recognized in British society at a subliminal level. If the psychotherapist was not private boarding school educated, it is possible that an unconscious deference may get in the way of challenging the powerful defence. If, on the other hand, the psychotherapist attended a boarding school it is possible that there is an unconscious recognition; a shared subliminal acceptance that it is not a problem. Clearly this is not always the case and many psychotherapists are not deflected from the suffering involved. However, there is enough evidence to indicate a need for further inquiry into why such highly qualified people sometimes miss the depth of trauma that follows early boarding. It may be that this would lead to a different technical approach to working with ex-boarders in psychotherapy.

Educational Advantage

Boarding is a legacy of British history that is regarded with incomprehension in nations, such as Scandinavia, where sending children away from home to school is practised only in exceptional circumstances. The educational advantages offered by most of these schools are considerable but the benefits need to be weighed against the long-term psychological damage brought about by the losses involved. Whilst many achieve significant social status, as a result of the educational advantages provided, there are casualties. The most severely affected are barely able to hold down a job or maintain intimate relationships.[4] For them being sent away from home may have been the final straw in the face of other factors or personal sensitivities. These people were unable to reap the rewards of the academic, social and sporting opportunities provided.

As already stated, those we meet in psychotherapy are usually the ones who struggled with boarding; however, others assert that boarding school was a positive experience for them. Often further discussion leads to painful memories with them too but these are not immediately recalled and the balance of positive experiences seems to outweigh the negative ones. Perhaps the difference lies in the age at which a person enters the school. Those who can take advantage of the educational opportunities, provided by committed teachers in academic studies, music or sport are often those who first went to school as teenagers. A child at 13 is more mature, psychologically, and physically, than the prep school child. At 16, some make an informed choice to complete their education away from home. Even so, many older children endure distressing episodes of loneliness, sexual abuse and bullying. It is now illegal to beat children but in the past, when many of our clients boarded, beatings (often sadistic) were ubiquitous; they were considered to be character forming. Age was no bar to this maltreatment.

There are some for whom school is better than their home. In these cases school is a sanctuary, offering relief from constant insecurity, neglect or abuse; as one of my patients expressed it: 'At school at least you knew where the punishment was coming from.' For this man, and others like him, boarding school was preferable to home because it offered stability which his parents, despite their material wealth, were unable to provide. Corporate identity and engaging in team games can give a real sense of belonging and of fair play and, as in the case described by Meredith Owen (2007), may compensate for the loss of the familiar environment.

The Unprotected Child: Tom's Story

I return now to Tom whom we met on the threshold of his prep school at the beginning of the article. Tom, a married man in his mid-30s, was referred by his GP for psychotherapy. He knew something was wrong but he could not understand what it was. He was clinically depressed but he did not want medication. Until recently, he had had a number of jobs in different countries but he had hated being employed. Now he was home and had set up his own small business. He had recently married and his wife had identified his emotional isolation. They slept in separate rooms, an arrangement which suited Tom. At boarding school he had shared a dormitory and now, free of school, he could choose to sleep in a space of his own; understandably his wife was unhappy about this arrangement.

Tom, the elder of two children, was sent to prep school when he was 6. His sister was born when he was 5 and after this his mother found his temper tantrums impossible to manage so it was decided that school would be good for him. It was a family tradition to send children to prep school, but usually at 8. Tom had accepted his parents' version of events – that he had been a difficult child. He had felt rejected but concluded that this was because he was bad. He was surprised when I suggested that he might have been jealous of his sister and this could have been exacerbated by being sent away. Sometimes it is not boarding school alone that has a negative impact, but the story the child is told associated with it. For Tom it had seemed that school was a punishment; he was banished for his badness.

This emerged in the early sessions but was passed over by him as unremarkable. The content of the sessions then stayed in the present and there was much about his work and home life. It was only when I asked him more about his school that he began to recount the cruel incidents of bullying he had suffered in his early days at school. This continued until he grew physically strong enough to stop it. He dismissed it as merely the type of initiation to which boys were subjected. However, as he became aware that I took these incidents very seriously, he began to do so himself. Then, in the fourth session, he told me the following story from his first days in prep school:

> As already stated, Tom was six years old when he was taken by his parents to his prep-school and left there in the care of strange adults. However, for Tom it was not the adults who mistreated him. One night, very soon after he arrived, an older boy appeared to befriend him. He took him by the hand and said they were going for a walk. Innocently Tom was led out into the dark night, a long walk from the school, and then the older boy told him he was going to kill him. Tom was terrified. The boy told him that his parents were not there and no one would hear if he cried out. Having duly frightened the child, he stopped; and then he told him he was only joking and led him, still by the hand, back to the school. Tom was unable to tell anyone what had happened.

This story of innocence abused reveals the trusting nature of a small child in the hands of someone only a year or two older. A casual witness might consider that nothing very much had happened; there was no dramatic assault and no physical damage. However, the psychological effects of this incident had lasted 30 years. Tom was in middle age and yet I was the first person he had ever told of this experience. This highlights the problem; even if staff members are kind, the child is exposed for many hours in the day and, even worse, in the night, to the impulses of other children. These children are themselves very young and may have little sense of the impact of their behaviours. Both these children were unprotected – the perpetrator, as well as the victim, in the grip of terrifying fantasies. The distinction between fantasy and reality, between symbolic thought and action, was not yet formed in their minds.

The older boy was apparently a sadistic abuser but he was also a small boy and he was out of control. He too was exposed because he could perpetrate an act that, had they known, adults would have prevented. Hypothetically, we might assume that he had been left in this school a year or two previously. He would therefore recognize Tom's insecurity. Taking charge of the smaller boy might alleviate his own insecurity, proving that he was no longer the youngest. It is possible that he regarded this to be a joke but it is likely to have had a more sinister, if unconscious, psychological motive. By terrifying Tom, it is probable that he was sadistically externalizing his own rage and fear; seeing them reflected in another he could feel in control, and powerful. Then, rescuing the younger boy, he could soothe himself and feel benign. One might speculate whether he felt guilt; if so there would be no one to whom to confess and to mediate his own rage and terrifying fantasies.

However, our concern is the lasting impact of his behaviour on Tom. For Tom the terrible thing had happened. He knew now how vulnerable he was and his trust had been violently shattered. There were no words for what he had experienced and no one to tell. In order to survive, in cases like this, a hidden compartment in the self is acquired where such experiences are locked away. This type of dissociation is a common response to trauma (Davies & Frawley, 1994; Wilkinson, 2006). This was a traumatic event in this child's life; Tom had learned that he could depend on no one. First his primary attachments had been broken and, subsequently, he was offered the potential friendship of an older boy, only to realize that he was at his mercy.

When he grew bigger Tom would intervene if another child was being bullied. This attitude continued into his adult life; Tom looked after his loved ones and was fiercely protective of them but he did not expect anyone to look after him. We might understand this in the light of Boarding School Syndrome. The boarder is trained in a similar way to an officer in the military; to look after his men and to care for others before himself. Consciously, Tom was friendly, kind and thoughtful but the unconscious opposite of this was that he was also furiously angry. His fear of his own violence kept him isolated; he kept separate to protect those he loved from the perceived danger of getting close to him.

This replayed in the transference. He was at first relieved to have someone in whom to confide. Gradually he began to understand how he had always cut off from people who came emotionally close to him. Banished by his parents, because of his rage, he continued to feel dangerous in relationships. In common with other ex-boarders he had, in the past, cut off suddenly from jobs and from girlfriends. This is a common form of self-harm in Boarding School Syndrome. The person makes a deeply dependent relationship and then severs his emerging tender feelings. Suddenly abandoning the loved object is an extreme form of self-abuse. Simultaneously it unconsciously expresses rage towards the present lover and those who abandoned him in the past.

As psychotherapy began to become important to him, Tom worried about how he would manage when, eventually, it ended. With ex-boarders, the breaks in psychotherapy apparently have little impact at first. The regular pattern of school holidays, followed by the return to school, arms the ex-boarder with a mechanism for coping with disrupted attachments; he is expert at cutting off. This Tom did for the first two breaks, telling me that he had been fine. However, after the third break, psychotherapy nearly came to an abrupt end when he left a message, telling me that he now needed to stop and work things out for himself. This is an occurrence that I have noted with men in psychotherapy with female therapists (Schaverien, 1997) and, in terms of working with Boarding School Syndrome, this is a common occurrence (Schaverien, 2002, 2004). Tom could not bear dependency and so he reverted to the previous method of dealing with attachments in his adult life; the impulse was to leave.

It is likely that Tom experienced the feelings that were emerging in the transference as intensely dangerous. The decision to leave was probably motivated by an unconscious need to protect us both from his potential violence. Steiner (1993) writes of the 'patient who is dominated by feelings of resentment and grievance' and suggests that such patients use a form of 'psychic retreat which operates as a defence against anxiety and guilt' (p. 74). Feelings of 'resentment and grievance' threatened Tom's previous self-image. His defences were breaking down and he was forming an attachment to me. As a result the sense of injustice and his previously unconscious wish for revenge began to become live in the present. Steiner describes this type of emotional turmoil: 'These patients feel wronged but are unable to express their wish for revenge actively by openly attacking the objects which have wronged them' (1993, p. 74). Some hold back for fear of retaliation but others are inhibited because of the 'fear that the revenge would be excessive' (Steiner, 1993, p. 74).

Consciously Tom was a caring man but he was beginning to realize that he was violently vengeful. His anger with his mother for abandoning him and his sister, for replacing him, were becoming conscious and replaying in the transference. He may have experienced me as another woman whom he had to look after; the fee often brings this to the fore. His impulse to leave was fuelled by conflicted emotions – a desire to make me suffer, as he had, but also the fear that he would wreak some terrible revenge. The 'psychic retreat' to which Steiner refers is an emotional retreat but with the ex-boarder it can be enacted as a concrete abandonment of the process. Tom returned to discuss his decision to terminate and eventually agreed to continue. Then the violence of his feelings was expressed; he was terrified of what he might do to me. It became evident that, no longer a victim, he was scared of his own power; now he could be the sadistic abuser. For a while he could not distinguish between his violent fantasies and acting on them; to imagine destruction was to have done it. It took a while for this to become separated out and for him to realize that his hateful fantasies were a form of attachment.

In the light of incidents, like the one to which Tom was subjected, the ostensible privilege of boarding might be viewed rather differently. It exposes the child to the unpredictable and, sometimes, harmful actions of others.[9] This story is far from unique and only one of many similarly damaging events that are reported. The deep scars left on the psyche may affect the person's ability to love. It is therefore troubling that this suffering may be dismissed as insignificant in comparison with the problems of material deprivation suffered by others.[10] This ignorance of the extent of exposure of such children seems to disregard the importance of emotional attachment. A child, of whatever social class, who feels neither physically nor psychologically safe is always vigilant and so their development may be adversely affected.

Boarding School Syndrome: In Conclusion

Boarding School Syndrome is a significant factor in the presentation of the ex-boarder in psychotherapy. As psychotherapy develops it becomes clear that the personality structure, acquired as a necessary protective shell at school, is still active. The child who learned to adapt continues to have unmet emotional needs that distort their development. These needs remain active in the adult. The intimacy of the mother–child bond can never be recaptured but the yearning for it, which begins with homesickness at school, may unconsciously dominate later life.

We have seen, through the stories of Philippa and Tom, how differently boarding school affects different children. The home situation is a factor. For Philippa the role models of her sisters, as well as their physical presence in the school, mediated her experience. Even so she was helpless and subject to painful 'initiation' which might well be reframed as group bullying. For Tom school was unfamiliar and the situation he was leaving at home, a little sister in his place, contributed to his distress and feelings of being abandoned. The bullying to which he was subjected was more sinister because of its one-to-one nature and because of the initial friendship offered.

The painful experiences of boarding, for many, inhabit the shadowy realm of split-off negative emotions. Secretly hidden they remain unconscious until the person is emotionally compelled to explore it. The transference can be complicated by the projected veneer of sophistication and confidence. This is the barrier that has to be overcome with the ex-boarder in psychotherapy. This is the reason there is a need for theoretical nomenclature such as 'Boarding School Syndrome'. Whilst further exploration is needed, and indeed planned, this may provide the beginning of a specialist framework within which to consider approaches to working with ex-boarders.

Acknowledgements

I am grateful to Dr Andrea Gilroy, Professor Helen Odell-Miller and Jane Schaverien, all of whom read and commented on earlier drafts of this paper; to 'Philippa' and 'Tom' for permission to tell their stories; and to Patrick Casement, Nick Duffell and Simon Partridge for permission to give details of their analyses.

Notes

1. An earlier version of this paper was given as a talk for the public programme of the Society of Analytical Psychology in Oxford in March 2009.

2. This article offers preliminary thoughts – a book on this topic is in progress.

3. I mean this in the sense of Winnicott's 'good enough mother' who, although good enough, also, at times, fails the child. This is a necessary developmental process (Winnicott, 1971, p. 11).

4. A campaigning group Boarding Concern was formed as an outcome of these workshops. Available from: http://www.boardingconcern.org.uk/

5. Fagging was finally abolished in the 1990s.

6. My own observations, from clinical practice, are confirmed in a personal communication from James Foucar, one of the Directors and Founders of Boarding Concern, who writes: 'We ... need to challenge the myth of "modern" boarding schools – my recent research shows that little has changed especially in boarding prep schools.' He quotes: *School Life – Pupils' Views on Boarding* (Department of Health, 1993); *Good Practice in Boarding Schools* (Boarding Schools Association, 2001); *Head to House: How to Run Your House Effectively* (John Catt Education Ltd, 2000).

7. Further research is planned to verify the actual percentages.

8. This is based on conversations with colleagues and observations from my own practice. The case described in Schaverien (2002) is one such example.

9. This is reminiscent of Golding's *Lord of the Flies*.

10. In presenting papers at professional conferences on this topic I have met this response on several occasions.

References

Beebe, B. & Lachmann, F.M. (2002) *Infant Research and Adult Treatment: Co-constructing Interactions*. New York, NY, London: Analytic Press.

Bion, W.R. (1982) *The Long Weekend: 1897–1919 Part of a Life*. London, New York, NY: Karnac, 1985.

Bowlby, J. (1969) *Attachment and Loss, Vol. 1. Attachment*. London: Hogarth.

Bowlby, J. (1973) *Attachment and Loss, Vol. 2. Separation: Anxiety and Anger*. London: Hogarth.

Bowlby, J. (1980) *Attachment and Loss, Vol. 3. Loss, Sadness and Depression*. London: Hogarth.

Brendon, V. (2009) *Prep-School Children: A Class Apart Over Two Centuries*. London, New York, NY: Continuum.

Casement, P. (2006) *Learning from Life*. London, New York, NY: Routledge.

Dahl, R. (1984) *Boy Tales of Childhood*. London, New York, NY: Puffin.

Davies, J.M. & Frawley, M.G. (1994) *Treating the Adult Survivors of Childhood Sexual Abuse: A Psychoanalytic Perspective*. New York, NY: Basic Books.

Duffell, N. (2000) *The Making of Them*. London: Lone Arrow Press.

Fonagy, P. (1991) Thinking about thinking: Some clinical and theoretical considerations in the treatment of a borderline patient. *International Journal of Psychoanalysis* 76: 639–56.

Fordham, M. (1967) Active imagination: Deintegration or disintegration. *Journal of Analytical Psychology* 12(1): 51–65.

Fordham, M. (1985) *Explorations into the Self*. London: Karnac.
Gerhardt, S. (2004) *Why Love Matters*. London, New York, NY: Routledge.
Golding, W. (1954) *Lord of the Flies*. London: Penguin.
Holmes, J. (1993) *John Bowlby and Attachment Theory*. London, New York, NY: Routledge.
Kalsched, D. (1996) *The Inner World of Trauma: Archetypal Defenses of the Personal Spirit*. London, New York, NY: Routledge.
Kaye, P. (2005) Homesickness. Unpublished MA thesis. Tavistock.
Lambert, R. (with Spencer Millham) (1968) *The Hothouse Society*. London: Weidenfeld & Nicolson.
Lanius, R. A., Vermetten, E. & Pain, C. (eds) (2010) *The Impact of Early Life Trauma on Health and Disease: The Hidden Epidemic*. Cambridge: Cambridge University Press.
Lewin, F.M. & Trevarthen, C. (2000) Subtle is the Lord: The relationship between consciousness, the unconscious, and the executive control network (ECN) of the brain. *Annual of Psychoanalysis* 28: 105–25.
McLeod, J. (1994) *Doing Counselling Research*. London, Thousand Oaks, CA: Sage.
Meredith Owen, W. (2007) On evading analysis by becoming an analyst. *Journal of Analytical Psychology* 52: 389–407.
Motion, A. (2006) *In the Blood: A Memoir of My Childhood*. London: Faber and Faber.
Paech, A. (2009) Impressions of boarding school from a non-boarder. *Boarding Concern Newsletter*, Spring 2009, p. 4.
Partridge, S. (2007) Trauma at the threshold: An eight year-old goes to boarding school. *Attachment* 1(3): 310–13.
Power, A. (2007) Discussion of trauma at the threshold: The impact of boarding school on attachment in young children. *Attachment* 1(3): 313–20.
Roth, A. & Fonagy, P. (1996) *What Works for Whom? A Critical Review of Psychotherapy Research*. New York, NY, London: Guilford.
Schaverien, J. (1997) Men who leave too soon: Reflections on the erotic transference and countertransference. *British Journal of Psychotherapy* 14(1): 3–16. [(2006) Chapter 1 in: Schaverien, J. (ed.), *Gender, Countertransference and the Erotic Transference*. London, New York, NY: Routledge.]
Schaverien, J. (2002) *The Dying Patient in Psychotherapy: Desire, Dreams and Individuation*. Basingstoke, New York, NY: Palgrave/Macmillan.
Schaverien, J. (2004) Boarding school: The trauma of the privileged child. *Journal of Analytical Psychology* 49(5): 683–705.
Steiner, J. (1993) *Psychic Retreats: Pathological Organisations in Psychotic, Neurotic and Borderline Patients*. London, New York, NY: Routledge.
Stern, D. (1985) *The Interpersonal World of the Infant*. New York, NY: Basic Books.
Stern, D. (1988) The dialectic between the 'interpersonal' and the 'intrapsychic': With particular emphasis on the role of memory and representation. *Psychoanalytic Inquiry* 8: 505–12.
Trevarthen, C. (2009) The intersubjective psychobiology of human meaning: Learning of culture depends on interest for co-operative practical work and affection for the joyful art of good company. *Psychoanalytic Dialogues* 19: 507–18.
Van Dijken, S. (1998) *John Bowlby: His Early Life*. London: Free Association Books.
Wakeford, J. (1969) *The Cloistered Elite: A Sociological Analysis of the English Public School*. London: Macmillan.
Winnicott, D.W. (1971) *Playing and Reality*. Harmondsworth: Penguin.
Wilkinson, M. (2006) *Coming into Mind: The Mind–Brain Relationship: A Jungian Clinical Perspective*. London, New York, NY: Routledge.
Wilkinson, M. (2010) *Changing Minds in Therapy: Emotion, Attachment, Trauma and Neurobiology*. New York, NY, London: Norton.

Television Programmes

The Making of Them (BBC film made by Colin Luke and broadcast in 1994)
Chosen (Channel 4 broadcast in November 2008)

Appendix V: Cognitive Behavioural Therapy

Cognitive behavioural therapy (**CBT**) is a talking **therapy** that can help you manage your problems by changing the way you think and behave. It's most commonly used to treat anxiety and depression, but can be useful for other mental and physical health problems.
15 Jul 2016 – NHS.UK

How does CBT work?
In CBT, you work with a therapist to identify and challenge any negative thinking patterns and behaviour which may be causing you difficulties. In turn, this can change the way you feel about situations, and enable you to change your behaviour in future.

You and your therapist might focus on what is going on in your life right now, but you might also look at your past, and think about how your past experiences impact the way you see the world.

CBT is learning to stop the cycle of negative thinking. I still have relapses now and it is the one tool that I use to get me out of the truly dark spots.
© 2013 Mind

LINKS:

https://www.rcpsych.ac.uk/mentalhealthinformation/therapies/cognitivebehaviouraltherapy.aspx

https://www.mind.org.uk/information-support/drugs-and-treatments/cognitive-behavioural-therapy-cbt/#.WZ8zQCiGNPY

http://www.nhs.uk/conditions/Cognitive-behavioural-therapy/Pages/Introduction.aspx

https://en.wikipedia.org/wiki/Cognitive_behavioral_therapy

Appendix W: School Report Summer 1979

Kesgrave Hall School (Lee Ellis):

Name: LEE ELLIS **Term:** SUMMER 1979
Form: 3

Subject	Term Work	Exam Mark	Remarks
English Language	Fair	—	Lee always appears to try
English Literature	Fair	39%	but finds the work difficult
French	Fair/Poor	45%	Lee finds languages difficult but
German	Fair/Poor	41%	usually does his best
History	V. Fair	50%	I think he is pleased with the result
Geography	Fair	31%	Lee works with interest
Scripture	Fair/Good	77%	[illegible]
General Science			
Biology	Fair	48%	A very pleasing exam result — Lee worked hard
Chemistry	Poor	33%	has no real interest in the subject but did a fair exam
Mathematics	Fair	31%	Tries hard but needs to make more effort with his work
Art	F. Good	42%	Lee has attained to an idea of quantity rather than quality, but still some good work
Music	Fair	—	Shows interest always
Woodwork	Good	51%	Good work
Technical Drawing	Good	—	Good progress
Physical Education	Fair	—	Tries hard but lacks skill
Games	Fair	—	Tries hard
Conduct	Immature at times		

General Progress: Although Lee has difficulty with several subjects he is always willing to try hard. With constant effort he can only improve the present situation.

.... A. Sutcliffe .... Form Teacher.

Headmaster's Comments: He finds the standard of work here difficult to cope with. However, he tries hard.

Appendix X: Kenneth Scott (Wheatley)

Media Links

Wikipedia: Kesgrave Hall School
In December 2012, former pupils of the school came forward to describe the abuse they had suffered there during the 1980s, and their call for a new investigation was taken up and successful.[4][5][6] In May 2014, after being questioned over allegations of sexual abuse, Kenneth Wheatley (Scott), a former care worker at the school and a convicted paedophile, was found dead.[7][8]

East Anglian Daily Times (Archant)
Convicted paedophile arrested in Kesgrave Hall and north Wales child abuse inquiries took his own life two days later, inquest told
The hearing at the Medico Legal Centre in Sheffield was told ex-Kesgrave Hall care worker Kenneth Wheatley - previously known as Kenneth Scott - had left a suicide not before walking in front of a train travelling between Silkstone and Dodworth, near Barnsley on April 12.
http://www.eadt.co.uk/news/convicted-paedophile-arrested-in-kesgrave-hall-and-north-wales-child-abuse-inquiries-took-his-own-life-two-days-later-inquest-told-1-3899644

The Daily Express
'Hope you die in jail' Victims confront vile paedophile teacher as he's sentenced
Wheatley, 62, committed suicide on a rail track near Barnsley two days after he was arrested by Suffolk officers and National Crime Agency detectives involved in the large-scale north Wales child abuse inquiry into the Bryn Alyn care homes.
http://www.express.co.uk/news/uk/670326/Die-in-jail-victim-tells-paedophile-teacher

Appendix Y: David Brockman Obituary and media

The Hunts Post: OBITUARY: Huntingdon radio stalwart David Brockman dies aged 59

http://www.huntspost.co.uk/news/obituary-huntingdon-radio-stalwart-david-brockman-dies-aged-59-1-3602088

Kesgrave Hall school sex abuse: Victim slept with 'one eye open'

By Andrew Woodger BBC News Online

'David Brockman, 59, who lived in Huntingdon, was questioned by police on suspicion of sex offences and died of natural causes'

http://www.bbc.co.uk/news/uk-england-suffolk-34504196

Printed in Great Britain
by Amazon